marked for life

HARMONY BOOKS
NEW YORK

JOIE DAVIDOW

A MEMOIR

marked for life

Grateful acknowledgment is made to **Viking Penguin** for permission to reprint an excerpt from *The End of the Affair* by Graham Greene. Copyright © 1951, renewed © 1979 by Graham Greene. Reprinted by permission of Viking Penguin, a division of Penguin Group (USA) Inc.

Copyright © 2003 by Joie Davidow

All rights reserved. No part of this book may be reproduced or transmitted in any form or by any means, electronic or mechanical, including photocopying, recording, or by any information storage and retrieval system, without permission in writing from the publisher.

Published by Harmony Books, New York, New York.
Member of the Crown Publishing Group, a division of Random House, Inc.
www.randomhouse.com

HARMONY BOOKS is a registered trademark and the Harmony Books colophon is a trademark of Random House, Inc.

Printed in the United States of Ameirca

DESIGN BY ELINA D. NUDELMAN

Library of Congress Cataloging-in-Publication Data
Davidow, Joie.
    Marked for life : a memoir / Joie Davidow.—1st ed.
1. Davidow, Joie. 2. Hemangiomas—Patients—United States—Biography. 3. Birthmarks—Patients—United States—Biography. 4. Hemangiomas—Psychological aspects. 5. Birthmarks—Psychological aspects. I. Title.
  RL793.D38   2003
  362.1'9699313'0092—dc21   2002153963

ISBN 1-4000-4741-2

10 9 8 7 6 5 4 3 2 1

First Edition

for my sisters

acknowledgments

My deepest gratitude goes to Michael Steffano of www.birthmarks.com and the members of his online newsgroup, whose stories are so like my own. I hope that I have managed to be true to us all. I owe a great debt to my fellow authors Eve Babitz, Hunter Drohojowska, and Esmeralda Santiago, who patiently prodded, encouraged, and corrected me through the writing of every page; to my friend, Robin Dresser, for believing I was up to the task; and to my agent, Jane Dystel, for believing in the book's potential. Special thanks to Becky Cabaza for her careful and insightful editing.

author's note

This story is no more than my memory of what happened and how it felt to me at the time. Although it is a true story, and all of the people in it are real, I have changed some of their names in an attempt to protect their privacy.

part one

THE ANGEL'S BLOODY HAND

The crimson hand expressed the ineludible gripe in which mortality clutches the highest and purest of earthly mould, degrading them into kindred with the lowest, and even with the very brutes, like whom their visible frames return to dust.

NATHANIEL HAWTHORNE
"The Birthmark"

If I had been born in another time, in another place, I might have been left out in the snow to die, a girl baby my parents couldn't afford to feed, a girl baby with a face so disfigured she'd never find a husband.

If I had been born in another time, in another place, I might have been the spinster aunt, the unmarriageable sister, taken in by her brother to help his wife with the housework, kept out of sight, always a burden, never in a home of my own.

If I had been born in another time, in another place, I might have died before I was forty. If I had lived to become middle-aged, the purple stain that marred my face might have grown, become thick, raised, nearly black in places like a slab of rancid meat. Swollen capillaries might have risen to the surface of my skin, erupting in bumps that became fountains of blood when lightly scratched. I might have turned so monstrous, I would have ended my days locked in an attic, or hidden in some remote convent cell.

But I was born in this time, in this place, where science and commerce conspire to make it ever easier for affluent women to fix up, chemically alter, surgically correct.

If a guardian angel really did touch my face when I was born, she's still hanging around.

"Whenever a baby is born," Mommy said softly, "a guardian angel *is sent down to earth to meet her new charge. If the baby is very beautiful, the angel is so moved that she can't help kissing it, leaving a tiny pink birthmark where her lips touched the newborn skin. But when your guardian angel saw you, she was so overwhelmed by your beauty, she couldn't resist touching your cheek, leaving a red stain in the shape of her hand."*

Mommy put her own hand over my face, covering my eye with her thumb and extending her fingers toward my mouth to show me where the angel had touched me. My birthmark did look like a hand, the size of a big grown-up hand on a five-year-old girl's little face. I could see it. So I believed my mommy, and when the other children called me cruel names, when every new child I met asked, "What's wrong with your face?" I remembered my guardian angel. But I soon found out that though the angel may have seen an irresistibly beautiful baby, the other children saw a freak. So I begged Mommy not to send me to school. I stayed in bed, pulled the covers over my head, and threw tantrums. But she picked me up and carried me screaming into the bathroom, bathed me, dressed me, and sent me off to face my life.

Miss Grape Juice Face

I was born at the end of the Second World War, at the beginning of what would be called the Baby Boom. My father spent the war as a lieutenant in the Judge Advocate General's Office in Washington, D.C. He came home to practice law in the little New Jersey town where he had been born and raised.

Millville is a factory town, midway between Philadelphia and Atlantic City—not a rural town, neither urban nor suburban, just a small town among other small towns. It's not even a particularly charming town, though it may once have been.

The Maurice River flows through the South Jersey salt marshes on its way to the Delaware, but it slows down to little more than a creek as it passes through Millville. The mill company that gave the town its name dammed the river and, at the turn of the century, excavated part of it to create Union Lake. Two miles wide, it was once touted as the biggest artificial lake in the world, a tourist attraction with an amusement park on its shores. But by the time I was born the park had long been abandoned. The carousel and bandstand were gone, and the scrubby forest had grown back. Local people put up summer shacks and boat docks on land they rented from the mill company. The bottom of the lake was filled with rotting leaves that turned the water a dark rusty color, staining our skin and ruining our bathing suits.

Millville was a white Protestant town, so unabashedly conservative that the local newspaper was the *Millville Daily Republican*. The town's few Jews were mostly merchants with small shops along High Street. Morris and Bea Friedman had the shoe shop; Maxie Zeitz had the delicatessen. Lou and Faye

Miller owned one drugstore; Bailey and Ada Abrahms, the other. The Ackerman family sold furniture. The Kleinmans sold toys. The Levensons sold groceries. There were a couple of Jewish doctors and a couple of lawyers, like Daddy. But no Jews worked in the factories.

In the 1950s, Millville's business district was a single street, High Street, just a few blocks of stores and banks, the post office and the Leroy Movie Theater, where we lined up on Saturdays for the twenty-five-cent Kiddy Matinee. All the stores closed at noon on Wednesdays so that the shopkeepers could make the trip into Philadelphia or New York City to restock their shelves.

My father's law office was on the second floor at the corner of High and Sassafras Streets, in a building that had once housed Davidow's Department Store, the crowning achievement of my grandfather's retail career. We lived only a block away, around two corners. My sisters and I could run back and forth between our house and Daddy's office even before we were old enough to cross the street by ourselves.

During Millville's boom years, at the turn of the century, some of the wealthiest people in town built homes on Second Street, where we lived. Half a century later, the street was just a row of middle-class homes, but remnants of the old architecture remained. Leaded-glass windows looked out onto front porches with lathe-worked posts and railings. Kitchens opened onto backyards neatly divided from the neighbors' by low fences.

Our house was half a double, a two-family structure built like Siamese twins. The two houses shared a common interior wall, and a low railing divided the porch in half. We had one side of the porch; the Brandriffs had the other. Chain-link fences, covered in the summer with honeysuckle vines, separated our little yard from two larger ones. On one side, Old

marked for life

Mister Brandriff grew roses. On the other, Old Man Friedman raised chickens and grew sunflowers.

Out our backyard gate, I take the shortcut across the empty lot. Hopping over mud puddles, I run through the narrow alley, holding my nose as I pass the big garbage bins behind the fish and vegetable market—and I'm on High Street where everybody knows I'm Daddy's daughter, one of the Davidow girls, the one with the purple-marked face.

I spend my allowance on a Three Musketeers bar at Miller's Pharmacy, handing my sweaty fistful of coins over to Faye Miller, who lives two porches away from us on Second Street. Daddy calls Faye Miller *Faygeleh*, which means little bird. But he never says that to her face, and I'm not supposed to say it, either.

Next to Miller's Pharmacy, I visit Friedman's Shoe Store, so I can put my feet into the machine that shows my bones. Morris and Bea Friedman live in an apartment over his father's house, next door to ours. Daddy calls Morris Friedman "the Chinaman" because his face is round and his eyes are slanty and his hair is black and shiny like patent leather shoes. His wife, Bea, dyes her long, curly hair bright red. She wears tight dresses and high-heeled shoes, even when she's working in the shoe store or doing the laundry. Whenever he sees Bea Friedman climbing the wooden stairs to her apartment, Daddy says, "There goes the *tschotschkeleh*." I don't know what it means, but he never calls her that when she can hear him.

On High Street, I'm safe—unless I run into a stranger, who might stare or ask questions about my face. I duck behind Mommy's skirt when she tries to introduce me. "Come on, Joie, can't you say hello to Ruthie's grandmother?" I look at Ruthie's grandmother sideways, showing her my good cheek, hiding the place where the angel touched me. I keep the birthmark cheek pressed against Mommy's knee, but Ruthie's grandmother probably sees it anyway.

~

Across Second Street, two massive nineteenth-century churches towered over us, their steeples thrust into the sky like arms raised in triumph. The brick First Methodist commanded one corner and the equally impressive gray stone First Presbyterian the other. Although we were Jewish, Mommy sent me to the Presbyterian nursery school, in that imposing bastion of white Protestant culture just across the street from our house, convenience trumping religious affiliation.

Westminster Day School was presided over by a very thin, very wrinkled, very white widow named Mrs. Shaw. A dozen four-year-old children assembled each morning at the grand porte cochere of the Presbyterian Church. In the colder months, we shivered under the covered walkway, holding tightly to our mothers' hands until Mrs. Shaw rang the opening bell. But in the morning sunlight of April and May, we raced around the little garden, running and dancing, shrieking under the flowering dogwood tree that dripped pink petals onto the grass.

Mrs. Shaw was a very strict teacher. For three hours a day, five days a week, she labored at transforming inadequately toilet-trained savages into miniature Presbyterian ladies and gentlemen. She knew that her task was formidable and she had no time for coddling and caressing or otherwise spoiling her unruly charges. Like a litter of puppies, we learned to understand and obey important commands such as "Keep to the right in a single file" and "Sit quietly with your hands folded in your lap." We learned that it was a very bad thing to get caught picking your nose or sucking your thumb. And we learned to raise either one finger or two when we had to go to the bathroom, depending on what it was we had to do when we got there.

We learned these things not because Mrs. Shaw kissed us or rewarded us or made us love her so much we'd want to please her. Nor did she ever hit us or punish us or even raise her voice to us. She was far too dignified a lady to stoop to any of that. She trained us with the calm skill of a lion tamer. Nothing we did ever fazed her. No snotty nose, no outburst of baby tears, no soiled panties ever so much as ruffled the folds of her perfectly starched handkerchief or caused a single hair to slip from the silky net that encased her head. Despite her physical frailness, she was imperious, rock hard on the inside, and we knew it. I feared her for no real reason, but I feared her mightily.

It was at Mrs. Shaw's school that I learned about Jesus. She told us that he was always watching us, every minute of our lives, even when we were asleep. He knew everything we did, everything we said, everything we thought. And even though we learned to sing "Yes, Jesus Loves Me," I didn't feel his love at all.

He was a scary man. I knew what he looked like. Mrs. Shaw showed us plenty of pictures of him and there were plenty more hanging all around the church. Jesus didn't look anything like any of the men I knew. I was afraid to undress or go to the bathroom because Jesus was watching me. I could see him there while I sat on the toilet, his hand raised in silent reproach.

And it was in my first weeks at Mrs. Shaw's school that I learned I was a strange child. "The little Jewish girl," I heard her whisper to another child's mother. "Such a pity about her face. They say the doctors can't do a thing for her."

Why? Why did something have to be done for me? What was wrong with my face? I stood in our living room and examined myself in the full-length mirror on the door of the coat closet. I saw the purple mark—not an angel's loving touch, but something wrong. Something shameful. Something pitiful. With the palm of my own little hand, I rubbed and rubbed, but I couldn't rub it off.

I couldn't face Mrs. Shaw again, couldn't face the other children, couldn't face being "such a pity." So I refused to go back to Westminster Day School. I begged and sobbed and clung to the blankets. But Mommy marched me back there, back across the street to the little school room in the great big church, where I now kept to myself in a corner, peering through the leaded-glass windows at our house across the street, wondering how long it would be before I could go home again.

I was a failure at nursery school. When we had to make lanterns from red construction paper, I couldn't cut the straight lines neatly with my blunt children's scissors. Mrs. Shaw made me do it over and over again, but I never got it right. When we had to play in the rhythm band, I was given sticks to bang together, the lowliest assignment, while pretty little Presbyterians Paula and Peggy got to play the toy piano and the xylophone I longed for. I was a child who could do nothing right. I even failed at raising one finger in time to be sent to the bathroom and piddled on the floor.

The entire curriculum of the Westminster Day School was an extended rehearsal for the elaborate commencement ceremony in May, when we would make Mrs. Shaw proud, another crop of little monsters tamed, ready to behave themselves, ready for kindergarten. On that Sunday afternoon, the boys were dressed in tiny suits and ties; and the girls, in frilly long white dresses. We each were called upon to demonstrate the impeccable deportment we had acquired under Mrs. Shaw's tutelage by reciting a poem from memory, then executing a flawless bow or curtsey. It was our coming out as proper children.

When commencement day finally arrived, I felt like a princess in the dress Mommy made for me, with puffy sleeves and a Peter Pan collar, my pigtails tied with white satin ribbons. In that long white dress, I was a beautiful lady, not a little girl with a pitiful face. And I would never have to go back to Mrs. Shaw's school again. The thought of kindergarten was terrifying, but that was months away, lifetimes away.

During the commencement ceremony I carried a basket full of flowers and recited Robert Louis Stevenson's lines, "Oh, how do you like to go up in a swing, / Up in the air so blue" from *A Child's Garden of Verses*. And when Daddy took my picture with his Brownie camera, the film was black and white, so the angel's bloody handprint looked like nothing but a shadow.

Our house faced the firehouse, a square, flat, one-room building hunched between the two great churches that flanked it. When there was a fire, an alarm went off loud enough to be heard by volunteer firemen all over town. All the kids on Second Street lined up on the porches. We punched our fingers in and out of our ears in rhythm, making our own music from the siren's deafening wail, while the grown-ups jumped into their cars to follow the trucks so they could find out where the fire was.

Behind the firehouse was the old brick Culver Elementary School, with separate entrances for boys and girls. I went to grammar school there, in the same building where my father had attended high school. Our house was so close to my school, I could run across the street at the last minute and slide in the girls' entrance seconds ahead of the bell. Better to be late, to cross the street after all the other children had already gone inside.

If I left my house too early, while the sidewalks were still crowded and noisy, I'd have to stand on the corner with the other kids, waiting to cross the street to the schoolyard.

On school days, Daddy stands at my bedroom door switching the lights on and off, yelling "Time to get up! Time to get up!"

But I don't get up. I just pull the blanket over my head. Not even five minutes later, Daddy comes back, pulls the covers off my body, and tells me, "Okay, time's up. Out of bed! You're gonna be late." I really hate Daddy when he does that.

Daddy doesn't understand that I really *have* to be late. It's not just an accident. Daddy never talks about my birthmark.

I'm standing on the corner waiting for the traffic monitor to let us cross. A bunch of older boys are walking along on the other side of the street. When they see me they yell, "Here comes the Bride of Frankenstein! Hey, Miss Grape Juice Face! Purple Face! Burn Face! Hey, Kool-Aid Face! Ketchup Face! Hey, Ugly Witch Face! Monster Girl! Girl from Outer Space!" Some kids look away from me. Some kids start laughing. I want to run right back home. Our front porch is only a few feet away. But Mommy would just make me turn around and go out again.

As soon as the bossy traffic monitor puts his stupid arms down, I walk across the street really fast so that I can get way ahead of the other kids.

Debbie, who lives on the corner, tries to catch up with me. I hear her say, "I think she's crying." But I walk faster and faster, as fast as I can without running. If I start to run, she'll know something is wrong. And I just have to pretend those boys didn't mean me when they yelled, "Bride of Frankenstein." I just have to pretend I'm fine.

Small-Town Housewife

In the 1920s and '30s, Millville's tiny population of Jewish immigrants lived clustered in a ramshackle row of wooden houses on Middle Street. My father was born and raised in that little ghetto. His parents gave him a Yiddish name, Yehudah Edel, but when his father registered him for school, the principal gave him an English name, Judah Peter. Then he named himself J. Peter, Pete. Judah sounded too foreign, too Jewish, too much like Judas, the betrayer of Christ. His mother sent him off dressed like a proper Ukrainian boy, in a blue velvet suit with knickers and white stockings, his long blond ringlets tied with ribbons. He was her baby, her youngest son.

On that first school day, little Edel discovered a hostile world. He learned that he was a strange child. The working-class gentile boys in overalls went wild when they saw this Jewish Little Lord Fauntleroy. They called him a mama's boy, a kike, a dirty Jew, and they beat him up. He came home to Middle Street bloodied, the velvet suit in shreds. After that, his two older brothers stayed close to him on the playground. They fought for him and they taught him to fight. Five years old, he learned to be fast on his feet.

He ran from the bullies on the playground, ran and ran until he became a football star, skinny but fast, good enough to be accepted by a team of blue-collar jocks. With a football scholarship, he ran all the way through law school.

After the war, when he came back to Millville and opened his law office, he joined the Rotary Club, the Lions Club, the Kiwanis Club, the American Legion, and the Veterans of Foreign Wars. He was a Thirty-Second Degree Freemason and a Shriner. He beat the bullies and joined them.

When Daddy was growing up, the Ku Klux Klan was active in New Jersey. Only five percent of the population of the state was African American in those days, so the Klan focused its attention on other undesirables, such as Jews, whom they accused of controlling the banks, running a white slave trade, bringing Russian Bolshevism to America, and generally undermining morality. The Klan's rank and file blue-collar workers feared that the influx of Jewish immigrants threatened their jobs and their solid white Protestant Republican majority.

Our Jewishness was a frequent topic at the dinner table. Daddy liked to repeat his points word for word, to make sure we got the message. He repeated himself over and over again for years, as though he had only a limited selection of phrases to choose from. He'd say, "Don't ever forget you're a Jew. You were born a Jew, and you'll die a Jew." Daddy thought that my sisters and I tried too hard to be like the other kids, like the Millville *goyim*. If we spoke affectionately of our school friends, he became derisive and repeated, "You may think they're such good friends, but someday you'll have a fight and they'll call you a dirty Jew." We heard that one a lot.

If Daddy thought we needed an extra special reminder that we were not gentile, he repeated the story about the time the Ku Klux Klan burned a cross in front of his house on Middle Street. Daddy never mentioned how scared he was, but he must have been. The whole family must have stayed inside the house, hiding in the closets or under the beds. Daddy's mother must have been hysterical. She left the Ukraine because of pogroms against the Jews, and there she was in Millville with a cross burning on her front lawn. When Daddy went back to school the next day, he must have wondered which of the other kids knew about the cross burning, which of their fathers had been at his house the night before disguised by a white hood.

At the dinner table, Daddy often repeated, "I can't trust anybody in this world but your mother. It's no good to be a lone wolf, but I guess that's what I am." He knew everybody in town, but Mommy was his only friend.

◦────◦

My mother, the former Frayda Schwartzmann, became Florence Schwartz when her father registered her for school. She liked to be called Florrie, but Daddy always called her Flossie, partly out of affection, partly because it annoyed her.

She grew up with two brothers and a sister in a Philadelphia townhouse with crystal chandeliers and stained-glass windows facing Fairmount Park. The neighborhood was elegant, but the language on the streets was Yiddish. Her father, an aspiring intellectual, had become a businessman in order to support his family. When his first child was born, he gave up his books and went to work, but he named the boy Lazar, Leon, after Leo Tolstoy.

Florrie was one of only two women accepted to the University of Pennsylvania Law School class of 1937. For the first month she thought she was the *only* woman, because she was too timid to lift her head and look around at the other students. She graduated at the top of her class, the fourth woman in the history of the university to make law review. But her fellow students barely tolerated her. She was taking the place of a man who would have to support a family, they told her, while she would soon get tired of playing career girl, marry, and have children.

She never thought she would marry. She suffered from severe acne, and even after her skin became clear, she still felt ugly. She thought that her nose was too big, her eyes were too small, her hair too fine. Her two brothers teased her constantly. When she asked them to fix her up with one of their friends, they laughed at her and said, "Who'd want to go out with *you*?"

But on March 9, 1941, she did a former classmate a favor by agreeing to a blind date with the girl's brother, who was visiting from out of town. And there was Pete, handsome, polite, driving a new Roadster. His hair was black and thick and wavy, his eyes pale blue green, and he'd learned to use his good looks to charm women. He had a reputation as a ladies' man—a playboy who took party cruises to Havana. He had never met a woman like Florrie. Twenty-eight years old, full of ambition, she had a steely will that could match his own and she shared his passion for the practice of law. If her brothers had utterly convinced her that she was ugly, Pete persuaded her that she was more than attractive. He admired everything about her, the way she dressed, the sharpness of her mind. He wrote to her every day, beginning his letters by discussing the cases he was working on and asking for her help and advice, but he always ended with a passionate declaration. "It was all I could do to work today. I keep thinking about you, seeing you, wishing you were beside me," he wrote.

On Saturday afternoons he closed up his office early, so that he could spend the evening and all the next day with her in Philadelphia. After three months he asked her to marry him. She lowered her eyes and buried her face in his shoulder.

"I am very seriously wondering where we are heading," he wrote. "You refuse to answer when I ask you to marry me. And when I look in your eyes, I always see the same pained, evasive expression. Why?"

She wrote back reviewing her position:

> Pete dear, what more can I say? I've begged you to give me arguments, to work out a plan. But you never do talk. And every time I try to broach the subject you get depressed and hurt. I've told you so often I believe you can tell it back to me verbatim.
>
> 1. I love to work. I'd hate to stop. 2. I am a member of the Pennsylvania bar. I am not a member of the New Jersey bar. I would despise studying and taking the examination. 3. If I were to continue working here and lived in Millville, I would ride on trains for hours every day. I'd be exhausted. 4. I love

marked for life 17

living in a big city. I doubt very much if I would like living in a small one. 5. I love you. And every day points one through four seem less and less important.

She dreamed of living in a Manhattan hotel where the doorman would greet her courteously at the end of her long workday, where she could go up to her suite and order room service, where the maid would turn down her bed each night. She thought she might become a judge, the author of important legal texts. She was sure Pete would compromise. Surely there must be someplace where they could live together happily. But he was incapable of leaving the little town where everyone knew him, where he could feel safe and important.

She broke off with him.

He wouldn't stop calling. He called her office at the Superior Court all day long. He called her at her mother's house in the evenings. She didn't take his calls. She tried to concentrate on her work, but at lunchtime she wandered the streets of Philadelphia in tears. Finally, he won, the way he would win every family battle, by stubbornly refusing to acknowledge any possible solution to the problem but his own.

By September they were engaged and Pete was ecstatic. He was the talk of Millville's tiny Jewish community. "Flora dearest (wife!)" he wrote. "My good friend, Mrs. Kane, must have put in a couple of hard days' work because almost everyone I've encountered has congratulated me and wants to know when I'm getting married. And the telephone has been quite busy with felicitations."

On the seventh of December 1941, while Florrie and Pete were parked in her mother's driveway, necking in the Roadster, her brother Leon began banging on the window. They thought he was just giving them a hard time and told him to go away.

"Turn on the radio!" he shouted. "The Japs have bombed Pearl Harbor!"

Pete had already tried to enlist, but he was deaf in one ear, the result of a childhood fever. The officer at the recruiting station decided to test his hearing by shutting him in a closed room, then firing a gun in the air, right next to his good ear. Pete instantly passed out and was designated "4F," exempt from service.

Now, with the United States at war with Japan, he had to face the possibility that he might be drafted, after all. Pete and Florrie were married three weeks later in the study of a Philadelphia rabbi. They tried to keep it a secret, but Florrie's mother and her sister, Evie, found out and showed up uninvited. Florrie wore a red crepe dress and hat and after the brief ceremony, they cut a cake she had bought on her lunch hour at the Horn and Hardhart bakery.

They spent their honeymoon driving along the Appalachian Trail, then temporarily settled in a bungalow in Millville. Florrie kept her office at the Superior Court library. She got up early and came home late, and used the time on the train to knit or read.

When Pete was called up by the Army, Florrie moved back into her room at her mother's house. The separation was unbearable. With her sister along for company, she took the long train ride to Ann Arbor, Michigan, where he was stationed, and stood outside the gates of the Army base for hours, until he could come out for a moment, to touch her fingers through the chain-link fence. After a year, he was commissioned a lieutenant and assigned to the Judge Advocate General's Office in Washington, D.C. Florrie joined him there. There was no war in Washington. It was a party. The life of an officer's wife was a round of shopping, dinners, teas.

After the war, she tried again to get Pete to compromise. She couldn't face going back to Millville. It was a fundamental difference between them. He was an independent, small-town guy who couldn't imagine how he would cope in the big city, swallowed up by a law firm. And he was not a compromising man.

Florrie, who dreamed of living in a cosmopolitan hotel, found herself in a semi-detached house in a town she thought of as the middle of nowhere. She was a curious figure in Millville. She dressed up in a well-tailored suit with matching hat and gloves to walk the few blocks of downtown High Street. Her old mentor, a judge, gave her a job as his clerk at the Circuit Court of Appeals in Philadelphia. She enjoyed the work, adjusted to the two-hour commute. She was married to her true love, and life was grand. Then disaster struck.

She was pregnant. How could this have happened? They were being so careful. She didn't want a baby, didn't want to have children at all. She locked herself in the bedroom and cried. She blamed Pete for being careless. He blamed himself for ruining her life. When her growing belly became an embarrassment to the superior court judge, she was advised that she could no longer handle her duties and that she should concentrate on motherhood. She was forced to resign from her job, and to resign herself to becoming a housewife, an extraordinary woman trapped in an ordinary little town.

Shayne Punim

One out of ten babies are born with strawberry birthmarks, often called angel kisses. These little stains gradually fade during childhood. But I was born with another kind of birthmark, not an angel's kiss but a touch. An angel's touch, which feels more like a slap, never fades but deepens over the course of a lifetime.

These birthmarks are commonly called port wine stains, not so sweet a shade as that of a strawberry, but the color of dark wine, spilled and spreading over a ruined white tablecloth. They are really bloodstains, pools of blood under the skin.

In a normal person, blood moves steadily through the body, carried by streams and tributaries, flowing clockwise from the head to the feet then back to the head, passing through the heart.

But under my skin, under the place where my face was stained by an angel's bloodied hand, the veins are dilated, like a widening in a riverbed. The steady stream of blood from head to toe and toe to head is arrested there. The blood stops. Time stops. The stream pauses to pool before flowing on again. Over the years, the engorged vessels grow slack. The blood has been collecting in this stagnant place for so long that the skin thickens over it.

―――

Florrie endured a hard labor on a blazing July day in a Philadelphia hospital without air-conditioning. She lay sweating in agony on a rubber sheet, birthing a baby she never wanted. She had chosen to suffer alone, had banished Pete, who had stayed

marked for life

at home in Millville while she spent the last weeks of her pregnancy at her mother's house. She was already in the delivery room when the doctor finally arrived and yanked me out of her body with forceps. She always said she fell in love with me the moment she saw me. I know that she did fall in love with me, but it could not have been love at first sight.

Before they brought the baby to her, a young intern came and sat on her bed. "Your daughter has . . ." What did he call it? A birthmark? A malformation? A facial deformity? Did he use a medical term she had to ask him to spell? He told her that no one knows what causes these birthmarks, and that there was no good way to treat them. The young intern told her that because the mark covered my forehead, the pooling blood might affect my brain. I might have seizures. Because the mark covered my left eye, I might have glaucoma. It would get worse as I got older. There would be darkening, thickening, spontaneous bleeding.

She was a fighter, like Pete. She had no patience for weakness. But after the intern left her, she wept silent tears. She was trapped with a baby, a baby with a stained face. It was her fault. Somehow, she had marked the baby she didn't want, the baby she had hoped she'd miscarry.

Florrie's mother felt sorry for her daughter, whose dreams were crushed by the birth of this unwanted child. But she was thrilled to have her first grandchild, Josephine, named for her beloved Joseph, my grandfather, the dead husband whom she missed so desperately. Grandmom scooped me into her soft, fat arms.

Together, they took me from doctor to doctor. The doctors peered at my stained face. They poked it with their fingers, shone bright lights on it, and put their big heads close to my tiny cheek, exhaling strange man's breath on me. The treatments the doctors offered were gruesome. One doctor wanted to implant radium under the skin. One wanted to freeze the mark off with liquid nitrogen. One wanted to graft clear skin from my buttocks or thigh over it. One wanted to stretch the clear parts of my face with a balloon planted under the skin in order to create enough extra flesh to graft over the excised birthmark.

Ever the efficient lawyer, Florrie did her research. She wrote letters, made phone calls. For months she searched and hoped—hoped to find a doctor who could remove the mark, hoped to save me from the day when I would be old enough to look in a mirror and see that something was wrong, hoped to save herself from my questions.

Why, Mommy? Why? Why does it have to be on my face? Take it off me, Mommy. Take it off me! Please, Mommy, please!

She consulted every doctor she could find. And then she gave up.

Once she realized that acceptance was her only option, she worked on it, shaping and molding it until it hardened into a rigorously enforced denial. As she walked along High Street, people bent over to peer, cooing, into my carriage. They lifted their heads, not knowing what to say. I looked like a battered baby, the victim of abuse or some unfortunate accident. "Will she grow out of it? Can't the doctors do anything?" She answered them politely, graciously accepted their sympathy, their unwanted advice. But still she managed to will the birthmark away. If she couldn't remove it from my face, she could remove it from her own mind. She would simply refuse to see it.

───────

My sister Jacqueline was born twenty-eight months after I was. Mommy's college courses in psychology had taught her about the perils of raising an only child, so she decided to get pregnant again right away. She'd get back to her career as soon as both children started school.

This time, no doctor came to sit on Mommy's bed before they brought the baby in. She unwrapped the receiving blanket and examined every inch of her second daughter, relieved to find only a tiny pink birthmark on the baby's scalp where it would be hidden by hair.

Although she thought of motherhood as a temporary detour in her career path, she was determined to be good at it. She baked cakes, sewed clothes. She wrote poems for Jackie and me.

We took the train to Philadelphia to visit Grandmom and stayed for days or even weeks at a time. The trip was always a happy occasion. Mommy sewed pretty matching sister dresses with Peter Pan collars, full skirts, and sashes that were supposed to stay neatly fastened in bows but always managed to come loose, so that she was constantly calling one or the other of us over to have them retied. We each had our own little suitcase and a hat and gloves. Mommy wrote a train song, which she copied onto lined paper in her even, angular handwriting and kept neatly filed in a three-ring binder with the other poems and songs she wrote for us: "The girls are all dressed up in their best clothes now, as they ride on the railroad train. Their suitcases are right beside them. They're off to Grandmom's house again. Choo, choo, choo. Can you hear that train? Whoo, whoo, whoo. There it goes again."

The song had a lot of verses, almost enough to keep us singing all the way to the end of the line in Camden, on the New Jersey side of the Delaware River. From there we took the subway through the tunnel into Philadelphia, changed trains, and rode on to Grandmom's house in the suburbs.

I'm six years old and Jackie is four. We're sitting with Mommy on the bench at the back of the train, the three of us huddled in a cozy row, merrily riding off to Grandmom's house. I love riding the subway, love looking out the window at the black tunnel, watching for the wispy trail of light that grows wider and wider until we roll into the next station.

The train stops and a scary man gets on. I want him to go away but he stands close to our bench holding on to a pole. He is a pale man with sparse gray hair, and his clothes are very wrinkled. Even if the only empty seat on the train was the one next to his, I'd rather stand up than sit close to this man. His face is half-covered with a deep purple birthmark. It's darker and bigger than mine, climbing down onto his neck, but I recognize it. He seems so sad and lonely, lonelier than anyone else on the train, because everyone else on the train is looking away from him, even me.

Mommy pretends not to notice. Mommy would never say anything about the man or his birthmark. But if Jackie sees him, she might point. She might say, "Look! That man has a purple face like Joie's!" And then everyone will look at the poor man and look at me. I slide closer to my mommy and put my head in her lap, hiding the birthmark side so that no one on the train will think I'm like that man.

The train pulls into the next stop. I shut my eyes tight. *Please, please, let him get off right now! Let him be gone when I open my eyes.* But the train starts up again and the man is still there. I have never seen anyone with a birthmark like mine before. I'm a nice little girl in a pretty new dress. It can't be possible that I'll be like that man when I grow up. I promise myself that the man has nothing to do with me. But for a long time I think about the ugly purple all over his face. I see him standing there, swaying, holding on to the metal pole, trying to be invisible.

After her father died, Mommy's family moved out of the townhouse on the park, so crowded with old memories there was no room left for new ones to grow. They bought a house for my grandmother's widowhood on genteel Chelten Avenue, in one of the quiet upper-middle-class neighborhoods that skirted Philadelphia's northern side.

Grandmom's house had a backyard full of shade trees and a hilly front lawn that dipped toward the sidewalk. I rolled down across the grassy slope over and over again, giggling wildly with that uncontrollable childhood laughter that would signal insanity in an adult, and sometimes gripped Mommy with fear that the dreaded seizures the young intern told her about had overcome me.

It may not have been such a big house, but to my little eyes it was enormous. The rooms had fireplaces, high ceilings, and tall windows curtained in deep red velvet. Persian carpets covered the polished wooden floors and the furniture was heavy, dark carved wood.

Mommy's younger brother and sister, Artie and Evie, in their early twenties, were both still living with their mother. I was their baby doll. They played with me, spoiled me.

The house was filled with voices calling to one another upstairs and downstairs, laughing, my grandmother's robust soprano booming, *"Achachoynia, achachoynia,"* the gypsy ballad "Dark Eyes." After dinner she opened the Victrola and chose something from her collection of 78s, recordings of the great opera singers of her day: Enrico Caruso, Amelita Galli-Curci, Feodor Chaliapin, Maria Jeritza, Alma Gluck. She had heard them all. I was amazed at these sounds, so different from ordinary singing. *How did they do it?* I warbled away, trying to imitate a coloratura cadenza. I wanted to be able to sing, to sound like Grandmom's records, and it made her so happy whenever I tried.

On the top floor of the house, in the room where I slept on a little cot, Grandmom kept an old upright piano. I was at that piano just as soon as I was big enough to pull myself onto the stool. It was the best toy in the world. I spent hours alone, experimenting with music, discovering parallel intervals, chords, and discords. And when I finally came downstairs to join the family, the grown-ups told me how nicely I had played. "So beautiful!" They could always get rid of me in a hurry by asking me to go back upstairs and play some more.

―――∽―――

Mommy was intellectual, determined, disciplined. But Grandmom was always laughing or crying. Her emotions were as unbridled as Mommy's were restrained. In Grandmom's arms, my face pressed against her enormous bosom, I was safe.

I ran to her the moment I woke up. Grandmom waited in her bed for me to patter down the hall and jump under the covers with her. Everything I did, everything I said delighted her. In her eyes, I was gorgeous. My marked face was beautiful to her, a *shayne punim*. "You mudder vas dreaming about vine ven you ver in her belly," she told me. "She vanted vine so much you vere born mit vine on you face." She covered my purple cheek with kisses. "So delicious," she murmured. "Such delicious vine."

Grandmom held me close against her big soft body, she rocked me, stroked me. Then it was time for breakfast. She wrapped herself in her kimono and held my hand as my little legs negotiated the steep back stairs that led down to the kitchen.

She had always been an ample woman. When she was a young girl, a voluptuous figure had been fashionable, the height of beauty. Now in her sixties, her size had caught up with her health and she had a bad heart. She wasn't allowed to eat eggs, or cakes, or sour cream. No more thick slices of dark bread rubbed with garlic and smeared with rendered chicken fat. Most of the dishes she liked to cook were forbidden, so she sublimated her love of food by watching me eat. "You'll let me make you some oatmeal?" "No, Grandmom, I don't want any." "You'll eat a *bagela* for me?" "No, Grandmom. I don't want it." "If I boil a nice egg, you'll eat it?" "An eggie, Grandmom, okay." She made it just the way she liked it, torn bits of buttered toast soaking up the runny soft-boiled egg, a little salt, a little pepper. Sitting by the windows in the breakfast room, I watched the squirrels chase each other across the lawn and through the trees, while Grandmom watched me eat. As each baby spoonful entered my mouth, she tasted it with me. I thought she was funny. Why would she want to watch me eat? *"Tokhtila,"* Grandmom said, "vatching somebody you love is better even than eating the food youself."

Then it was my turn to watch her get ready for the day. I bounced on her bed as she stuffed herself into her corset, rolled up her stockings, and fastened them with garters. I watched her pull a silk slip over her head, and then a dress. I watched her at her vanity table, dusting her face with the fragrant powder she kept in a porcelain jar, rubbing her cheeks with rouge from a tiny golden compact, and carefully coloring her lips. She put on her earrings and then her shoes, and finished by lifting the glass stopper from a round bottle and dabbing Ma Griffe perfume inside each wrist, behind each ear, behind each knee, and in the deep pocket between her breasts. I loved all the jars and bottles, the hand-painted porcelain, the cut glass. And I loved the mirrors that showed your reflection from three sides.

If I sat at Grandmom's vanity table and looked out of the corner of my eyes at the mirror on the right side, I saw a perfect little girl with a perfect little cheek. But if I shifted my eyes and looked at the mirror on the left side, I saw a blotchy purple face, a purple eye, the angel's handprint. So I looked only to the right. I looked at myself in profile, and imagined I was perfect.

Grandmom was impeccably groomed. But she had no patience with her hair, which she wore very short in a mannish cut. I watched her slick a comb through it. Two, three strokes and she was done. When she was younger, heavy dark brown waves fell below her waist. One day she got so sick of having to put it up and so tired of having hair pins sticking into her scalp, she grabbed scissors and impulsively chopped it all off.

When my grandfather came home, he found her locked in

the bathroom, sobbing—not because she mourned the loss of her beautiful tresses, but because her hair was an uneven mess and she was afraid that her beloved husband would be horrified at the sight of her. He made a humiliating call to his barber, asking him to discreetly come to the house and salvage Grandmom's botched haircut. No one cut women's hair in those days. When Grandmom walked the streets of the Jewish neighborhood with her short hair, people muttered, "Here comes the Communist." But she never let her hair grow out.

She didn't care what other people thought about her, but as she aged and her beauty faded, she no longer liked the way she looked, so she cut her face out of family photographs. Our albums were full of pictures with holes in them where her head should have been.

Grandmom talked funny. She said "buhdday" instead of "birthday," no matter how hard my sister Jackie and I worked to teach her to say it right. "It's not a bird day, Grandmom, it's a birthday! Say birth, Grandmom, like this." "Burr-thththth," she'd say. "Now say 'day.'" "Day." "Okay, birthday, Grandmom, say it." "Buhdday."

She had weird ideas about what words meant. If we came downstairs in our nightgowns, she'd ask us why we were "naked." She was brave and wise in many ways, but foolish in others. She'd grown up in a small town with horses and buggies and never got used to riding in motorcars. She became so frightened when we were driving on the highway, she'd crouch down on the floor in the backseat and hide her face in her hands.

Her name was Bronya, but in America she became Bertha. Bertha Schwartz. She was born in Kalarash, a town of nearly three thousand Jews and less than a thousand gentiles, not far from Kishinev, the capital of Bessarabia, which was once part of Romania and is now its own country, Moldova.

marked for life

In turn-of-the-century Bessarabia, Jewish girls were not permitted to go to school, not even to the temple *schul,* so a tutor was hired to educate Bronya and her sisters. He was a young man from a good Jewish family, who passionately discussed the French and Russian novels and philosophy books he was forever reading. Teenaged Bronya fell in love with this tutor, whose name was Schwartzmann, black man. His hair was very black and his skin was very white. His eyes were deep-set and very pale blue and his nose was long and narrow, like my mother's.

A man who had been to America returned to Kalarash full of exciting stories. He taught Bronya a song in English: "I got a girl in Baltimore. She got carpets on the floor. I got a girl in the marketplace. She got whiskers on her face." Many years later, Bronya taught it to her grandchildren, just the way she had heard it. She sang it with a bouncy klezmer rhythm, adding a lot of bum dee-dee yah-yah, yah-yah-yah verses. It was not the sort of tune that would put a child to sleep, but it was our favorite lullaby. The only English words Bronya knew, when she landed in Baltimore herself, were the lyrics of that song.

She came to America, a teenaged girl, with her brothers, my great-uncles Leb and Velvel, who was a cantor; her sisters, my great-aunts Tante Fanna and Tante Dora; and Josef Schwartzmann, the tutor. The man they paid to smuggle them out of Bessarabia led them on a long walk through the woods and eventually, by train to Hamburg, Germany. When it came time to board the ship that would carry them over the ocean to Baltimore, the man disappeared with nearly all their money so they were forced to scrape together what little they had left and travel in steerage.

Later, they sent for their parents, Motl and Yenta. Baba Yenta had to sell her prized pocket watch to pay for the trip. But she kept the heavy gold watch chain, and always wore it across the voluminous skirts of her long black silk dresses, so that no one would know she didn't have a watch at the end of it.

They traveled just ahead of a dark cloud of anti-Semitism that would culminate in the bloody storm of the Kishinev Pogrom of 1903, which was memorialized in a Yiddish folk song:

> *Dem ersthn tog peysach*
> *Hobn yidelech gants freylech farbracht.*
> *Un demletstn tog choge*
> *Hot men Kishenev chorev gemacht.*
> *Keshenv arumgeringlt*
> *Azoy vi a bonder di fas.*
> *Tates un mames un kinde*
> *Aynen gefaln in gas.*

> (On the first day of Passover,
> all the Jewish people were full of joy.
> And on the last day of Easter,
> Kishinev was destroyed.
> Kishinev was surrounded,
> like a barrel circled by staves.
> Fathers and mothers and children
> died in the streets.)

The pogrom took place on the first day of Passover, the last day of Easter, when anti-Semitic fervor was always at its height because of an ancient myth that Jews slaughtered gentile children so that they could use their blood in the Passover seder ritual. Gangs of enraged and drunken peasants overran the Kishinev ghetto, raping, beating, and murdering the Jews.

Bronya, her brothers and sisters and the tutor, Schwartzmann, made their way from Baltimore to Philadelphia. Having no money, they crowded into a tenement and took whatever jobs they could find. Bronya, who was used to choosing her favorite styles for the family dressmaker to copy, got a job in a sweatshop snipping the loose threads at the ends of seams. On the first day, her scissors slipped and she cut a hole in a garment. She stood up and quietly walked out of the factory. Josef Schwartzmann lasted much longer. In Bessarabia he had been a socialist. In America he became a union organizer. In America, he became Joseph Schwartz.

Bronya's sister Dora had an arranged marriage to a man she didn't like. When she became pregnant, she spent months staring at herself in the mirror so that the baby would look like her, not him.

Bronya was destined to be married off, too. Her brothers had found a husband for her. They didn't approve of Schwartzmann, who they thought was too intellectual, too much a dreamer to support a family. But Bronya was desperately in love. She went to him and begged him to marry her. She didn't care that they might starve. "If a woman loves a gypsy, she'll follow him into the woods," she said.

When their first child was born, Schwartzmann gave up dreaming. He became determined to earn a good living for the sake of his new son and struggled through a series of entrepreneurial failures. With a partner, he bought a gas station to service the first automobiles, but they never managed to turn a profit. Then he invented a machine that shaped the brims of felt hats. Soon after his patent came through, styles changed, and the machine became obsolete before he could recoup his investment.

Schwartzmann and Bronya had four children by the time he got the idea to open a movie theater. It was an enormous undertaking. He booked vaudeville acts, installed a pipe organ, commissioned muralists to decorate the walls. It was the Depression, Hollywood's golden age. Everybody went to the movies. Business boomed.

Mommy and her brothers and sister worked as ushers and

ticket takers. They saw every movie dozens of times. Mommy sat in the lobby studying, but when Al Jolson sang "Mammy" in the first talking picture, she ran inside the theater to watch those five minutes, over and over again.

My grandfather opened a second movie theater in Atlantic City. Every year my grandparents rented a house there, spending their summers by the Atlantic Ocean just as they had spent childhood summers in Odessa, by the Black Sea—sitting on the beach with other Jewish families, playing cards, wading into the water.

Atlantic City was a segregated resort with "restricted" hotels. The Ambassador, the President, and the Traymore were big and lavish and patronized exclusively by Jews. The Marlboro-Blenheim, the Chalfonte-Haddon Hall, and the Ritz-Carlton were just as big and lavish and just as exclusively gentile.

Even after my grandfather died and the movie houses were sold, Grandmom made the trip to Atlantic City each summer, living in rented houses or hotel suites. Mommy brought my sister Jackie and me to stay for a week or two at a time. Our uncle Artie and aunt Evie brought their friends. Daddy came down on Saturday afternoons after he'd closed up the office in Millville.

Mommy makes a bed for me on the living room couch of Grandmom's suite at the Ambassador Hotel. Very early in the morning I stand at the window looking down at the big machines that sweep across the beach, cleaning the sand, combing it into wavy patterns. I keep checking the bedroom doors, listening for the sound of Mommy or Grandmom or Evie stirring, desperate to get into the ocean. When I can't stand it anymore, I climb into Grandmom's bed to wake her up, and we tiptoe out together, being very careful not to wake up baby Jackie. The hotel elevator takes us down below the lobby, under the boardwalk, and out onto the sand. Grandmom wears a black bathing suit made of stiff material that drapes in folds across her big belly and breasts. She takes me by the hand, walking slowly into the water, stooping to splash her armpits, laughing when I do the same. We wait, her two hands holding both of mine, until a wave comes and she lifts me up and we are both wet, both shrieking with delight.

Because Grandmom's bad heart prevents her from strolling on the boardwalk with the rest of the family, in the evenings, she takes me for long rides in a Rolling Chair, a wicker carriage propelled by a driver who pedals from behind.

The driver helps us into the carriage and tucks a blanket over our laps. I feel so important, so regal. I am Cinderella in her magic pumpkin carriage and Grandmom is my fairy godmother. I am a princess rolling along, looking at all the lights, all the people. I sing my favorite Mario Lanza song for Grandmom, "It's the Loveliest Night of the Year." Really, it is. Happy sounds sing out of the shops and restaurants, out of the Nosherei delicatessen, where every table is set with a jar of kosher dills and pickled cherry tomatoes; out of Fralinger's Salt Water Taffy store, where costumed ladies stand in bright windows, churning tubs of shiny pastel candy; out of the Planter's Store, where a giant, monocled Mr. Peanut stands bowing and waving his cane; out of the Ferris wheel on Million Dollar Pier, the roller coaster on Steeple Chase Pier, the ballroom on Steel Pier; out of the penny arcades where the mechanical voices of the gypsy fortune-telling machines and the guess-your-weight machines compete to be heard over the bells of the pinball machines.

And to one side of our carriage, just beyond the reach of the boardwalk lamps, just beyond the festival of color and noise, is the dark ocean, the waves unfurling onto the sand, harvesting the daily crop of ice cream wrappers and lost sandals under a black sky.

Television killed my grandfather. He worried so much that this new invention on the horizon would put the movies out of business. He worried himself to death. He had one heart attack, then another one. Grandmom was only in her forties when he died. She might have remarried but he was the love of her life and she never stopped grieving for him.

Sometimes she held me on her lap hugging me tightly, weeping, "Josephine, Josef, mein Josef, Joe. You have his name." Frightened and confused, I wondered how I could take the place of this grandfather, whom I had never even met. But then my uncle Artie or aunt Evie or Mommy thought of something funny to say and in an instant Grandmom began to laugh just as hard as she had been crying, wiping away tears of laughter with the same damp handkerchief she had just used to mop the sorrow from her eyes.

Grandmom could make a doll from a dishrag and tie a babushka six different ways. She could knit and embroider and cook. Her house was always full of food, wonderful Bessarabian Jewish food she wasn't allowed to eat: *mamaliga*—creamy cornmeal topped with melted butter and pot cheese; *prakas*—cabbage envelopes stuffed with meat and raisins, baked in a sweet-and-sour tomato sauce; kugel—rice pudding with almonds. On the vestibule table by the front door, she kept a plate of strudel—dried fruits and shredded coconut, wrapped in a papery crust. She never let anybody leave her house without a little bag of strudel in case they might get hungry in the car on the way home.

She was a great believer in the healing power of sunlight,

marked for life

which she thought was essential to good health. On sunny summer afternoons, she lured Jackie and me out of the house and onto the front porch by telling us stories. She settled her round fleshy body on the metal glider, while we sat at her feet for hours, begging her to tell us another story, and another one. She told us about growing up in Bessarabia, about the hills covered with flowers in springtime. She told us about the gypsies who camped nearby, announcing their arrival with music so beautiful she ran into the woods to find them. She told us about coming to America with her brothers and sisters and our grandfather, walking for days and days, crossing the ocean in steerage, sick in the airless, crowded, smelly bunks.

We loved her Arschel Strapola stories the most because they were about naughty things like farting and caca and taking off all your clothes, and they always made us laugh and laugh. We thought Arschel Strapola was someone only Grandmom knew about, someone she made up just for us. But Mommy said he was a Jewish folk hero who played pranks on rich and haughty people.

"Once dare is a princess mit a sad, sad face. She neveh smiles. She neveh laughs. She just sits dare. The king, her faddeh, promises if any man could bring a smile to his daughter's lips, he could marry her. Princes come from all over de voiled to give it a try. Dey bring clowns un comics un dey spend all kinds uff money on fancy tricks. One prince brings a whole lot of elephants covered mit jewels. Clowns ride on de elephant's backs. Dey stand on de elephants' heads un swing on dare long, long noses. But de princess just sits dare mit de sad face.

"Anudder prince brings a great big golden cage filled mit monkeys dressed up like kings and queens. Dese monkeys are sitting on velvet couches, pouring tea in glasses mit out spilling—not even a drop. But still de princess just sits dare mit de sad face. Den comes a prince who flies into de king's palace on a tousan balloons. One by one, he lets go de balloons until he lands like a fedder by de princess' feet. But still she just sits dare mit de sad face.

"Vhen Arschel Strapola hears about dis, he knows *for sure* he could make dat princess laugh, even dough he don't have money for an elephant or a monkey . . . not even one balloon. So he goes to de king's castle and shakes de gates till dey let him in. Dat king don't want some poor Jew in his castle, but he's desperate.

"Arschel Strapola tells de king's men, 'Bring me a barrel *full* mit fresh buttuh.' So dey bring de barrel full mit fresh buttuh into de great big room vheh de king is sitting un de princess is sitting right next to him, mit de sad face. Arschel Strapola comes in un starts to take off his close. Now dese kingsmen are really, *really* angry. 'Vhat are you doingk? You don't take your close off in front of a king!'

"But Arschel Strapola keeps taking off his close. He takes off his torn old coat; he takes off his dirty old jecket, his shoit, so old its like a *schmata*. Un den . . . he pulls down his pants un he stands dare in his *verschtunkene*, smelly old undevare, he's been varing all vinter . . . *right* in front uff de king. An den . . . he takes off even de undevare un he stands dare showing de king his *nachete tuchas*. Dat king is so *angry!* But vhat's he gonna do? His daughter is still sitting dare mit de sad face.

"So now . . . Arschel Strapola starts schmearing de buttuh all over his body, so much good, delicious buttuh he schmears over his *verschtunkene* skin. Vhen he's all buttuhed up, he puts his greasy *tuchas* on de king's marble floor and he slides—zoop!—from vun end uff de great big room to de udder end—until he lands right on top uff dat princess mit de sad face. Her eyes open vide. Her mout opens vide. Un den she starts to laugh; she laughs un laughs until she cries."

And so did my sister, and so did I. I laughed until my whole face turned so red my birthmark almost disappeared.

What Happened to Your Face?

> At school I learned that the port wine stain was either a curse-mark laid by God on the cobbler as a punishment for his drunken dissolute past or else some awful disease he had contracted before coming to the village. Like leprosy, it was highly contagious and any contact with it might prove fatal.
>
> PATRICK BOYLE
> *The Port Wine Stain*

At night, while the house sleeps and no one can catch me at it, I get out of bed and kneel before the mirror. I stare at my face, robbed of color by the darkness. Now and then, white lines move across the ceiling as a car passes on Second Street. Headlights bleed through the windows, flash across the mirror, and I watch the purple stain spread over my left eye and cheek, extending in streaks, long fingers reaching for my mouth. I'm seven years old. I need to see what the other children see.

How hideous am I, really? How can they bear to look at me?

I stretch the skin over the mark. I push hard on it with my finger. The stain fades for a moment, and the skin looks normal, the color of the "flesh tone" crayon in my Crayola box. But as soon as I let go, it turns purple again. If I pull my pigtails tighter, tighter, tighter, maybe my skin will stay stretched and I can go to school with a clear face.

In the mornings, I rub and rub my left cheek with my washcloth, trying to scrub the stain off. There must be something that will make it go away.

Why won't Mommy take me to a doctor? Why can't she fix it?

"It's nothing," Mommy tells me. "I have a big nose; you have a birthmark. Everybody has something. Don't make a Big Deal."

"No, Mommy, it's not the same! Big noses are normal. I wish I had been born with a big nose instead of a birthmark. Plenty of people have big noses. Nobody asks you why your nose is so big. But people are always asking me what's wrong with my face. I look like a monster from outer space!"

"Cut it out, Joie. You're getting yourself all worked up over nothing," Mommy says. "When you get older you'll just put a little extra rouge on the other cheek. No one cares that you have a birthmark. Nobody's looking at you."

They are, too. I know they are. A little extra rouge on the other cheek won't make it go away. I just want to look like everybody else.

In the summer, Mommy gives us fresh strawberries and sour cream. I twirl my spoon in the bowl, watching the sweet red berry juice bleed into the white cream, leaving a lovely pink trail. Strawberries are pretty. Lots of people have strawberry birthmarks. I pretend that's what's on my face. Nobody has ever heard of a port wine stain, anyway.

"What's that on your face?" a little girl asks me.

"Oh, I have a strawberry birthmark there," I say, looking down at the ground.

"My sister had a strawberry birthmark on her belly when she was a baby, but it went away; maybe yours will go away, too."

"Maybe it will. Do you want to play jacks?"

"How did you get burned?" a little girl asks me.

"I fell asleep in the sun with a towel over my face, but the towel slipped."

"Oh, it looks like it really hurts."

"No," I say, looking down at the ground. "It doesn't hurt too much."

I hope I'll never see that little girl again, never have to explain why the bad sunburn doesn't fade away.

⁓

"My, my, what happened to your face?" the lady asks me.

"It's just a birthmark," I say, looking down at the ground. "I was born with it."

"Perhaps you'll grow out of it, dear."

"No, I'll never grow out of it. It just keeps growing with the rest of me."

"Really? What do the doctors say?"

"The doctors told my mother that they can't do anything."

"Well, the Lord must have had something special in mind for you when He put that mark on your face. I hope you don't let it bother you."

"No. It doesn't bother me. It doesn't hurt or anything. It's just there," I say.

I really want to say, "I'll bet it would bother *you*, you dumb lady! How would you like to have a big purple mark on *your* face?" But that wouldn't be polite.

⁓

I try to make the birthmark funny. If I make it funny, maybe nobody will feel sorry for me. If I make people laugh, maybe they'll like me. I make jokes about the birthmark at school. I name its shape, the way some children are taught to name the shapes of clouds. I study maps looking for a country shaped like my birthmark.

I say my birthmark is like North and Central America. Alaska is on my temple and connects to Siberia under my scalp. Guatemala and Honduras cross my cheek. Newfoundland covers my eyelid.

I say we can use my birthmark to report the weather. It turns dark purple when it's cold outside, red when it's hot.

In school, I sit at my desk, my head resting in my left hand, hiding the birthmark. Anyone who walks into the room will see a normal little girl, lost in her own thoughts, imagining herself somewhere else, imagining herself perfect.

I live safe and alone inside the misty haven of my own mind. On my report card, my second-grade teacher writes, "Josephine appears to be constantly in a fog. She is always day dreaming."

Mommy pulls my hair back in two neat ponytails, wrapped in rubber bands and decorated with ribbons. But as soon as I get home from school, I pull it free and turn my head upside down to fluff it out so I can toss it over the left side of my face and hide the birthmark behind a veil of hair.

Two-Colored Hands

We were the last family on our block to get a television set. Daddy kept saying television hadn't been perfected yet. While we waited for television perfection, we had to be happy with our combination radio and record player. Whenever the voice on the radio said, "Let's give them a big hand," I held my hand up like a cop stopping traffic. I couldn't understand why Mommy and Daddy thought that was so funny.

As soon as we could walk, Jackie and I starting showing up at *Faygeleh* Miller's house every afternoon to watch *The Howdy Doody Show* with her daughter, Ruthie. Daddy finally got so embarrassed he broke down and bought us a set of our own. When I watched Ed Sullivan say, "Let's give them a great big hand," I still didn't get it. Why didn't he say let's give them *two* hands if he wanted the audience to clap?

My favorite radio character is Aunt Jemima. I love her because I know what she looks like from the box in our kitchen. She's smiling as though she is just so pleased that you're about to mix up some of her delicious pancakes. Aunt Jemima is all by herself on the box, but she has a whole family on the radio.

At Woolworth's, a counter is piled with black rubber baby dolls. They stare at me through the cellophane covers of boxes bearing that very same picture of Aunt Jemima, grinning her ecstatic pancake grin. I ran up and down the aisles, calling for Mommy. But Mommy won't buy one for me. She says, "You have so many dolls at home already. Why do you need this one?" And then she turns around to look at something else. I know Daddy's father is just outside the store, on the corner, where he spends every afternoon, leaning on his cane, kibitzing with other old Jewish men.

"Come here, Grandpop." I grab his free hand and try to drag him away. "I want to show you something." I take a doll from the top of the pile and start marching toward the cash register. Grandpop is right behind me, opening his wallet. But he keeps asking Mommy, "Why does she want a *schwartze* baby?"

The Garland sisters, Gail and Darlene, are the only black children in all of Culver Elementary School, grades kindergarten through six. Their father died in the war, so their mother has to work cleaning houses, but she always gets time off to show up at school events. She is a plump, pretty lady who keeps her handbag pressed close to her belly. I once overheard someone tell Mommy that Gail and Darlene's mother is a lovely woman because she sends her girls to school clean and well dressed and she "knows her place."

"What does that mean, Mommy, 'knows her place'? What's a place? Do I have to know *my* place?"

Mommy tried to answer my questions. She said that some people think they are better than other people just because they have white skin, and that those same people might think they are better just because they are Protestants and not Jews. But I still didn't understand.

Gail and Darlene come to school in pretty dresses and white socks and Mary Jane shoes, just like Jackie and me. But when we all hold hands in a circle on the playground, the other little girls whisper that if you hold Gail's or Darlene's hands, their color will rub off on you. I know that isn't true.

marked for life

Rose Love comes to Grandmom's house to help her clean and do the laundry. Rose is as glamorous as her name. She's always dressed in high heels and stockings, as if she were on her way to lunch at a nice restaurant, even when she's mopping Grandmom's kitchen floor, or listening to soap operas on the radio while she irons. A lot of Rose's clothes once belonged to Mommy's sister, Evie. When Evie brings a new outfit home from the store, Rose asks her, "When you gonna give me that, Ev?" Rose and Evie are always laughing and talking in low voices so I can't hear what they're saying.

When we stay at Grandmom's house, Rose is our baby sitter. I like to sit on her lap and hold her hands, turning them over. They're beige on the palm side and brown on the backside and I think they are beautiful. "I wish I could have two-colored hands like yours, Rosie," I tell her. "No you don't," she says. "No you don't." Rose paints my fingernails dark red, like hers, but the brown color of her skin never rubs off on mine.

There are Italian and Puerto Rican children in Millville. They go to the Catholic school where the teachers are all nuns, so I never see them. There are two other Jewish girls in my class, twins who are so good at playing sports nobody minds too much that they are Jewish. But there are no other children with faces that are two-colored white and purple like mine, two-colored like Rosie's beige and brown hands.

The Sound of Female Weeping

Daddy's mother, Sarah Davidow, lived alone in the same dilapidated wooden house on Middle Street where she'd raised her four children. Grandpop moved out years before I was born. We didn't see her very often, but sometimes on Sunday afternoons, Jackie and I had to keep Daddy company when he went to visit her. Mommy never came along. "She's your grandmother," she told us. "She wants to see you. She doesn't need to see me."

Mommy put up with Daddy's father, our Grandpop, but she had no use for his mother, who was not at all like her own mother, our soft, warm Grandmom. Everything about this grandmother seemed bleak and mean—the shapeless cotton dresses that hung from her shrunken body, her thin hair, too tightly wrapped in a tiny bun at the nape of her neck. She never greeted us with smiles or hugs.

⁓

"Siddown, siddown," she says, waving us onto the couch as though sweeping us out of the way. Jackie and I perch on the edge of the frayed old upholstery. The windows are all shut tight so it's hard to breathe. It smells funny, like an attic. I don't want to look at this grandmother. She has a witchy face with a curved nose that bends down toward her chin and her lips are thin and pressed together. I look at my dress-up patent leather Mary Jane shoes, swinging next to Jackie's. I look at the faded carpet, the scruffy wooden floor.

"You vant some sodavoda?" She offers soda water. Coke, Pepsi, root beer—it's all sodavoda to her. Our Uncle Sam, who drives a truck for Frank's Soda Company, keeps her supplied with big wooden cases of it.

There's never any real food in this grandmother's house, but she always has a glass bowl full of mints on the table. "Eat some kendy," she says. I don't like those mints. They have yucky red or green jelly inside. But I know I have to be polite, so I take one and put it in my mouth. Maybe I can suck on the white mint part until I get down to the yucky jelly, then spit it out in my hand while nobody's looking.

Daddy's mother sits on her hard wooden rocking chair. She heaves her chest, taking enormous loud breaths. Her shoulders go up and down like she's shrugging. "Oy, I soffer. Oy, I soffer." She says it over and over again. Daddy tries to talk to her.

"The girls are doing very well in school."

"Yeah? Dot's gut. Gut."

I can tell she doesn't really care how we're doing, and maybe Daddy can tell, too, because he doesn't say anything else.

Silence. Horrible, uncomfortable silence. Her breathing even quiets down.

Then she starts in, chest heaving. "Oy, I soffer. I soffer."

Daddy tries again. "Sam says he comes to see you."

"He don't come here. He brings me sodavoda, dot's all." Daddy looks miserable. He can't find anything she wants to talk about. Maybe I can tell her something she'll like.

"Grandpop came over to play with us last week. He watched me and Jackie practice dancing."

Her mouth curls down in disgust. "Oy! Dot teddible, teddible man!"

Why did I have to say that? Why did I have to say anything? She is so mean she even hates Grandpop!

I have to go to the bathroom, but I hold it in. Now that this mean grandmother is angry at me, I'm afraid to ask if I can go.

Finally, Daddy stands up.

"The girls' mother is waiting for us at home."

Oh, hooray! We're leaving!

Daddy bends down to give his mother a hug. Daddy is not good at hugs but his mother is even worse. Her stick arms reach up to him. She starts whimpering. "Edel," she calls him. "Edeleh."

The whole time we were here she could hardly even talk to him and now she's crying when he leaves! If she loves him so much, why couldn't she have been nicer?

"I'll be back to see you soon, Mom."

"Iz a'righ'. Iz a'righ'. You busy. You have a family. You don't hef no time fo me."

I don't want to hug her. Daddy has to tell us, "Girls, kiss your grandmother good-bye." Then Jackie and I race down the rickety front steps of her house and into the car. Daddy doesn't say a word until we get home.

———

Grandpop first saw her while he was making the rounds of the Jewish settlements in South Jersey in a horse and wagon, selling dresses to the wives of immigrant chicken farmers, a business he eventually parlayed into the little department store on the corner of High and Sassafras Streets. Her thin frame was graceful then, her pointed chin and nose were delicate. Newly arrived from the Ukraine, her cousins married her off to a man she learned to hate.

On Friday nights Grandpop went to the synagogue and came home late. Maybe he came home drunk, demanding his conjugal rights. Daddy woke up in terror to the sound of his mother crying and screaming. "He's killing me! He's killing me!"

There were three sons: Izzy, Sam, and Pete, my father. Rivka was the only daughter, the baby of the family. When their children grew up, Daddy's parents separated. Grandpop moved into a house just a few steps down the street from his wife but they never spoke to each other again. Rivka, who arranged the blind date between Mommy and Daddy, changed her name to Evelyn, made a good marriage to a doctor, and moved to Philadelphia. The three boys all stayed in Millville. Izzy, the oldest, became a lawyer, like Daddy. When Daddy graduated from law school, he thought he'd go into practice with his brother. But Izzy told him to get his own office. Sam got a job with the soda company, and resented his more affluent and educated brothers.

Daddy grew into a man unable to bear female weeping; it conjured up those terrifying nights when his mother screamed as though she were dying. If Jackie or I ever started to cry while he was at home, Mommy hustled us out the kitchen door. It didn't matter why we were crying. We always thought we were crying for a good reason. But she always threw us outside and told us we couldn't come back in until we'd pulled ourselves together.

I wandered aimlessly around the backyard, sobbing, scandalizing the neighborhood. If Old Mister Brandriff peered over the fence to see what the noise was all about, if Old Man Friedman came out to feed his chickens, if his daughter-in-law, Bea the *tschotschkeleh*, appeared on her second-floor landing to ask what was wrong, I struggled harder to stop crying, full of shame, hiding my face, always hiding my face.

Sometimes, when I start to cry, Mommy locks me behind the door that leads down to the cellar. I cling to the narrow landing, crowded with the vacuum cleaner, mops, and brooms. It's pitch black and I can't see a thing. I can't tell where the landing ends and the stairs start, and I'm scared that if I step back, I'll fall all the way down into the basement, full of spiders and cobwebs and who knows what else. I can't stop crying, no matter how hard I try. I'm too lonely and too frightened and too mad.

"Mommy, please, please, open the door. I promise I'll stop

crying. I promise. But I can't stop crying till you let me out. It's too dark in here. Just let me out, and then . . . I'll . . . stop . . . crying—I hold my breath, gulping air, so I can hear Mommy's answer. But she doesn't answer. I can't hold my breath anymore and when I let it out, I'm crying harder and louder than ever.

I stand on tiptoe, stretching up to reach the light switch, but I'm too short. I try jumping, just a little jump. *What if I jump and land on the steps and fall down into the cellar?* I press my body against the door to be sure I don't step back too far. If I can't stop crying, I might be locked in the dark for hours.

"Let me out, Mommy, please, please! I want to stop crying. I really want to but I can't stop till you let me out." And I hold my breath again, listening. All I hear are Mommy's footsteps walking right past the cellar door and into the living room and then up the stairs to her bedroom where she won't hear me no matter how loudly I yell.

Sometimes, if Jackie or I start to cry when Daddy is home, he just runs out the front door and doesn't come back for hours. Mommy almost never cries.

I Don't Have to Stay Here with My Stained Face

A book could swallow Mommy in one big gulp. She always read the last page first, so she'd know how it ended before she started it. But once she found a book she liked, she never looked up until she'd read it straight through. If I tried to talk to her while she was reading, she couldn't hear me. When a book swallowed Mommy, our whole house came to a complete stop. Once someone asked her how she could sit there and read a book when her house was such a mess. "How can I clean my house when there's a book to be read?" Mommy asked back.

I never saw a book swallow Daddy, but he bought books, new books, used books, old books, more books than he could ever read. Wherever we went on family trips, Daddy found a local bookstore and spent hours going through the marked-down tables. Our attic was crowded with stacks of books, cardboard boxes full of books. Daddy collected art books and back issues of *Art News* magazine. He had complete sets of the works of Dickens, Shakespeare, Thackeray, Jane Austen, the Brontë Sisters, Shakespeare, Chekhov, Dostoyevsky, Gogol, Tolstoy, Victor Hugo, and Guy de Maupassant. Daddy had nowhere to keep them properly and no idea what he owned, so he often bought the same book over and over again.

Daddy's father had taught him that education was more important than food, more important than shelter, more important even than health. In the Ukraine, Jews were barred from secular schools, forbidden to study with the gentiles. Daddy's father was determined that his American children would be educated. So Daddy bought books.

In the winter, when it was too cold to throw me out in the

backyard or onto the cellar landing, Mommy banished me to the attic "until you can stop crying." Locked up with so many books, I started to read. I escaped into other worlds, into the world of Emma Bovary, of Père Goriot, of Jane Eyre, of Silas Marner.

When I was very little, I begged Mommy to teach me to read. I wanted to know what words and letters meant. I wanted to read street signs and cereal boxes. I wanted to read the comics in the back of the newspaper and I was desperately jealous of everyone who could read them. By the time I got to kindergarten, I could sound out words. Now eight years old and in the third grade, I could read the ninth-grade books that our neighbor Debbie's brother brought home from school.

Sitting on the dusty wooden attic floor, I read until my legs, curled under me, got so numb I couldn't stand when I tried to get up. When Mommy called that I could come down now, I stayed in the attic, reading.

"She'll read anything she can get her hands on," Daddy often repeated. He said it in a way that let me know he was proud of my reading. As long as I kept reading, I didn't have to stay in Millville with my stained face. I could go away, far away, wherever a book would take me.

One of Pete's Girls

Our name is engraved in the sidewalk at the corner of High and Sassafras Streets where Grandpop's department store used to be. I bend down and trace my finger over the letters that spell "Davidow," Grandpop's name, Daddy's name, my name.

When he got old, Grandpop gave up the little department store but kept the building. The basement, which had been the shoe department, was used for storage. The first floor was rented to a woman's clothing shop, and the second floor was rented to Daddy. The entrance to Daddy's office, squeezed between two storefronts, is a wooden door with a pebbled-glass panel painted in gothic letters and a silhouette of a hand with a finger pointing upward:

J. P<small>ETER</small> D<small>AVIDOW</small>
C<small>OUNSELOR-AT-</small>L<small>AW</small>
2<small>ND</small> <small>FLOOR</small>

The reception area at the top of the steep steps has a green linoleum floor. A row of chairs waits in line outside the door to Daddy's private office. Framed paintings of young girls with enormous eyes, dark curly hair, and straw hats hang on the wall behind the chairs. Daddy says that those pretty girls look just like Jackie and me. I stare hard at the paintings trying to believe him, but I'm sure he must know that isn't true.

Daddy works in the biggest room on the floor, at the front of the building with windows facing High Street and Woolworth's Five and Ten Cent Store. The office smells like Daddy, like Old

Spice aftershave lotion and Camel cigarettes. Daddy smokes all day long. His fingers are stained dark yellow from smoking. Whenever I ask him about his yellow fingers, he says, "It's a dirty habit I picked up in the Army, a dirty, filthy habit."

He sits behind a wide desk on a leather-covered chair, the chair of a very important person, so big I have to climb onto it knees first. If I can get somebody to give me a push, I twirl around and around in it. The floor of Daddy's office is covered with a Persian carpet and the walls are decorated with diplomas and certificates with gold stamps. On one wall, he keeps a mounted deer's head, given to him by a client in exchange for legal advice. I love the deer's gentle expression, its glass eyes so calm and accepting, seeing nothing, expecting nothing. Sometimes Daddy lifts Jackie and me up so that we can take turns petting the furry nose.

If I have a special request, like extra allowance money, I have to make an appointment with Daddy. I wait in the reception area, just like a regular grown-up client, sitting under the picture of the pretty girl who really doesn't look like me, practicing what I'm going to say, until Daddy opens his door and comes out with one of his clients. "I'll be with you in just a minute," he says to me, and he walks the client out into the hall where they keep talking forever. Then he comes back into the waiting room, which is a really good name for it, because now I still have to wait some more while he talks to his secretary. Finally, he remembers me and says, "Go on in, I'll be right there." Inside Daddy's private office, I climb onto the client chair and lean over the wide desk, studying the old postcards and photographs that are stuck under the glass desktop. There's a newspaper clipping with a picture of Grandpop announcing the close of his department store, and one with a picture of Mommy announcing her engagement to Daddy. There's a picture of Daddy wearing his Army uniform, and postcard pictures of Moro Castle in Havana and the boardwalk in Atlantic City.

When Daddy comes in, I get off the desk in a hurry and sit up straight, my feet dangling high off the ground, ready to present my case to the important man in the big leather chair. "So what can I do for you?" he asks.

For eight years Daddy was Millville's magistrate, presiding over the municipal court every Monday night. He took me along to watch, hoping to inspire me to become a lawyer. Daddy looked very grand in his robes, sitting high up on the platform, banging his gavel. But I was bored, stuck there for hours listening to people get worked up over things that didn't seem worth arguing about. The bailiff decided to take me on a little tour of the courtroom and introduced me to all the lawyers, plaintiffs, and defendants. I had to shake their hands politely and watch their eyes shift from my left cheek to my right and back again.

Only in the Eyes of Strangers

I love the comic strips at the back of the *Philadelphia Evening Bulletin* and the *Daily Inquirer*. Daddy hands over the comics pages as soon as he brings the newspapers home. I always read *Brenda Starr, Girl Reporter* right away, before *L'il Abner* or *Steve Canyon* or *Rex Morgan, MD*. Brenda Starr is my idol—beautiful, courageous, and too independent to marry her boyfriend, the handsome and mysterious Basil St. John. The amazing stories Brenda Starr covers for her newspaper, *The Flash*, take her all over the world. Each story goes on day after day for weeks, and then a new one starts.

I spread the pages out on the living room floor. Lying on the blue Chinese rug, my chin in my hand, I happily settle in with a fresh story. But this time, Brenda Starr is not flying off to the tropics or some other exotic place. The world-famous girl reporter has discovered a poor little girl who hides in her house and never goes outside, because she has a big mark on her face. I look at the picture of the little girl's stained face for a long time, trying to convince myself that this little girl's mark is not the same as mine, but finally, I have to admit that it is.

Why does this little girl have to be so pathetic? Why does she have to be in the newspaper that everybody reads? What if the kids at school see the comic strip girl and think of me that way? I want to go on dreaming of myself as the fabulous Brenda Starr. I never want to be like the pathetic little girl with the tragic marked face.

I take the paper into the kitchen.

marked for life

"Mommy, I have something to show you."
"Not now, dolly. Show me after dinner."
"No, I have to show you now."
Mommy turns around, bends down to look at the paper.
"This little girl has a birthmark like mine! Well, she does, doesn't she?"
Mommy is taking too long to answer. Finally she straightens up and turns back to the stove. "Maybe it is a little bit like your birthmark."

It's just a comic strip, but it's my only source of information about my birthmark. For the rest of the week I stand on the front porch every night, leaning over the railing, watching for Daddy to come around the corner from Sassafras Street carrying his big briefcase, the newspaper tucked under his arm.

For several days the strip tells the story of the invention that would be the poor child's salvation. Lydia O'Leary had a birthmark too, like the girl in the cartoon strip, *like the man on the subway, like me.* Unlike beautiful reporter Brenda Starr, Lydia O'Leary couldn't get a good job. She had a degree in chemistry, but no one wanted to hire a woman with a birthmark from her forehead to her chin. So she worked where no one could see her, painting flower patterns on porcelain plates. One day, her brush slipped, and she fixed the mistake by painting over it, covering a darker color with a lighter one. A lightbulb flashed over her head! Why wouldn't this work with her birthmark? She found a way to cover her dark purple stain with a lighter flesh tone and she called her invention Covermark. It was the first cosmetic to be granted a U.S. patent.

In the next day's cartoon strip, Brenda Starr, triumphantly bearing a jar of Covermark, rescues the little girl by covering her birthmark with makeup. The last frame shows the girl beaming, her face clear and radiant. No longer pathetic, she leaves her house, looking normal at last.

I run to show the comic strip to Mommy. I want to wear Covermark makeup, too.

⁓

Mommy sits at her vanity dresser, where she stores the mysteries of womanhood—lipsticks, nail polish, fragrant bottles and jars—and in the bottom drawer, a stack of neatly folded Kotex. When I ask her what they are, Mommy tells me she uses them to set her hair in a pageboy style.

"Mommy, look! Brenda Starr showed this girl how to cover her birthmark with makeup! Why can't I do that? Am I too young to wear makeup to school?"

From its hiding place behind the Kotex pads, Mommy brings out the Lydia O'Leary Covermark set she bought when I was a baby—a pink plastic jar of flesh-colored makeup, smaller jars of white and brown for blending, and a cardboard box full of white powder. Mommy studies the directions. Slowly, she begins to work on my face, patting and pressing the thick pigment onto my cheek and eyelid with her fingertips.

She tells me to keep checking in the mirror until I am satisfied that the stain is covered. Blending the colors on the back of her hand, she pats layer after layer of makeup on my cheek and around my eye. She dips a cotton ball into the cardboard box and blankets my face with a great blizzard of white powder. We have to wait for ten minutes while the powder sets before she can brush off the excess and sponge my face with water for a "natural" finish.

I run to the mirror, hoping to see a beautiful princess, but I look like I'm wearing a Halloween mask, disguised as a ghost. So Mommy adds some of her own rouge and eyebrow pencil.

"Mommy, I look more horrible than ever! If I smile, my face will crack!"

Mommy sits quietly.

marked for life

"That's why I never showed it to you," she says. "You're not ready to wear makeup yet. You can wear it when you get older, if you want to."

In the bathroom at the end of the hall, I wash my face, scrubbing hard with a cloth to take off all the makeup. Then I go into my room and lay down on my bed, paralyzed with disappointment.

Why didn't it work? Why didn't I look like the comic strip girl? When I get older I'll have a choice of looking like a strange lady with a big purple stain on her face or a strange lady who wears thick, awful makeup.

⌒⌒⌒

Jackie and I play with the other girls who live on our block. Jackie plays with Ruthie, who lives next door to Mr. Brandriff. I play with Debbie, who lives on the corner. We screw roller skates to the soles of our shoes with keys we wear around our necks. We play jacks and jump rope and hopscotch on the sidewalk. We never play with boys, although boys play with us. Boys are nasty creatures who get into fights on the playground, who tease and torture girls. Ruthie's older brother offered to take us for a ride in his toy wagon, then let go of the handle and watched us roll downhill screaming. He hid behind his fence and sprayed us with the garden hose as we walked by. Boys call me Bride of Frankenstein, Grape Juice Face, and Purple People Eater. They are not nice.

I have play friends and one real friend, my first best friend. Her name is Louise, but she calls herself Weezer. And my name is Josephine, but I call myself Joie, spelled J-o-i-e because J-o-e-y is a boy's name.

We both have curly dark hair and we both wear pretty skirts and blouses or dresses to school. We are the same size, so short we stand next to each other at the front of the room when the class lines up in order of height. Weezer has cute little freckles on her face and I have a big ugly birthmark on mine, but we are alike enough to see ourselves in each other.

We save our allowances and buy matching silver friendship rings at Woolworth's. After school, we go to my house or her house to play paper dolls or Monopoly. Weezer's mother makes tuna casserole, macaroni and cheese—dishes we never have at home. When I tell Daddy what I've eaten at Weezer's house, he screws up his face and says, "*Goyishe molchulem, chozzerei*— gentile food." But I know it's just regular American food.

Late at night, when I get out of bed to stare at my face in the mirror, I think that Weezer must be the most generous girl in the world to have chosen me as her best friend. I can't imagine why anyone would want to look at me long enough to carry on a conversation. I need to know how horrible my face is and Weezer is the only person I can ask. I practice the words, but I can't say them to her. I can't even say the word "birthmark" out loud, can't mention the thing Mommy has taught me I have to ignore.

No one talks about it in our house. Everybody knows it's wrong to make a Big Deal. Daddy, who says the same things a zillion times, never says even one word about my marked face. Now I'm going to make a Big Deal about it with Weezer, and I'm very ashamed, but I can't help it, I just have to know how I look to other people. As we walk toward her house after school, the question repeats and repeats in my head until I can't hold it in anymore and it escapes from my mouth. Then I freeze.

"I just don't see it." Weezer says. "Maybe the first time I met you, I saw it, but that was when we were in kindergarten, so I don't really remember. It's like it's not there."

It's like it's not there! How can that be true?

Weezer might have said that just to be nice. I asked the question out loud once. I can do it again.

The next day, while we're tightening our roller skates, I ask Debbie. Blond, beautiful Debbie is not a girl who would lie to spare my feelings. "I guess I got used to it," she says. "I don't see it unless you point it out to me."

I decide to trust this truth. It's easier to go to school believing that my birthmark is visible only to strangers.

A Birthmark Proves You've Been Born

Mommy's belly started to get bigger. I stared in the mirror, not at my face, but at my own little tummy, imagining, hoping that mine was growing, too, that I might have a baby in my belly like Mommy.

At school, I announced during Show and Tell that my mother was pregnant and my third-grade teacher, Mrs. Riley, was so shocked she sent home a note.

"What did I say wrong?" I asked Mommy.

"Little girls aren't supposed to know words like 'pregnant.' They want you to say that the stork is coming to your house," she told me. "Don't pay attention. It's stupid. Storks don't bring babies. If a husband and a wife love each other, a baby grows in the wife's belly."

Just because they love each other?

I didn't get it. I couldn't understand how the husband had anything to do with the baby. As far as I could tell, that meant Daddy wasn't actually related to us at all, which meant I wasn't related to that nasty old grandmother.

Mommy couldn't give birth in a Millville hospital, couldn't trust the small-town doctors. In the final weeks of her pregnancy, she moved in with Grandmom and Evie. When the baby was two weeks old, Jackie and I went to Philadelphia with Daddy to meet our new little sister. Mommy met us at the door and Daddy gave her a long, passionate kiss on the lips. I was amazed to see my own parents locked in what Jackie called a "television kiss." They never touched each other at all in front of us. Sometimes Daddy put his hand on Mommy's head, and she'd say, "Cut it out, Pete." And sometimes, Mommy tried to

marked for life

put her arms around Daddy, but he'd pull away from her and say, "Not in front of the *kinder*." I had never seen them kiss before.

⌒

The curtains are closed because the baby is sleeping. Jackie and I stand at the door. We really want to see the baby, but we're afraid of getting too close. Mommy says we're allowed to look but not touch and no talking.

We tiptoe up to the crib. "Hello, baby," I whisper. "Hello, new sister." I was supposed to have been Joseph, not Josephine. When Mommy went to the hospital to have Jackie, she told me she was going to bring home a baby boy named Jonathan. This time, Mommy and Daddy said we were going to have a brother, for sure. But we got Julianne instead, with white-blond hair. She doesn't even look like us.

She's much smaller than my baby doll, and she has a funny thing coming out of her belly button that reminds me of yellow poop. "*That's* it?" I whisper to Jackie. "That's the baby?" I can't find a birthmark anywhere, not one purple patch on her body. *She must have one under her diaper.* Grandmom says everybody has a birthmark somewhere. She says a birthmark proves you've been born.

⌒

When the baby first came home, she was really boring. We had to be quiet all the time because she was always sleeping. Except at night. As soon as I fell asleep, she woke up screaming. I ran into the back bedroom and talked to the baby in her bassinet. "Shhh. It's okay. Go back to sleep." Then Mommy showed up and told me I was the one who should go back to sleep. If the baby wouldn't stop crying, no matter what time it was, Mommy called Grandmom in Philadelphia and put the phone to the baby's ear. "I got a girl in Baltimore. She got carpets on the floor." Grandmom sang the song she learned in Bessarabia and the baby fell asleep.

After a while, Mommy said she just couldn't stand to stay home any longer. If she couldn't go back to her job in Philadelphia, she could at least go around the corner and work with Daddy. She would be close by and we could call her—but only in a real emergency. She hired Mrs. Ralph Lee to take care of Julie and watch over Jackie and me when we came home from school. Lee-Lee was a widow, a grandmother who kept her gray hair short like Grandmom and wore loose, tailored dresses and heavy black lace-up shoes like our school principal. I loved her because she was kind and fair and a great Monopoly player. She taught me the importance of buying Baltic and Mediterranean Avenues early in the game.

Now instead of coming home at lunchtime, like most of the other kids, I got to walk downtown to the sandwich shop owned by a man everyone called Nick the Greek. I felt very grown up and liberated sitting in an old wooden booth at Nick's with Susie Dobson, one of the few girls at school whose mother also worked. Every school day we split a grilled cheese sandwich and a black and white milkshake made with vanilla ice cream and chocolate syrup. And every school day Nick teased us and gave us extra potato chips for free.

The Saturday before Christmas, Weezer and I are sitting on chairs outside the door to Daddy's office. I have come to collect my Christmas shopping money. Mommy says that Christmas is a national holiday. She thinks it's mean to deprive Jewish kids of Christmas. We have a tree and presents, but we celebrate at Grandmom's house with Evie and Uncle Artie and Uncle Leon, and all of our cousins. Mommy says that everybody in Millville doesn't need to know we have a Christmas tree.

marked for life

Weezer and I wait for a very long time. When Daddy finally opens the door, his face looks bad.

He is usually too busy with important work to pay much attention to me, but he always has time to be charming to anyone outside the family. This time, he hardly notices us. He just hands me five dollars without demanding any explanation other than my plea for spending money, without even teasing Weezer.

Holding hands, Weezer and I walk down High Street to the big new five-and-ten-cent store, Grant City. I keep seeing the bad look on Daddy's face, but I'm fighting it. I have to concentrate on my Christmas shopping. Millville is called the Holly City. At Christmas, High Street is decorated with branches from the holly farms outside town, and arches of colored lights. Speakers outside the stores play "I Saw Mommy Kissing Santa Claus." The plastic pin I'm wearing on my winter coat is in the shape of Santa's head, and when I pull the little string, the nose glows bright red. I don't want Daddy's bad face to ruin my Christmas spirit.

I have a shopping list folded up in my pocket, but it's very hard to decide what to buy each person and how much to spend, especially because I've just started to learn subtraction and I'm really bad at it.

Weezer and I take a lot of time, circling two counters full of cheap gifts—tiny bottles of perfume in glittery boxes, folding paper fans, plastic jewelry, all Made in Japan. I pick things up, carry them around for a while, look some more, change my mind, put them back again. I want to buy Grandmom a wooden box with a picture of a pagoda painted on the top, but it costs three dollars, and I have only five dollars altogether.

I pick out a pink cotton handkerchief with an orchid printed on it for Mommy and a white handkerchief embroidered with a red initial "D" for Daddy. I find a plastic rattle for the baby, earrings for Evie, and erasers shaped like animals for Jackie.

Weezer and I huddle in the corner of the store and add everything up, checking each other's addition, to make sure. I think I have enough money, but I'm still scared when we get to the cash register. Grandmom's box is the most expensive gift I've ever given anybody.

On the way home, I start to worry about Daddy's bad face again. I open the front door. "I got all my presents!" Nobody answers.

Mommy is sitting at the telephone table in the dining room, crying into the receiver in a way I've never heard anybody cry before. "Oh no!" she keeps wailing, "Oh no!" It's only four o'clock, but Daddy is already home. He is standing with his head down, talking out loud to nobody. "I just didn't have the courage to tell her," he says. "I just didn't have the courage."

I stand next to Mommy, still clutching the big bag from Grant City in one hand, stroking Mommy's arm with the other, waiting for her to hang up so I can ask her: "Mommy, why are you crying? Who were you talking to?"

"Grandmom died."

Uncle Artie called Daddy at the office while I was waiting with Weezer. He asked Daddy to tell Mommy, but Daddy just didn't have the courage, so Artie had to call the house and tell Mommy himself. Grandmom had another heart attack that afternoon and died, sitting in her favorite chair.

Mommy is crying so hard I'm afraid she might have a heart attack, too. Jackie is on the floor, screaming and banging her arms and legs. She had a fight with Grandmom just last week. Now she'll never be able to say she was sorry.

I am crying, too, but this time, Mommy doesn't send us up to the attic. This time, even Daddy is crying.

I'm still holding my bag of Christmas presents from Grant City. I don't know what to do to make Mommy feel better. So I show her the wooden box with the pagoda painted on the lid.

"Do you think she would like it?"

"She would love it. Grandmom loved you very, very much."
"What should I do with it now?"
"Keep it, Dolly. Every time you look at it you'll think of her."

I kept it for years. I kept it until it fell apart, and then I kept the pile of painted wooden sticks.

───

Until Grandmom died, I didn't know that the people I needed and loved wouldn't be there forever. People could die without warning. Anybody could be dead from one minute to the next, just like Grandmom. If Mommy's mother could die, my mother could die, too. I needed to know where Mommy was all the time to be sure she wasn't dead.

I had nightmares every night. I dreamt that my bed was crawling with bugs. Even when I woke up, the bugs were still there, covering the sheets. I ran down the hall and knocked on the door to Mommy and Daddy's room. They slept in twin beds pushed together to make one big bed. Sometimes Jackie was already sleeping with them by the time I got there, so I'd lie down in the crack between their two beds. As soon as I got in bed next to Mommy, the nightmare disappeared and I was safe; I laid in the dark and watched her chest move up and down, listening to be sure she was breathing.

The Voice Has Me

I stand in front of the mirror, pretending to be one of the singers on the *Voice of Firestone* television program. "Aaaaah . . . sweeeet . . . mystery of life, at last I've found you!" I mouth the words, lift my arms in grand operatic gestures. I'm wearing long white gloves and a floor-length silver gown. My hair is piled on top of my head in a chignon and diamond earrings dangle to my shoulders. I don't have a big ugly birthmark on my face. I am beautiful. I am glamorous. I am famous. I am Roberta Peters. I am Risë Stevens. I am Patrice Munsel. My voice is big, powerful—like an opera singer's. Jackie runs into the dining room and back out to the front porch. "Mommy, Joie's making faces in the mirror again!" Jackie is a big pain. "Cut it out, Joie," Mommy calls to me. "Everybody's waiting in the car for you."

Mommy took me to see the movie *The Great Caruso* starring Mario Lanza. When the great Caruso was just a little boy, his dying mother told him, "God gave you a great gift and you should use it." If only God would give me a voice, I would use it, treasure it, sacrifice for it, like the great Caruso. "I don't have the voice. The voice has me," the great Caruso keeps saying. "I don't have the voice. The voice has me." My voice could have me! I would be like a nun, devoted to my voice. I begged Mommy for singing lessons.

marked for life

On Sundays, Nancy Johnson was a soloist with the choir at the First Presbyterian Church. From Monday through Friday she was an executive secretary at the Wheaton Glass Company, and on Saturdays she gave singing lessons in her living room. Since her divorce, she had lived with her mother in a two-story unit at the Charlene Village Garden Apartments, where there were no gardens at all.

Starting when I was in the fifth grade, Mommy dropped me off there every Saturday morning. Nancy sat at her piano in the same outfit, week after week—red corduroy capri pants, a black and white striped T-shirt, and flat black shoes. She was young and attractive, her dark straight hair cut in a bob. We sang simple exercises to warm up the voice, and we spent the rest of the lesson working on a song. We worked on only two songs a year, one for each of the two student recitals Nancy held at the Presbyterian Church.

Nancy always ended the sacred recitals by singing the Lord's Prayer. The program read, "The Lord's Prayer will be rendered by Nancy Johnson, Contralto." I thought it looked very important and professional, very artistic, better than Nancy Johnson, Ph.D., or Nancy Johnson, M.D., or even Nancy Johnson, Girl Reporter.

She stood on a platform in the middle of the congregation, closed her eyes, and started singing very softly. "Ow-uh fah-thuh. Who art in heh-vehn." Little by little, she sang louder and louder until her deep, dark contralto voice thundered out, "And Thine is the kingdom, and the pow-uh and the glow-ree, FOR EH-VUH!" Then suddenly, almost whispering, "Ah-ah men." At the exact moment when she sang the "men" part of "amen," the church bell in the steeple began to ring, and all the people in the audience—except for Mommy and Daddy—thought it was "very moving."

My first assignment was "Brahms Lullaby," which is not

really sacred, but solved the problem of what to give a Jewish girl to sing at the Presbyterian Church. On the Sunday afternoon of the recital, we were told to meet in the vestry. I had no idea what a vestry was, but it turned out to be a dressing room, with long closets full of choir robes. All Nancy's students wore their best birthday-party dresses or suits to the vestry room, only to have to hide them under long dark red robes. Nancy handed out mimeographed programs with our names and the names of our songs, so we would know when it was our turn to sing. It made me very nervous to see my name there in print, "Josephine Davidow," even without "contralto" or "soprano" after it. People in the audience would be expecting something from me, something good. This wasn't just making faces in the mirror, or rehearsing in Nancy's living room. People would be listening—a lot of people. I wasn't so worried about my birthmark. But I was very worried about singing well. If I couldn't look beautiful, maybe I could sound beautiful. Lots of people had pretty faces, but only a few people had really pretty voices.

Nancy told us to line up single file in the order in which we were to sing, and we silently marched into the choir loft. We stood facing the congregation, until we were all filed in—then we could be seated.

From the choir loft I look out over the church. *So this is "the sanctuary."* It looks very old and very grand. The soaring vaulted ceiling reminds me of King Arthur and the Knights of the Round Table. All around the sanctuary enormous stained-glass windows filter the afternoon light through panes of brilliant blue, ruby red, and gold. *No wonder they call this the House of God.* I look out at the congregation. Mothers and fathers and brothers and sisters fill the polished wooden pews, expecting something, something good. *What am I doing in this great Protestant castle, facing all these people?* I lower my head so that I can sneak a peek at the other children out of the corners of my eyes. They don't look nervous. Maybe a little bored. *It's only me. I'm the only one who is petrified.*

Mr. Walden Cox is seated at the church organ, waiting for us to begin. I know Mr. Cox. His wife was my kindergarten teacher. He's short and bald. I shouldn't be afraid of nice Mr. Cox, but I am. How can such a little man play such a big pipe organ? It's at least three stories high.

Each of the children stands up in turn and sings a song, but I'm not listening. I'm trying to remember the words to the "Brahms Lullaby." I know I can't do it, can't stand up and smile and sing, like the other children. There are only four children ahead of me. Only three. Only two. The girl next to me finishes her song and sits down. She looks very pleased with herself. I hate her.

I grip the brass railing of the choir loft and pull myself up. Mr. Cox plays the introduction. The enormous pipe organ sounds like the Lord Himself, roaring at me. It fills the sanctuary, all the way up to the top of the high, high vaulted ceiling. *How will my little voice be heard over that bellowing sound?* Mr. Cox plays the introduction again. My mouth is frozen shut.

Nancy Johnson, sitting below us in the first pew, hurriedly changes her position so that she is directly in front of me. She gives me encouraging little nods and smiles. Mr. Cox turns on his bench and looks up at me. He plays the introduction a third time. Nancy Johnson is making frantic lifting motions with her arms. The sleeves of her choir robe are flapping like the wings of a big red bird, trying to get off the ground.

Maybe I could just sit down. Maybe I could trample over the legs and feet of the children in the row beside me, escape back to the vestry, and hide in the closet. But Nancy Johnson is looking straight at me. Mommy and Daddy and Jackie and Julie are all there, waiting for me to sing, expecting something, something good.

My voice sounds thin and creaky. "Luh-uh-luh. Bah-ee." After a couple of measures, Mr. Cox catches up with me. The lullaby is long, so long. Two long verses, but I keep singing one note after the other. And then it's over. "May thy sluh-uh-uh-uhm-buhr . . . beeblessed." It's a sacred recital, so there's no applause. Probably, I would have just gotten "boos."

My knees collapse and my tush is back on the bench. Sunk below the rail of the choir loft, I stare at my feet and try not to cry while the rest of the children fearlessly sail through their numbers.

Back in the vestry I get rid of my choir robe as fast as I can, without looking at anybody. As we're leaving the church one of the other fathers tells Daddy, "She didn't do too bad once she got started." I hope nobody else will say anything, especially not to me, but Jackie says, "You looked like you were really scared, Jo. You were really scared. Weren't you? Weren't you?"

For my second recital appearance, six months later, I was assigned a setting of "Christopher Robin is saying his prayers," from *Winnie-the-Pooh* by A. A. Milne. This time I was not going to freeze up again. This time I was going to be like the Great Caruso. "I don't have the voice. The voice has me." I practiced and I practiced, and one day, I knew that if I just sang the words, I wouldn't be afraid. After all, Christopher Robin wasn't scared. He was just saying his prayers.

Josephine Davidow, the girl with the purple-stained face, was not in the choir loft that day. Christopher Robin had taken her place. I imitated the picture on the cover of the sheet music— sweet little Christopher, kneeling by the side of his bed, his hands clasped, his head bent. When I sang "If I open my fingers a little bit more, I can see Nanny's dressing-gown on the door," I spread my fingers and concentrated so hard I really saw Nanny's dressing gown. "It's a beautiful blue, but it hasn't a hood. Oh!" I sang, as if suddenly remembering, "God bless Nanny and key-eep her good."

I was the hit of the recital. This time, when we were leaving the church, the other parents told Mommy and Daddy, "She's quite a little actress." After that, all I ever wanted to do was sing.

Beautiful Queen Esther

The Beth Hillel synagogue was a plain square brick building, not at all grand like the Presbyterian Church. The sanctuary was just a room with two rows of wooden benches and a platform where the torah was kept. On either side, stained-glass windows depicted lions holding the Ten Commandments, which were engraved in Hebrew on stone tablets. There was a little balcony at the back of the room. Nobody ever went up there during services, but it was a good place to play. Mommy told me that the women used to have to sit in the balcony behind a curtain so that the men couldn't see them while they were praying. A big basement room with a stage was used for meetings of the B'nai Brith and the Sisterhood, and for Saturday-morning Hebrew lessons.

We had to get all dressed up to go sit in that little square building. In September, when Mommy bought us clothes for school, we also got fancy new outfits for the High Holidays. Yom Kippur was a fashion show at the Beth Hillel synagogue. The women wore the very best clothes they could afford—wool suits, silk dresses with matching hats and shoes and purses—and, if at all possible, a fur. Any piece of fur a woman owned came out of the closet for Yom Kippur, no matter how hot it was that day. *Faygeleh* Miller, Bea the *Tschotschkeleh* Friedman, Ada Abrahms, Harriet Ackerman—all the women who worked in their husband's stores on High Street day after day—turned into glamorous ladies for the holidays. I loved to watch them make their entrances, walking down the aisle, all done up and perfumed, winking and nodding at their friends. I loved whispering with Mommy about what the other women were wearing.

Otherwise, it was torture. We had to keep standing up and then sitting back down on those hard wooden benches for hours and hours, while the men swayed and prayed in a language I didn't understand. I tried to keep from going crazy by reading along in the English translation, but even that didn't make much sense to me.

There was no pipe organ and no choir. The Beth Hillel congregation was too small to afford a full-time cantor to sing the Hebrew songs and chants. But on the High Holidays, somebody was hired to come from Philadelphia or New York City. Sometimes he had a horrible voice, but sometimes he sang very nicely. When it was the congregation's turn to join in, I sang out, pretending to know the Hebrew words, faking it with all the other kids.

Mommy's father, the socialist intellectual, had been opposed to organized religion. He never allowed his children to set foot in a synagogue. Mommy told us that religion was for people who were too stupid to behave honestly and ethically, so they had to be scared into it with stories of heaven and hell. But she didn't want to embarrass Daddy by staying away from the synagogue, which would have been a disaster in Millville. Being Jewish was bad enough. Nobody would have trusted a lawyer whose wife had no religion at all. Mommy even joined the Sisterhood and baked sponge cakes for their monthly dinner meetings in the synagogue basement.

Although she had no faith in organized religion, she firmly embraced Jewish culture. She thought we should know about our Jewish heritage, so for a while, Jackie and I went to Hebrew school on Saturday mornings. Round, pretty Miss Nathan, who was my fourth-grade teacher, taught the class in the synagogue basement. We learned to sound out Hebrew letters without understanding what any of the words meant, and we read about the history of our culture in a book called *When the Jewish People Was Young*. The title bothered me. I thought it should be *When the Jewish People <u>Were</u> Young*. I imagined that it must have been written by someone with a Yiddish accent. *"Ven de Jush Pipple Vas Yungk."* It was just a story about shepherds in the desert, without any information about the bad things I'd heard of like pogroms, Hitler, and Atlantic City hotels that didn't admit Jews. Maybe those things happened later, *When the Jewish People Was Old*, or at least middle-aged.

At first I was glad to have something to say back to Weezer, who was always talking about what she did at her Lutheran Sunday school. "We have Sunday school, too," I could say. "We just go to it on Saturdays, instead." I was afraid that the few interesting things we did, like making little paper baskets to hold dried breadfruit and dates from Israel for the holiday Shavuot, would seem too weird to Weezer. She always needed a long explanation when I tried to tell her about them. Whoever heard of dried breadfruit, anyway? I couldn't possibly explain to her what it was, let alone get into the story of Shavuot. I could barely pronounce it.

At Beth Hillel, the boys had Bar Mitzvahs but there were no Bat Mitzvahs for girls, who were deprived of the big payoff for learning all those meaningless Hebrew letters. Mommy understood that I needed my Saturday mornings for ballet classes and for singing lessons with Nancy Johnson, so I dropped out. But not before I got my chance to play Beautiful Queen Esther.

―――

Each year, to celebrate the holiday Purim, the children of Beth Hillel put on a play in the synagogue basement. The heroine of the story, and star of the show, was Beautiful Queen Esther, who had been chosen in ancient times to become the wife of the King of Persia. The king was looking for a queen, so he held a contest, something like the Miss America Pageant. Esther was so beautiful that the king chose her as his bride over all the other girls in the land, even though she was Jewish. And like Miss America, she was more than just beautiful. She was a very brave and clever girl who saved the Jews from Wicked-Wicked Haman, the king's chief advisor.

With so few Jewish girls in Millville, I knew it was just a matter of time until my turn came. The only other Jewish girls my age were twins. They couldn't pick just one of them, so they had to pick me. But I still clung to the hope that, like Beautiful Queen Esther, I had actually been chosen because I was the prettiest.

My costume was a lavender dress with a satin bodice and a skirt made from layers of net sprinkled with glitter so that it looked like dewy flower petals. I had already worn the dress at a ballet recital, but I had no trouble believing it was Beautiful Queen Esther's royal robe. I didn't mind wearing it again. I deeply longed to wear it every day. As Beautiful Queen Esther, I also got to wear a silver foil crown and carry a cardboard scepter. For one night, Miss Grape Juice Face, Bride of Frankenstein, Purple People Eater would be a beautiful queen.

Two days before the Purim play I started to feel sick. It was the worst thing that could have possibly happened to me. I tried to hide it from Mommy, but on the night when I should have been appearing onstage, I was throwing up in the toilet and running a high fever. I knew that I had missed my turn forever. Next year, some other little girl would be chosen to play Beautiful Queen Esther.

As soon as I got better, Mommy and Daddy tried to console me by taking a picture of me in my Beautiful Queen Esther costume. They didn't have a flash camera so the picture had to be taken outside, and since Purim falls in early spring, it was cold. They made me hide my royal lavender gown under my old winter coat. I wasn't even allowed to take it off just for a minute because I might get sick again.

I looked more like a disgruntled little girl with a foil crown on her head than a beautiful queen. But at least Beautiful Queen Esther doesn't have a birthmark in that picture, because I already knew how to pose.

My school pictures were taken almost in profile, hiding the birthmark. Year after year, the photographer said, "Turn your head all the way to the left. Now look just a little bit back at me. That's it. Show me your good side. Right there. Now smile!"

I learned to stand that way, sit that way, always at an angle, until without thinking, I kept my head tilted down and to the side, never looked strangers in the eye, never made them see my birthmark.

Just Ignore Them

I wasn't the only freak at Culver Elementary School. Phyllis wore braces on her polio-stricken legs. She'd even done time in an iron lung. But her parents made it up to her. They gave her a swimming pool, a canopy bed, the prettiest clothes, and the most elaborate dolls. I'd kill to get invited to play at her house.

Two of the boys in my class had accents. The sons of war brides, they spent summers with their grandparents in England. Their crisp pronunciation jarred the ears of kids who'd learned how to talk in South Jersey, where every vowel was a diphthong. Whenever the English boys said "bean" instead of "been" and "a gain" instead of "again," the rest of the class roared with laughter.

Fat Lou Ann was always the brunt of jokes, so she tried too hard to be likeable, which just made her obnoxious. She had a fat mother and a fat father and when the other kids made fun of her whole fat family, she got really upset. Mommy liked to use Lou Ann as an example whenever I made a Big Deal about the birthmark. "Lou Ann is fat; you have a birthmark. Everybody has something," she said. But Lou Ann had hope. She could lose weight. I couldn't do anything to loose the birthmark. Fat was understandable. Lots of people were fat. No one had a purple face but me.

One of the girls was so poor she wore the same dirty blouse and skirt to school every day. Even in the dead of winter she wore her beat-up loafers without socks. You didn't want to sit next to her because she looked like she never washed her hair and smelled like she peed in her panties. She had black rings under her nails and black splinters in most of her fingers. On

Monday mornings, when we handed in our weekly milk money, the poor girl never had the twenty-five cents we all brought from home. She got excused before the lunch bell rang so she could earn her milk by working in the kitchen. When the class had to join hands in a circle, nobody wanted to stand next to her because she obviously had cooties. The other kids shoved me next to her. "Let Purple Face get cooties." The girl's hands were so rough they felt like cardboard.

The relentless teasing I endured, the name calling, didn't make me a bit more tolerant of other kids. I joined right in when somebody else was getting it. I knew how wrong it was. I knew how much it hurt to be tormented. I felt guilty, but I did it anyway, because I was desperate to be included and because it felt good to be the one doing the teasing for a change.

In the sixth grade a brother and sister moved to Millville from some other town. They were the weirdest kids any of us had ever seen, very thin and very white, without a lick of color in their skin. They both had black, stringy hair. The boy wore his plastered to his head and the girl wore hers like Olive Oyl, which was one of the names we gave her. They were black and white kids with black and white clothes. The girl always wore a white blouse and a black skirt; the boy, a white shirt and black pants.

He got the worst of the teasing. None of us had ever met a really effeminate boy before. We knew tough boys who were terrors on the playground. We knew boys who were good at sports and we knew a couple of boys who were nerdy, but we had never met a boy who talked like a girl. The other boys never stopped calling him a sissy. When they knocked his books out of his arms, his sister stood quietly beside him and helped him pick them up. She never said very much. I knew their lives were a living hell, so sometimes I talked nicely with the sister, but only if none of the other girls were around to catch me.

The school social hierarchy was no longer organized around

coupled-off best friends. Having one friend, my steadfast Weezer, wasn't enough to protect me. Girls ran around in cliques now, and I fit in nowhere. I was called the Purple Cow. In my prepubescence I had been transformed from a kid so skinny Daddy used to say he was going to cut me down for a weed, to a tubby girl with a potbelly and buckteeth. Mommy and Daddy were both busy being lawyers, so they had gotten into the habit of taking us to Howard Johnson's for dinner almost every night. For months I lived on HoJo's hot roast beef sandwiches with mashed potatoes and gravy, and brownies with vanilla ice cream and hot fudge sauce.

So the other kids had something new to tease me about. I wasn't just ugly; I was fat, too. Some kids sang out "Here comes the Purple Cow" whenever I was in earshot. Some made low "moo" noises. When I complained to Mommy, she told me to "just ignore them," so I always looked straight ahead and kept walking. But I wasn't just ignoring them; I was ignoring the hurt, too. I wasn't just pretending the other kids weren't there; I was also pretending that I didn't feel bad about myself, that I didn't feel fat, disfigured, and ugly.

It's Friday afternoon, one minute after the final bell, and the whole school is crowding the doors that lead to the playground. The sixth-grade girls are bunched together in a giggling clump. They are the coolest kids in school, and they know it. I am standing on the edge of the clump, eavesdropping, pretending to be part of the clique. The weird black and white kids are the last to come down the steps. They stand there, in back of the crowd, hesitating, not daring to plunge in. One girl raises her curly blond head from the tangle of sixth-graders and spots them. "Here comes the fairy!" And I am pushed aside, as the girls stampede the black and white boy, knock him around, and make him drop his books on the gray-painted cement floor.

They'd never dare to do that to any of the other boys, or even any of the other girls. A boy might beat them up. A girl might scratch their cheeks and pull their hair. But they know that this weird girlie boy won't fight.

He doesn't raise a hand to defend himself. But he lifts a finger, wagging it at the girls, scolding. "That's not very nice!"

"That's not very nice!" his sister echoes.

The girls lisp back at them, mimicking. "That's not very nice! That's not very nice!" And I'm there, too, pretending to be one of them.

The weird boy spies me among his tormentors. "You, of all people!" he said. "You should know better!"

He's right. The other girls have had their fun and now they scatter, running out onto the playground, laughing. But I can't run with them. He has singled me out. I don't have a chance of melting into the group now. I know I'll hear "The Purple Cow should have known better," over and over again for days.

I bend down to help him pick up his things, muttering, "I'm sorry, those girls are stupid," trying to distance myself from them, feeling like a little hypocrite. "Thank you," he says, amazed, and I understand that no one but his sister has ever helped him before. "It's okay," I say. "You should just ignore them when they tease you."

The movers came to Second Street while I was at school. Before I left the house for the last time, I walked through the rooms and said good-bye. I said good-bye to the living room where I once lay all day on the sofa, crying after Mommy chopped off my long braids. She did it because I screamed every morning when she combed out the tangles. But she had cut off my veil of hair and I couldn't hide my face behind it anymore. I said good-bye to the dining room where Grandmom once sat at the table, teaching me gypsy card tricks. Grandmom was dead and I'd never live in that house again.

I came home to a house that Mommy and Daddy had built in a new development near the lake. It was a much bigger house with a much bigger backyard. Mommy had designed it herself. If she had to spend the rest of her life stuck in Millville, at least she'd have a really nice house. Our furniture was all there, and the rugs were on the floor, but the familiar, comforting clutter was missing. Mommy was sitting on the floor staring into the fireplace. Beside her were packets of letters, tied with ribbons, love letters Daddy had written while they were separated during the war. One by one she threw them into the fire and watched them burn. "That part of my life is over now," she said.

It was impossible for me to imagine Daddy writing love letters to Mommy. At the office it was easy to tell that they were partners, working on the same cases. But at home they were always bickering, arguing—not romantic at all.

It seemed to me that Daddy just made our lives less fun. Mommy could laugh until she cried. She came home from the office and stood working at the stove, still wearing her hat, jumping and kicking her legs, doing what she called the "kitchen dance." Daddy never did anything like that. We had to be careful to stay out of his way because Mommy said he was "under a lot of pressure." "Try not to do anything to upset your father," she told us.

Daddy was very proud of Mommy. At the dinner table he often repeated, "Your mother is a very bright woman. She's a tremendous help to me in the office." Mommy always rolled her eyes and made a face. She said she was a lawyer. She didn't like the idea of being Daddy's helper.

I no longer raced across the street to slide into the girl's door at Culver Elementary School just as the last bell rang. Now I took a bus to Bacon Junior High School. I wasn't a little girl anymore. I was twelve years old. I had my own bus pass and my own locker. At Culver Elementary School, all the teachers had known me since kindergarten. At the new school there were students and teachers who had never seen me before. I had to answer *the questions* again. I wasn't surprised by those questions anymore. I expected them and I was ready with answers. No, it's not a burn; it's not a scar; it's a birthmark. No, it doesn't hurt. No, it isn't going to go away. Strange boys called me Scar Face, Purple Face, Grape Juice Face. I'd shot up and slimmed down, but I looked worse than ever, because there were braces on my teeth, and I had to wear glasses to see the blackboard.

The "nice" girls, whose fathers were "professional people," formed a tight little clique. I followed them around, carefully copied their uniform—ponytail, saddle shoes, white socks, straight skirts, cardigan sweaters worn buttoned up the back. I tried to sit with them at lunch. They made room for me, but they paid more attention to the ketchup bottle.

At school dances, the girls sat in a line of folding chairs, and the boys sat opposite them in another line. Sometimes I danced a "fast dance" with another girl, but most of the evening, I just sat there, waiting, as the boys crossed the room and held out their hands to every girl in the line except me. I watched jealously when a boy danced with a girl he really liked, closing his eyes and burying his nose in her neck, whispering her name. I wondered if any boy could ever feel that way about me, could ever look at my purple-stained face as though it was the most adorable thing in the world.

I scanned the row of boys for a victim I could pounce on when "Lady's Choice" was announced, somebody too nice to say "No thank you." It took all the courage I had to ask a boy to dance, but I had to do it, or what would I tell Mommy when she wanted to know who had danced with me? I couldn't duck out early because Mommy and Daddy were always waiting in the car. I didn't want Jackie and Julie to know their big sister was a dog. So I dressed up and went to the dances, and I kept my shame to myself.

All's Right with the World

I found refuge in the classroom of the music teacher, Miss Nau, a skinny young woman with a Buster Brown haircut and thick glasses.

Most people in Millville thought classical music meant Liberace or Mantovani and His 101 Strings. They enjoyed listening to something called semi-classical, which meant anything played on a grand piano or by an orchestra, like Broadway musicals, or even the music on *The Lawrence Welk Show*. But Miss Nau knew what real classical music was.

She told us that composers of classical music were all geniuses, and that the musicians who played this music were all near-geniuses. Only one person in many millions was capable of composing classical music, she said, and only about one in a million was capable of really playing it well. When she taught us about opera, she told us that the operatic voice was a freak of nature, a rare combination of facial cavities and muscles that revealed itself late in puberty. I was devastated. What chance did I have against odds like that?

But because Mommy had taught me to read music, in Miss Nau's glee club I was a section leader, and because I had a "strong voice," I was a soloist. I was even excused from the humiliation of mandatory lunchtime basketball games, so that I could rehearse. I had no talent at all for sports.

Junior high school commencement was a momentous rite of passage, the first time girls were allowed to wear stockings and lipstick—not red lipstick like Mommy's, but Tangee lipstick from Woolworth's that looked orange in the tube, then magically turned pale pink when you put it on your lips. I was thirteen, an official teenager. All the girls wore white dresses and their fathers gave them their first corsages. Mommy made me a beautiful dotted Swiss dress with a sheer bolero jacket. She took me to Belle Godet's store two doors down the street from Daddy's office to buy my first garter belt and stockings. Belle pulled out box after box looking for a garter belt small enough to hug my narrow hips without slipping down around my knees.

And Mommy bought me my first pair of high heels, white leather pumps. I walked around my room in them, my ankles buckling under me, practicing on the rug before I dared to try walking on the slippery floor in the hallway.

On the day of the graduation Daddy brought home a wrist corsage—yellow roses attached to a clear plastic bracelet and decorated with a glittery mesh butterfly.

I would be on stage, singing with the glee club, and then I would perform a solo, "The Year's at the Spring," Robert Browning's poem "Pippa's Song" set to music by Mrs. H. H. A. Beach. Miss Nau and I had rehearsed it over and over. She taught me to honor the dynamic markings, to sing through the vowels and to enunciate clearly. The song was very old-fashioned, written more than half a century before I sang it, but I loved it, because the poem was joyful and the music rose to a dramatic ending when I could let my voice fly.

It's time for my solo, but I'm not scared. I step forward from the front row of the glee club and walk to the center of the stage. I plant my feet so I won't wobble on my high-heeled shoes, and I angle my head to hide my "bad" cheek. Miss Nau, at the piano, nods on the downbeat.

I look out past the rows of folding chairs on the gymnasium floor, up past the top row of the bleachers all the way in the back. The audience doesn't exist. Mommy and Daddy, my sisters, the other parents, the girls who ignored me, the boys who were mean to me, all disappear. I am alone with the music, inside the music, surrounded, protected by the sound of my own voice. "The year's at the spring and day's at the morn."

The song builds to its crescendo. I take a really good breath and just let my voice go. "Ah-ah-ll's raaaa-eet with the world!" The sound fills the gymnasium. It rolls over the ceiling, sails across the audience, echoes all around me. It's bigger, much bigger than I am, the voice of someone large and powerful. But it's mine, my ship, and I can steer it, make the sound swell and then ebb, open my throat to ride the crest of a high note, like a wave breaking over the top of my head. The sound surges through my whole body, loud and strong. My sound.

The Girl I Could Become

High school. More new people, more questions about my face. I learned to get past the questions quickly, learned to explain what that mark on my face was all about very fast, then change the subject, case closed. No further discussion. Kids from towns even smaller than Millville were bused to the senior high school. And since there was no Catholic high school in Millville, I met kids who had studied with the priests and nuns through grade eight, Catholic Italian and Puerto Rican girls, and Eastern Orthodox girls whose parents, like my grandparents, had come to South Jersey from Russia and the Ukraine. I had to find a place for myself in this larger social order.

I tried to fit in with the clean-faced girls who lived in our new neighborhood, the girls who were going on to college, the girls with freckles and cute noses, girls who spent Sunday mornings at the Presbyterian or the Methodist Church, the Lutheran Church or the Episcopalian. Millville was a little town with big churches.

I adopted the preppy high school uniform—pleated skirts, Oxford cloth shirts with buttoned-down collars, penny loafers with knee socks. The pretty girls, the popular girls, the cheerleaders, the girls with boyfriends on the football team belonged to the Tri-Hi-Y. They met on Tuesday nights at the YMCA. They wore their club jackets to school. They spoke, in a code I couldn't understand, about club meetings and parties. The cute boys, the good clean boys, the popular boys, the football boys they dated belonged to their own Tri-Hi-Y club. They wore their club jackets to school. They walked their girlfriends home—high school sweethearts, teen angels in their matching club jackets, holding hands.

I was dying to join the Tri-Hi-Y. It was my passport into the inner circle. An invitation to join the Tri-Hi-Y would prove that I wasn't so strange, after all. It would prove that I was just a regular girl, that my birthmark really was no Big Deal.

I walked to school every day with blond, freckle-faced, blue-eyed, button-nosed Protestant Paula, who lived down the street. Paula and I were in and out of each other's houses every day. I spent summer weekends at her grandparents' beach house. I helped decorate her family Christmas tree.

Paula was a Tri-Hi-Y officer. She talked about it all the time. She knew how much I wanted to belong to that club. Paula held my fate in her hands. I needed her to sponsor me, to argue for me, to vote me in. The night the Tri-Hi-Y met to decide who would be invited to join, I didn't sleep at all.

The next morning when I showed up to walk Paula to school, I was so anxious I could hardly breathe, but I didn't dare ask. I didn't have to. She said, "I'm going to tell you the same thing I'm going to tell the twins. You just wouldn't be happy in Tri-Hi-Y." The twins were the only other Jewish girls in the freshman class, the same girls who had once been my competition for the role of Beautiful Queen Esther. I knew why we "just wouldn't be happy." It was the Young Men's *Christian* Association, after all. But I didn't say anything. I looked straight ahead and kept walking.

Paula and I stayed friends all through high school, but now I knew that she saw me as an outsider, a Jew. I didn't feel especially angry about it. I had been treated that way all my life. But the next time she came to our house, I told her with a straight face that the silk rug Mommy had just hung on the brick wall on the other side of our fireplace was a sacred Jewish artifact we had received from Israel and that we asked all visitors to please kneel down before it in a moment of respectful silence. When Paula obediently got on her knees, I fell apart laughing. "Jewish people don't really do things like that!" I said. "You think we're so strange, but we're not."

Excluded from the preppy sorority, I decided I could be like the tough girls who teased their hair, rimmed their eyes with shiny black liquid liner, and painted their lips pearly white. The girls who wore impossibly high-heeled shoes and indecently tight skirts. The girls whose purses were loaded with cans of hairspray and packs of cigarettes. The girls who were learning to type and take shorthand. The girls who dated beautifully muscled boys, boys with dark, slicked-back-in-a-ducktail hair. High school sweethearts, teen angels in their matching motorcycle jackets, necking in the halls.

I longed for such a boy, a boy who would steer me into the shadows where he could stare into my eyes and press his legs against mine, a boy who would call the radio station and dedicate a song to me. *Each night before you go to bed, my baby.* A blue-collar boy Mommy and Daddy would fear and loathe.

At the Orange and Blue Hub across the street from school, I slid into a crowd of girls who always sat at the same booth, eating cheeseburgers and fried onion rings and drinking cherry Cokes, smoking Kents or Newports, putting coins into the little jukebox on the table, waiting for their songs to come up, the same songs their boyfriends dedicated to them when they called the radio station. *This is dedicated to the one I love.*

But by the end of freshman year, I still belonged to no group. No matter how hard I tried to copy the fast girls or the good girls, I was still just the strange girl who didn't fit in anywhere.

Mommy worried that her daughters would grow up thinking Millville was the world. She said we had to "broaden our horizons." We took riding lessons, ballet lessons, art lessons, singing lessons, piano lessons, flute lessons, clarinet lessons, guitar lessons. She left the office early so that she could spend afternoons as well as Saturdays driving us around to our lessons. Nothing in Millville was good enough—not the teachers, not the schools, not the doctors, not the shops. So Mommy drove all the way into Philadelphia for anything that really mattered—dentists, eye doctors, nice clothes.

For years she took us to the Saturday-morning Philadelphia Orchestra Children's Concerts. Mommy never missed a concert—not even when Julie was a baby on her lap and she had to run out into the lobby if Julie started to cry; not even when she had walking pneumonia and had to run out into the lobby, coughing. We all dressed in our best big-city outfits and climbed up to the top balcony of the Academy of Music to sit in the cheapest seats. We had to climb so many flights of steps, Mommy said we were climbing up to heaven. There were binoculars attached to each seat, and if you put a quarter in the slot, a long wire cord would be released, so you could hold them up to your eyes. Mommy used just one quarter, so Jackie and I had to sit on either side of her, leaning over to take turns looking through the binoculars, navigating our heads around baby Julie on her lap. Without binoculars, the orchestra looked like a bunch of ants sitting on the stage.

After the concert, we descended all the way to the street, and found Mommy's sister, Evie, waiting for us in the lobby of the Bellevue Stratford Hotel. Evie, wonderful Evie, single, independent Evie worked for the Philadelphia school system. Her official job title was home and school counselor, but she laughingly called herself a glorified truant officer. To me she was the height of sophistication, always elegant in a cashmere sweater and skirt, a silk scarf tied around her neck, her wrists loaded with scarab bracelets, her hair streaked blond. Evie was always

marked for life

cheerful and full of pep. She seemed to be having much more fun than anybody else in our family.

We always went someplace nice for lunch—the tearoom at Wanamaker's department store or Schrafft's restaurant. After lunch Mommy and Evie shopped for hours while my sisters and I waited around, watching them try on clothes, dying of boredom, wondering when they'd make good on their promise to buy something for us.

─────

Mommy and Daddy liked to toss Yiddish words around. I found this practice embarrassingly unsophisticated and mean-spirited, because they most often used Yiddish to denigrate somebody else. The vast majority, from which we were excluded, were *goyim*, non-Jews. Black people were, of course, called *schwartzes*, a Yiddish word identical to the German for the color black, the same word that had given the name Schwartzmann to my grandfather's dark-haired family. Italian people were *lokshen*, which means noodles or pasta. Jews from Galicia in Poland or from Lithuania, where they were particularly downtrodden and uneducated, were considered low-class and backward by the Russian and Romanian Jewish intelligentsia. They were called Galitzianers and Litvaks. In my parents' mouths, all these terms were insults.

Daddy used the word *gonif*, which means thief, to describe anybody who sold him anything. *Bubkes*, which is a word for an amount less than zero, meant what Daddy got paid when he "broke his back" for a client. *Shlepper*, a word that literally means someone who drags or pulls something, such as a porter, was used to describe people at the bottom of the social scale.

According to Mommy and Daddy, Millville was crawling with *shleppers*, stupid, uneducated, ill mannered, and amoral. *Shleppers* didn't maintain their homes, didn't pay their bills.

Shleppers didn't read books. They were afraid that my sisters and I would fall under the influence of the local *schleppers*.

A boy from a *shlepper* family could get a nice Jewish girl in big trouble. He could ruin her whole life. Most of the boys in Millville were *shleppers*, and almost none of the boys were Jewish. If their daughters were going to date, it would have to be a European Jewish boy from an educated, affluent family with liberal politics. Nobody too Jewish, nobody too religious. No Galitzianers or Litvaks. In short, somebody just like us, and there was nobody just like us in Millville.

Mommy decided that it was time for Jackie and me to go away to summer camp and "broaden our horizons" before we fell under the spell of some *shlepper* boy, before we became real Millville girls. She studied the advertisements in the back pages of the *New York Times Sunday Magazine*, sent for brochures, and chose a theater arts camp run by some of the teachers at a boarding school in Lenox, Massachusetts.

The school was a beautiful place, a once-grand estate with acres of lawns. The rich furnishings that must have filled the main house had been replaced by metal beds and dressers. But even in its echoing emptiness it was still magnificent, its paneled rooms and corridors shielded from the summer sun by heavy leaded-glass windows.

On that first day, while Jackie and Julie explored the grounds with Mommy, Daddy and I stayed behind in the great hall, sitting on one of the carved benches that lined the walls. I watched the other students come in with their parents. No one looked at me strangely. They were all strange, each in his own way. A handsome boy named Kim came into the hall with his black father and his Jewish mother. A tall thin boy with a bad complexion had the long, strong fingers of a concert pianist. A slender girl with masses of orange-red hair wrapped around her head walked by, her shirt stained with oil paint.

All of those kids would have been freaks in Millville. But they were proud to be freaks. They cultivated their freakishness. They were regular students at the boarding school. Or they were kids from Manhattan, students at New York's High School of Music and Art or at private schools like New Lincoln, where there was no Tri-Hi-Y and the students called the teachers by their first names.

My birthmark was no more remarkable to them than an interesting tattoo. They asked about it in the most casual way possible. No one ever insinuated that my face was ugly or disfigured. I slept in a big room with three other girls. My best friend was Jane, a ballet dancer. My other roommates wanted to do portraits of my dappled face.

For the first time in my life, I thought I might fit in. I copied my newfound friends as slavishly as I had copied the popular girls in Millville. I borrowed their ethnic jewelry, wrote home asking for some of Daddy's old white dress shirts so that I could wear them over black leotards like the other girls. White shirts flapping, earrings dangling, carrying our ballet shoes, we hurried across the lawns on our way to dance class in the mornings like a flock of nuns. We studied dance all morning with beautiful Elfriede. Jane and I adored her, revered her, wanted to be like her—chic, European, sure of herself, her deep throaty voice still lightly accented from a German childhood.

I met older kids who had been adopted by the headmaster, refugees from the failed coup in Hungary. I learned to weave and spin from a Dutch woman and her rosy-cheeked daughter. I sang Schubert songs, accompanied at the piano by the boy with the strong slender fingers.

The French class presented Moliere's *Le Malade Imaginaire*. The drama class presented García Lorca's *Blood Wedding*. The modern dance class presented a work set to Satie's *Gymnopédies*. We saw Pete Seeger and Odetta at the Music Barn. We saw *The Skin of Our Teeth* at the Williamstown Playhouse. Millville would never look the same to me again.

"Dear Mommy and Daddy," I wrote.

> *I am fifteen years old today. I can't remember fifteen years ago when I was born, but you can and it must seem like a long time to you. A great deal has happened to me since then. I have become a person, and I have come to expect to be treated like one. I have learned to say things and read them and write them, with words and with music. I have learned to discuss things and to think them out, and to learn from the thoughts of others. I have learned to get along with other people and with myself. A year has passed since my last birthday, and in addition to being older perhaps I am wiser. There is that hope.*

It was my declaration of independence.

───⌒───

It's the last day of camp. I'm sitting on the staircase in the main house, surrounded by friends, saying good-bye, trading addresses, while the parents talk to one another, to their kids, to their kids' friends, to the camp directors. Some of them chat in German or French, laughing easily. Some of the mothers wear flowing dresses, their long hair piled on their heads or in braids that hang down their backs, swaying behind them as they walk. Some of the fathers wear shorts and socks with sandals. I have never seen grown-ups dressed that way in Millville.

Mommy and Daddy come in with Julie, smiling, looking a little nervous, almost shy but happy to see Jackie and me. I force myself to smile back. I can't hurt their feelings. But I'm not glad they're here. It means camp is over. My happiness is

marked for life

over. It means that I'll have to go back to Millville, pulled out of the light and returned to the darkness.

Mommy looks me over carefully, taking in my newly pierced ears and dyed red hair, not so happy to see me now. "Who was supervising these kids?" Daddy asks her.

Why did we need to be supervised? This is my body to decorate or mutilate. It's nobody's business but mine. The holes in my ears and the red in my hair are my own uniform, my club jacket, my emblem of not belonging in Millville, of not wanting to belong, after all.

My friends are looking forward to going home, to going back to school. They are making plans that can't include me. "See you next week in the city." They're free. They ride subways and buses all over Manhattan. Their parents are accepting, amused, even proud of anything they do.

Mommy and Daddy aren't like that. They aren't interested in finding out who we are. They have strong ideas about who we should be and they think it's their job to make sure that's who we become—Jewish but not too religious, stylish but not ostentatious, intellectual but practical. They want us to be lawyers and to marry lawyers, to live in Millville or very close by. They want us to grow up to become them, exactly them.

I can't be Mommy and Daddy's dream daughter. I don't even want to try. I am going back to nowhere, to a place where nobody is like me, where no one will understand what I did this summer.

There are no buses or subways in Millville. There is no place to go and no way to get there, no one to see. New York City is a three-hour bus ride and Mommy and Daddy won't let me go there by myself, anyway. I can't even drive. I wasn't allowed to get a learner's permit with the rest of my high school class because Daddy said it was too dangerous.

Mommy and Daddy had no idea what the camp would mean to me. They thought they were just sending us off for a little cultural enrichment. But that summer, a great door opened and I saw what was on the other side of the wall, only to be forced back inside.

⁓

I am a prisoner, exiled to a bleak world. When I write to my summer friends, I don't have much to say. They go to concerts, to Broadway plays. They meet in Washington Square on Saturday afternoons. Jane is continuing her ballet lessons with Elfriede in the City. The City. The forbidden emerald city where I belong. I have been ripped out of the sky and flung back to earth, to suffocate in the airless confines of this lonely wasteland. It's all a terrible mistake. I don't belong in Millville. I belong in the City, with parents who trust me to find my own way.

I lock myself in my room. Decals from Woolworth's, black and gold butterflies, are plastered everywhere. They flutter across the desk, alight on the telephone, on the windowsill, encircle the big mirror that hangs above the old mahogany dresser. I undress and face myself in that mirror, a nymph among the butterflies. I'm changing. I have nice breasts. I have a tiny waist. I have Mommy's great legs, and between them, curly black hair that wasn't there before the summer.

I look carefully at my face. I bring my cheek very close to the mirror to examine the birthmark, hoping that it might be changing, too, hoping it won't keep up with me as I grow. But it still covers my temple, my eyelid, spills mottled red and purple all over my cheek. It's neither larger nor smaller, darker nor lighter than before.

I look straight ahead and take inventory: clear complexion, just a couple of pimples hidden under my bangs, pale amber eyes, long dark lashes; nose not too big, not hooked, not crooked; lips nicely shaped, not too thin, not too full. Not too bad. If I have a guardian angel, then maybe this nice face is her way of compensating for the birthmark, her way of settling my account.

A Woman Now

Maybe I shouldn't call him a boy. He was already a young man of twenty-one who had just graduated from college. Not an especially handsome young man, he had a strong nose and full lips, and his dark hair was already beginning to recede from his forehead. He was short and he walked with a funny gait, his head cocked to one side.

On the first day of the second summer at Lenox, Daddy and I waited again on the wooden bench in the long, cool great hall of the main house, talking about nothing much. It was Daddy's way of saying good-bye without actually saying it, a rare moment when I felt that Daddy and I were friends.

The boy ambled past us, looked at me. Five minutes later he passed us again, looked at me again. And a few minutes later, he came through for another look. Now Daddy noticed and became annoyed. "What is it with that guy? He keeps walking by here and giving you the once-over." I noticed the boy's eyes, more green than blue. I didn't think much of him except to think he might like me, the way he kept walking past us again and again.

He was a nice Jewish boy from Ohio, a graduate of the school, one of the lucky ones whose parents had sent him away. Maybe they knew he wouldn't have survived high school in Ohio. At the camp he taught Russian, tennis, and drama and he had his run of the girls. He went through two or three others before he got around to me. He boasted that he had a photographic memory and could speak thirteen languages, which impressed most of us. He didn't have much competition, anyway. There weren't enough boys at the camp that year to keep the girls supplied with summer crushes.

At first he just talked to me, found me in the dining room, sat next to me on the bus when we went to concerts. I was flattered by the attention, thrilled to have been chosen from such a wide selection of girls. Like the King of Persia who chose Beautiful Queen Esther even though she was Jewish, the boy chose me even though I had a birthmark. He would never call me Monster Girl, Bride of Frankenstein. The blotch that stained the left side of my face meant nothing to him.

The boy had his own room in the house where the boys slept, on the other side of the campus from the room I shared with Jane in the main house.

After dinner, in the still-bright light of an August evening, we walk across the rolling lawn. He holds my hand, and when we get to the door of his building, he asks me to come inside.

"I can't. I'm not allowed in there."

"It's okay. It's okay. No one will see us."

Upstairs, miniature bottles of vodka are lined up along his windowsill, the little bottles you get on airplane trips. He closes the door and we're alone. We sit close together on his narrow cot. He takes one of the bottles from the sill behind us, opens it, takes a slug, and then passes it to me. I throw back my head and gulp it down. It's nasty, burns my throat. It's my first real drink, my first taste of being alone with a boy. I lean into him when he puts his arm around me. We speak very quietly, whispering as though we're in a library, listening for a noise in the hall. The boy puts his finger to my lips. Someone is using the bathroom.

The sound of the toilet flushing, a door closing, footsteps, the all-clear signal. The boy looks at me and smiles a naughty smile. He kisses my mouth, pushes his tongue between my lips. It feels strange, tingly. *French kissing, television kisses—I'm doing it. I'm really doing it, me, just like a grown-up woman!*

marked for life

He moves his tongue around, across the roof of my mouth. I'm very still, clutching his shoulders, wondering how to kiss properly. "Do what I do," he says. I'm not sure I want to. But I try. I concentrate on the strange dance of tongues, the same way I have to concentrate when I try to do the fox-trot, trying to oblige, to get it right. His hand moves down, reaching under my T-shirt. I pull it away. I know that boys will try to pet below the neck and that I have to stop them or they won't respect me.

The boy keeps an eye on the clock by the cot. He can't be late for rehearsal. The school is short on male students so he has a walk-on part, playing a courtier in the first and last scenes of *A Midsummer Night's Dream*, staged outdoors on the lawns where the slope of the hill makes a natural amphitheater. When it's time to go he says, "Look what you've done," showing me the bulge in his jeans. "I have to relax a minute before we can leave. Otherwise, I'll have to tell people, 'Joie did that to me.'"

I wait on the bed while he opens the door, making sure no one is in the hall, no one in the bathroom, no one on the stairs. "Okay, go now," he whispers. "You go first. I'll look for you later, after it gets dark. I'll find you as soon as I can get away." And I obediently tiptoe down the steps and rush out of the building.

I am so proud, so different from the girl who stole into that boy's room just an hour ago. *I'm a woman now. I'll never be the same again.* Late summer's cool, sweet twilight rushes over me as though a window has been opened, a heavy curtain has lifted. My life is beginning, full of possibility, full of love.

I stumble up the path and find a hiding place behind the bushes. On the lawn below, the campers are gathering for rehearsal. The director claps her hands, calling, "Places! Settle down!" Someone presses a button on a tape recorder. The ascending chords that begin Mendelssohn's overture float up from the loudspeakers and land on the hill where I nervously wait and watch for him. On the damp grass, clasping my knees in the lingering light, in the ripening New England summer, I sit and wait for darkness, wait as the dawdling sun reluctantly sets.

I lay back on the grass, watching the sky slowly fade to black, trying to sort it out, trying to be sober again, remembering the kisses, the funny feeling of his tongue in my mouth, my tongue in his, our mouths connecting. *Did it really happen? Did we really do that? Will he really come and find me here, waiting?*

The sun surrenders one more day. Flutes tremble over the last lingering chords of the overture. The scherzo begins, flutes and violins urgent now, hurrying. And he's there, creeping among the bushes in the dark. "Joie? Joie?" whispering my name. *My lover has come back to me.* "Here I am. I'm over here." "Sshh!" he whispers. "We have to be careful. We can't let anyone see us." Down on the grass beside me, he is kissing me, kissing me. Television kisses didn't look like this at all. Our chins are covered with drool. But I want him to kiss me more, keep on kissing me. He kisses me and kisses me and we roll in the grass, staining my shorts and shirt a guilty green, until the drums pound through the loudspeakers, one two three four, one two three four, and the strings leap joyously as the clown's melody begins. The boy leaps up, too, and hurries back down the hill to become a courtier again when the Wedding March trumpets blow. And I am alone, spinning in the dark.

It's a miracle. When he looks at me, I'm something precious. When I look at him, I see my mate. He and I are like two birds flying side by side. In the afternoons, we walk the lawns with arms wrapped around each other. At night, after curfew, we meet in secret. We whisper and kiss—in the back stairwell, behind the bushes, on the cot in his room. We read through a duet from Mozart's *Magic Flute*, my girlish soprano chirping over his rough baritone. "*Mann und Weib und Weib und Mann.*" "Man and wife and wife and man," we sing.

I have been blind all my life. I am just now discovering the world. For the first time I see the August shadows, the patches of light the afternoon sun smuggles through the trees.

A rainy afternoon is beautiful. The gray sky is beautiful. The narrow, muddy trail, the soggy leaves under our shoes are beautiful. Rain had always just been rain, wet and annoying. But this is warm, cozy rain, beautiful, wonderful rain.

We spend a rainy afternoon in the main house, in my room with my girlfriends where he isn't allowed to be, painting my toenails, painting his toenails, then walking, skipping, leaping through the rain into Lenox for ice cream sundaes.

We are like Hermia and Lysander, Helena and Demetrius, Romeo and Juliet. But we speak only of our friendship, say only that we like each other very, very much.

At the end of the summer, the boy went home to Ohio. I went home to New Jersey. In two weeks, he would be starting graduate school. I would be starting eleventh grade. He would be studying Chinese and Sanskrit in Philadelphia, only an hour by car from Millville. This time I could say, "See you in the city." It wasn't over at all.

We wrote every day. He wrote that he missed me, that he was sad. For fourteen days, I read his letters, reread his letters. I wrote him back, tore up what I wrote, wrote it over again, copied my letter one last time on pretty stationery. I lit a stick of sealing wax and dripped a golden blob onto the back of the envelope, pressed a little rose seal into it. I borrowed Mommy's Stoplight Red lipstick and pressed my lips to the paper, leaving a kiss there for him, beneath the gold rose. Then in purple ink, I wrote S.W.A.K., Sealed with a Kiss.

On Labor Day weekend, the boy flew from Ohio to New York City, took the bus from New York to Philadelphia, and called me from the bus station as soon as he arrived. I told him to get on the next bus to Millville.

I am ecstatic. *I'm going to see the boy again! Today! This afternoon!* I'm not worried about what Mommy and Daddy will say. They're always glad when my friends come to visit. He's a nice Jewish boy from a nice family. And he's very educated, very smart. He's just the sort of boy they hoped I'd meet in Lenox. They'll like him.

Mommy will be thrilled when she sees how happy I am. Maybe she'll say, "Oh Joie, that's wonderful! You must be so excited!" Of course, that's what she'll say.

But Mommy isn't thrilled. Her face tightens up. "I don't know, Joie," she says. "I'll have to talk to your father." *Don't know! What doesn't she know! What's not to know?*

Mommy finds Daddy watching a baseball game on television in their bedroom. She closes the door behind her. Jackie hangs around in the hall, trying to eavesdrop on them. Something is going on and she wants to know what it is. But I'm too happy to be worried, too desperate to be with the boy again. I go outside and wait on the back patio. I don't want to hear Mommy's and Daddy's voices.

Mommy comes out of the bedroom first. It's always Mommy who speaks to us. We never want to ask Daddy for anything. He'll give us a hard time for sure, and at the end of all our pleading, all our carefully planned arguments, he'll say no. Not just an ordinary no, but a "How could you have even thought of asking such a thing, you ridiculous, pathetic excuse for a daughter?" That kind of a no. The worst words Mommy ever says to us are "You'll have to ask your father."

Mommy says that she is very annoyed with me and that

Daddy is really upset, but that she'll take me to meet the boy's bus. We'll bring him back to the house and then Daddy wants to drive down to the shore. I try to explain to her that the boy and I would like to just stay home and hang around the house or go for a walk or to the movies while they all go to the beach, but Mommy says, "That's out of the question."

I'm in trouble but I'm too delirious to care. The boy will be here in only an hour, only fifty-nine minutes, fifty-eight minutes, fifty-seven minutes. "Maybe we should leave now, Mommy. How long will it take us to drive to the bus station? What time should we leave?"

In the car on the way to the boy, Mommy tells me that I live in a family with other people and that I have to take their plans into consideration before I make plans of my own. She says I should have asked her before I told him to get on the bus. Now it's too late and there's nothing she can do about it. I wonder what happened to her old rule of "This is your home, and your friends are always welcome here." I wonder why she isn't delighted that a nice Jewish boy is interested in me. But I know better than to try to defend myself. I can never win a case against Mommy. She's a good lawyer. Besides, I don't want her to be in an angry mood when the boy arrives. I don't want her to be mean to him. I don't want her to ruin everything.

When the car pulls up at the station I see a bus. *I see him! He's here! He's here!* I want to jump out of the car. I run to him, hug him. He's grinning at me. Mommy is leaning against her station wagon, not smiling. She shakes the boy's hand as though she were being forced to shake hands with the opposing attorney after she'd already lost the case.

The boy throws his bag in the backseat. I sit next to Mommy in the front. He sits next to me. I can't stop looking at him, trying to see the boy I remember, the boy in the afternoon shadows, the boy in the dark, in the grass behind the bushes, the boy in the rain, in the mud puddles. Here he is in my world now, in Millville, in Mommy's car, the same boy. It's too amazing. He's right here beside me on the front seat, his leg against my leg with Mommy on the other side of me, Mommy not smiling, no matter how hard we smile, no matter how hard the boy tries to be charming.

When we pull up at the house, Jackie is peering out the window. Nosey Jackie is in Julie's room, which faces the driveway. She must be standing on Julie's bed. The boy looks at the rotting real-wood trim on Mommy's old second-hand Rambler station wagon, and notices that it's sprouting. "That's an interesting fungus," he says. Mommy doesn't say anything. She just walks up the flagstone path, then turns around to make sure we're right behind her. She must think he's insulting her car. Now she really doesn't like him. Jackie's face is still at the window, but it disappears when I point it out to the boy.

I try to explain to the boy why we have to go the beach with my family, why there's no possibility that they'll let me stay home with him and just go to a movie or something, why we can't even spend the afternoon at the home of one of my friends, so Mommy and Daddy won't think they're leaving us alone together. He doesn't understand. He thinks Daddy is being unreasonable. He's twenty-one years old. He gets to do whatever he likes. I'm a teenaged prisoner who has to do whatever her parents say.

On the way to the beach, the boy and I are squeezed into the backseat with both of my sisters. Mommy and Daddy are sitting in the front, not talking. The boy takes my hand. I smile at him, blissful. "Mommy!" Jackie yells. "They're holding hands!" Jackie keeps up a running commentary. Mommy doesn't need to have eyes in the back of her head. She has Jackie. "Mommy! They're whispering in each other's ears!"

I've never had such a horrible time at the beach. Jackie trails

marked for life

us like a hunter and reports every move back to Mommy. My sister was very friendly with the boy when we were all at camp, but you would never guess that by the way she's acting now.

On the boardwalk, we eat cole slaw, French fries, and fried clams in little red plastic baskets lined with grease-soaked paper napkins, while we swat monster mosquitoes. The boy says these are the biggest mosquitoes he's ever seen in his life. When the bill comes, the boy tries to pay for himself, but Daddy wordlessly waves him away, as though the boy were a bum on the street reaching out to get money from him, not give it. I want to punch Daddy in the nose for being so mean and rude. He's not even trying to hide his hatred of this boy, this boy he doesn't even know. I'm sure we would have eaten at a nicer restaurant if the boy wasn't with us. Daddy would rather eat greasy *chozzerei* than treat that boy to a decent meal.

On the ride home nobody says anything. Not even Jackie.

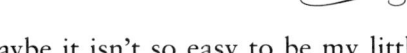

Maybe it isn't so easy to be my little sister. I have a big birthmark on my face that nobody is supposed to notice. Jackie has to pretend it isn't there. I used to play big-sister tricks on her. I gave her Indian burns and pinned her to the floor so I could tickle her until she begged me to stop. When we ate our TV dinners on tray tables in front of the TV, I always got to watch *The Mickey Mouse Club*, even though she wanted to watch *Ramar of the Jungle*. When we were really little I got her to trade a dime for two pennies. "I'll give you two monies, if you give me one money," I said. Her little hand clutched the pennies. "Ooh! I have two monies!" That wasn't nice. I never let her tag along when I played with my girlfriends. Tag-a-long Tallulah, I called her. That wasn't nice, either.

I was always the oldest. I always got there first. I got to wear a bra first. I got my period first. I went to high school first. She had to wear my hand-me-down clothes when I outgrew them. I got to wear a grown-up long strapless gown to our cousin's wedding, when she had to wear a little-girl birthday party dress.

Now I've crossed an invisible line, and she can't follow me. She's stuck on the other side at thirteen going on fourteen, while I'm a young woman of sixteen, holding hands with a boy. Nobody has to explain it to me. She says it herself. "Mommy, Joie's acting like a teenager with a boyfriend!" She's tormenting me when I need her to help me.

―――

Back at the house, Daddy announces that we are all going straight to bed. The boy whispers, "Your family will never let us have any privacy. Sneak into my room later so we can talk." We haven't managed to be alone at all.

Overnight guests always sleep on the sofa bed in the little room between the kitchen and the garage where we watch TV. It's the room where I practice singing and play the upright piano that once belonged to old Mr. Brandriff's wife, Claribel. To get to that room from my bedroom I'll have to go out into the hall, pass the living and dining rooms, and cross the kitchen.

I make a big show of saying "Goodnight. See you in the morning." "See you," the boy answers. Then we all go into our rooms. I close my door and put my nightgown on over my underwear. I put my bathrobe on top and button it up. I'm not going to visit the boy half-undressed. He might get the wrong idea. I turn out the lights and get under the covers. I hold my breath, listening for sounds in the house. I hear Daddy walking around. He's turning out lights and checking to make sure the doors are all locked. I can't tell how much time has passed. Every second feels like a minute. Every minute feels like an hour. I strain my ears, hoping to hear Daddy snoring. I go over my escape route, mentally practicing how I'll silently close my door, tiptoe across the floor, stand in the kitchen, in the dark,

marked for life

whispering to the boy until his door opens without a sound. I imagine sitting on the foldout couch with him, talking softly, so softly. Maybe we'll kiss wet television kisses.

I lay in my bed for ten, twenty, thirty minutes. *That should be enough. Everybody went to sleep more than half an hour ago. Anyway, I can't lie here any longer without losing my mind.*

I get out of bed, straighten my bathrobe. Carefully close the door behind me, without making a sound. I tiptoe into the dining room, head for the kitchen. Then I hear Daddy's voice. "Going somewhere?" It isn't a question. It's a nasty accusation. Nobody can be as sarcastic as Daddy. *What's he doing here?* Daddy is standing by the living room fireplace in his pale blue cotton pajamas, a ghostly specter. Even in the dark, I can see his lips curled in a familiar sneer. *I can't afford to fall apart. Daddy couldn't have seen me jump out of my skin.*

"I thought I'd make myself a cup of tea. Do you want some?" *My voice didn't shake, I'm sure it didn't. I sounded perfectly normal.*

"A cup of tea?" Daddy mimics me. "Go ahead. Have your tea." He doesn't follow me into the kitchen, he just stands there staring, which is worse. I turn on the light, turn on the electric burner under the teakettle. The boy is five baby steps away, just on the other side of the door, listening. But I can't go to him. I have to sit at the kitchen table and drink that whole cup of hot tea, sit there and not cry, sit there and not shrivel up and die while Daddy watches me.

"Why are you awake, Daddy? Aren't you going to bed?"

"Nooo, I think I'll just stay down here on the couch."

He sat there all night.

The next day, as soon as it could be politely accomplished, the boy was returned to the bus station.

I am in Mommy and Daddy's bedroom, summoned there like a criminal. Daddy is a wild man, screaming, sobbing hysterically. He is exploding, insane with rage. I have never seen him like this. He has been arrogant, despotic, but never out of control. The house, where I have sometimes felt trapped, has always been a safe place, a sanctuary as well as a cage. Now the walls are shaking. Jackie and Julie are hiding in their rooms.

"How could you do such a thing? How could you?" He is crying, choking. "I go over it and over it in my mind, but I just can't understand it. How could such a thing happen in this house? What did I do to deserve such behavior? All I ever did was sacrifice for you, for all the girls. Look how upset your mother is! You know her health isn't good. You could kill your mother! Is that what you want? Would it be worth it to you if you killed your mother over that boy?"

Daddy can't stay like this forever. In a few hours, he'll calm down. He'll turn back into his old grouchy self. I just have to wait. If I can figure out what he wants me to say, maybe I can get out of this room.

"I'm sorry, Daddy. I don't want to upset you. Honestly, I didn't do anything bad."

"Anything bad? You don't think you did anything bad?"

"Please, Daddy, please don't be mad. I don't understand what I did wrong. Explain it to me. Please. Just explain it to me. Just tell me what I did wrong and I'll apologize for it."

Sweetness isn't working.

"Apologize! You'll apologize! You can't apologize for this! What kind of a girl are you that I have to explain right from wrong? That boy wants one thing from you and one thing only, and the sooner you understand that, the better. I forbid you to see him again. I forbid it! You're not to talk to him. You're not to write to him. I forbid you to be in touch with him in any way."

Mommy is sitting on the blue velvet easy chair, silently

watching, clutching an embroidered white handkerchief, twisting it in her hands.

He cannot keep me away from the boy. Nothing can keep me away. The more Daddy screams, the more defiant I become. I shout to be heard over Daddy's tirade. "I will, too, see him! You can't stop me! I didn't do anything wrong! What do you think I did that was so horrible? Tell me! Tell me!"

Daddy grabs me by the hair with one hand, and with the other he slaps my face hard. "You filthy liar. You little whore! You're nothing but a cheap slut, a prostitute! You don't deserve to live under my roof!"

I'm still a girl, taking her first timid, thrilling steps toward becoming a woman. And I'm alone, for the first time in my life, without Mommy and Daddy to protect me. I have to defend myself against my own father, while Mommy just looks on, wiping her eyes. I crumble. Then I fight back.

"How dare you call me a whore, Daddy? Why can't you believe me when I tell you that nothing bad happened with that boy? You've known me ever since I was born, but you're acting like I'm a complete stranger!"

Daddy reaches for me again. He is a strong man. But I push him away and run down the hall toward my room, while he chases after me, smacking the back of my head. I lock my door against Daddy, who stands just outside, pounding, threatening to break it down and give me the beating I deserve. *Am I really a whore? Am I really so bad?* And Mommy, my mommy! Mommy must know that I would never go all the way with a boy. She must know that Daddy is wrong. I wait for her to comfort me. But she never comes.

House Arrest

Mommy got rapid heartbeats. She called them "episodes." Her heart would suddenly begin to race. She had to lie upside down, her head hanging over the edge of the bed. She had to suck chips of ice. Sometimes these things worked and the racing heartbeat stopped. Sometimes it continued racing for hours. The doctors said Mommy's heart was strong, that the rapid heartbeats were more frightening than life threatening. But every time she had one of her episodes, we were all made to think this one might kill her. She got them at the most inconvenient times. When I wanted to go to the bonfire at the high school after the football game, when I wanted to go to a party, Mommy got rapid heartbeats. So I had to stay home, in case this one turned out to be serious, in case this time she had to be rushed to the hospital, in case this time she died.

Daddy had episodes too. Every night he took belladonna drops for his "sour stomach," his "gruesome heartburn." My sisters and I were made to understand that anything we did could cause Mommy and Daddy to have episodes, terrible physical suffering, even death. Now Mommy was getting rapid heartbeats every day. Daddy felt like his "stomach was on fire." And it was all the fault of the filthy little whore they had raised. The ungrateful child they had nurtured and cared for was determined to kill them.

I was a pariah without allies. My sisters spoke to me in whispers. I had made them miserable, too, turned the house into bedlam, ruined the normalcy of their lives. Daddy avoided me, but whenever he saw me, he looked at me with utter revulsion. Mommy hardly looked at me at all. She turned her head away when she told me that I would not be allowed out of the house for any reason except to go to school. I would be driven to school each morning and would have to report to Daddy's office immediately after my last class. I would be driven home when Mommy or Daddy was ready to leave the office.

I was under house arrest. On the first day of school, when Mommy drove me home from the office, I leapt out of the car, even before she turned off the engine, and raced her to the mailbox. There was a letter from the boy! I tried to quickly hide it between my schoolbooks but Mommy was right behind me. "Give that to me!" She demanded. She snatched it out of my hands, but I got it back and tore it, unopened, into little pieces that scattered over the flagstone walk.

For months, if Daddy spoke to me at all, it was only to berate me, to call me a filthy whore. At the dinner table, while my sisters miserably stared at their plates, he endlessly repeated to me that the boy was interested in one thing and one thing only. I knew what that "thing" was, something unspeakably shameful. Over and over again he would ask the rhetorical question, "What kind of a twenty-one-year-old messes around with a girl like her? He must be sick. A real sick-o."

"It's not like that, Daddy. We have a lot in common. We talk about books and music. He's Jewish; he's smart. Why don't you like him? Why do you think he's only interested in my body? Why couldn't he be interested in my mind or my personality? We didn't even do anything bad!"

But Daddy just sneered at me. "You'd better get it through that thick head of yours that that boy doesn't care about you or what happens to you. He got what he wanted and that's all he wanted."

I thought Daddy might believe that no boy could want me because of the birthmark, that the only explanation for this boy's interest in me was that I must have given in to him sexually. I understood that he might have considered the boy too old. But neither of those explanations justified the violence of Daddy's reaction.

Daddy was a tough and judgmental father whose approval I constantly sought and rarely received. I never spent time alone with Daddy. Once, when I was eleven, we walked together in the woods near our house and he stopped to peel the bark off a fallen branch so that I could have a walking stick. Once, he took me to a record store and after he had browsed through all the albums, making a few selections for himself, he treated me to a recording of the opera *Lucia Di Lammermoor* starring Maria Callas. These two incidents were so out of character that they stayed in my mind as special days, like graduation days or birthdays.

Still, when he was pleased with me he called me "JoPo." And sometimes he added a few lines to the bottom of the letters Mommy sent me at camp. Nothing in his past behavior prepared me for the way he shunned me now.

Mommy and Daddy's constant vigilance wasn't enough to keep me from writing to the boy. If I couldn't get to the mailbox first, I prevailed on Paula to get there for me.

The boy wrote that he missed me very much followed by three exclamation points, and he underlined the word *very* four times. He plotted ways that we could see each other, contrived ways that he might make Mommy and Daddy like him.

He wrote about his violin and piano lessons, his photography, about his walks around the city. He sent me copies of the photos he'd been taking. He sent me books: Antoine de Saint-Exupéry's *The Little Prince*, Thomas Mann's *The Magic Mountain*, Franz Kafka's *Metamorphosis*, which I kept hidden in my room and read behind a locked door. I sent him copies of the poems I'd been writing, smuggled out of the house between the pages of my schoolbooks, mailed from street corners at lunchtime.

I used my lunch money to call him from the pay phone at school. He told me to call collect. "I hope the phone rings," he wrote,

> and that it's you. The phone is good for me. It stops your image from floating away. Call me. Please.
> Whenever I am supremely happy, I start to sing Bach fugues in my head (especially the one in C minor, from "Book II" of the Well-Tempered Clavier). I'm feeling sad right now, so I'm going to see if it works in reverse. I'm putting Wanda Landowska on the HiFi. I miss you . . . P.S. It's working!

The boys at Millville High could never have competed with that.

The boy was the only person in the world who understood me, the only one who was really on my side. I survived on his letters, scanned the scrawl-covered pages for evidence that he cared for me, unable to breathe until I found "It hurts not to see you" or "I feel very lonesome for you tonight, Joie." Then, only then, I could start at the beginning of the letter and read it all again and again. I kept all his letters locked up in a box with his photographs, the necklace he gave me.

I survived on furtive telephone conversations, whispered intimacies interrupted by operators demanding an additional thirty-five cents for the next three minutes. I leaned into the telephone in the old wooden booth at school, clinging to the receiver as though it were the body of the boy I loved, as though his voice kissed my ear through cold black plastic lips. And with the final click of the last good-bye, I began my incessant review, fearful that even one word might slip away before I could memorize the conversation. As I lay awake at night, I reviewed it over and over, treasuring, analyzing everything he said.

Madame Opens the Door

Daddy was on a rampage, liable to blow up whenever something reminded him that his oldest daughter was a whore. Anything could reignite his rage. He was completely unpredictable. My sisters and I were constantly on guard, tense, waiting for the next explosion.

"I feel like a spurned lover," Mommy told me. "You never talk to me, never so much as put your hand on my shoulder." I was too angry, too hurt that she hadn't defended me. Maybe Daddy didn't trust me, didn't care who I was. But Mommy, my Mommy, had deserted me. She used to tell me, "I love you with all my heart and soul. You're my flesh and blood." She must have known that I wasn't really a whore.

Mommy never told me that she was sorry. That wasn't her style. And she would never admit that Daddy might be wrong. She found another way back to me. She wrote to the Curtis Institute of Music in Philadelphia and arranged an audition with a famous singing teacher there. My clever Mommy had contrived a brilliant strategy. It would be impossible for me to stay angry while she was so obviously trying to help me. And she was sure that the singing lessons would get my mind off that boy.

Mommy picked me up at school on a Friday afternoon, but instead of taking me to her office and holding me hostage there until she was ready to go home, she drove me into Philadelphia to audition for Madame. I wore my first grown-up suit, a narrow skirt and a fitted, double-breasted jacket in bright blue and

marked for life

green tweed wool. Mommy and Evie chose it for me from the designer salon at Wanamaker's department store, where I'd spent so many boring hours, waiting and watching while they tried on clothes. To wear with the suit, Mommy bought a bright blue hat, trimmed with a green ribbon and shaped like a lampshade; blue gloves; a necklace of chunky blue and green beads with matching button earrings; and blue suede pointy-toed pumps.

I had worn the fully accessorized outfit to school because there would be no time to go home and change. It was early October, still too warm for wool, so I kept the jacket in my locker. But I was sweating in a white nylon blouse and my feet throbbed from staggering through the school halls in high-heeled pumps. By the time I slid into the front seat of Mommy's old Rambler station wagon, I felt wilted and sore.

Since the day Mommy showed me Madame's reply inviting her to "bring the child so I can hear her," I had been scared out of my wits. Mommy said that Madame would determine whether or not I had talent. If she said no, I had to give up my obsession with singing. And if she said yes, well, then we'd see. Maybe Madame would suggest a suitable teacher for me, someone not far from Millville.

I practiced nonstop. I knew only one classical selection well enough to sing it at an audition, *"Dank sei Dir, Herr"* by Handel. It was a short song, often given to students as an exercise in breath control. The first note must be held for more than three measures, ten slow beats, begun softly then gradually building in a long, even crescendo. I woke up extra early so that I could practice for an hour before school. I practiced before dinner and after dinner. I sang that long first *"Daaaaaaaaaaaaank"* again and again. I was determined to make it sound as smooth and clear as a clean black line slicing through white paper, narrow on one end, growing wider in a perfectly calibrated arc until it connected with the next note, a third above it, then neatly narrowing again to softly finish the phrase. *Dank sei dir, Herr.* Thanks be to you, Lord.

On the day of the audition, I was just a body in the school building. Handel was playing so loudly in my head, I couldn't hear anything the teachers said. At lunchtime, I called the boy from the pay phone. I would be so close to him, in the very city where he lived, but I wouldn't be able to see him. He said he could sit in the park opposite Madame's apartment building, hoping to catch a glimpse of me. But it was too risky. If Mommy saw him there, I could forget about singing lessons forever. He said that he believed in my talent and that I had to believe in it, too. And when he said that, I thought that maybe, maybe I'd pass the test. Maybe Madame would like me.

Madame's apartment is in one of the majestic old buildings that border Rittenhouse Square. Everything about it is imposing: the marquee that shades the entrance, the white-gloved doorman who announces Mommy and me, the wood-paneled elevator with its shiny brass fixtures. We stand outside Madame's door. *This is it. My whole life will be determined by what happens in the next hour.* "What are you waiting for?" Mommy asks. "Ring the bell."

My hand weighs five hundred pounds. It takes all my strength to lift it up and push the button. The white nylon blouse is moist under my smart suit jacket. Under my narrow skirt, my stockings are stuck to my legs. My bright blue lampshade hat is suddenly much too tight, crushing my head.

Madame answers the door herself. She is a short, compact Italian woman with neatly curled white hair, a strong nose, and dark eyes whose piercing gaze seems to contradict the warmth of her welcoming smile. Her large living room is filled with elaborately detailed antique furniture, a carved Italian armoire, upholstered chairs. A wall of windows at one end of the room overlooks the park below. The piano is covered with framed photographs of opera singers. "My pupils," she explains. "Sit anywhere you like." She motions toward Mommy. "Make yourself comfortable." But Mommy doesn't look comfortable at all, perched on one of Madame's chairs, her hands clutching her purse on her lap, her feet crossed at the ankles. I continue standing, not knowing what to do. Madame sits at the piano, lifts herself just off the seat, pulls the stool in a bit, and sits back down.

"All right," she says, looking at me expectantly. "The child may sing, but let her first take off her hat. She shouldn't have to sing with a hat on." *She called me "child." My grown-up outfit hasn't fooled her at all.* I take off my hat, look around for someplace to put it, place it on an empty chair a few steps away. Then I position myself in the crook of the grand piano, facing Madame, open my music, and hand it to her. Madame waves it away. She is not interested in Handel. She plays a simple five-note scale. "Sing this for me, child." My mouth is dry. My lips are stuck to my teeth. I was so ready to dazzle her with Handel. How can I show off my voice with this little scale?

"Just sing that?" She looks at me impatiently. "Yes, child, sing what I play. Just what I play." *Now she thinks I'm so ignorant I can't recognize a scale. I can't afford to fail.* I remember Christopher Robin. I'll have to become someone else, someone unafraid, someone who sings scales in elegant apartments every day, someone like Maria Callas. I clasp my hands over my breasts, take a good breath, lift my head, open my throat, and sing that scale as though it were the greatest aria ever written, connecting the five notes together in an even line. "Ah-ah-ah-ah-ah. . . ." Madame plays the scale over and over in ascending keys, finding the limits of my range as I sing my heart out. Then she plays intervals. "Do-ME-do," I sing; "do FA do; do-SOL-do."

After only a few minutes, she swivels on the piano stool so

that she faces Mommy. "The child has a voice," she says. *I have a voice!* Mommy looks skeptical. "It's a very good voice, a beautiful voice. Don't you hear it? You must hear it yourself!" Madame challenges her. "I will teach her. But she must work for me. Child, will you do that?"

I am so in love with Madame, I want to promise her anything she asks. But I just nod, mute. *What if she didn't say what I think she said? What if I didn't hear her correctly?* "Answer me, child! Will you work for me?"

"Yes! Yes! I promise!"

Madame looks triumphant. She speaks seriously now to Mommy, leaning toward her, conspiratorial, enlisting her in their shared goal of my glorious career. I will study privately with Madame until I finish high school. I must study solfeggio and music theory, as well. I will study with Madame at Curtis Institute when I'm ready. Then I will be sent to Rome to study some more, to be coached, to learn roles. And finally, I will make my debut. "Perhaps if she works very, very hard, she will one day sing at the Metropolitan Opera like some of my other pupils," she turns to me, twinkling. "She can do it! But she will have to be willing to give up everything, to sacrifice everything for the voice."

I swear to Madame with all my heart that I will do that. I swear with the fervent faith of a novitiate taking her vows: I don't have the voice. The voice has me.

Mommy was not happy. Things were not going according to her plan. Madame had offered to teach me herself. She had "filled my head with big ideas." Mommy was suspicious. Why should she believe what Madame said about my voice? Maybe Madame has offered to take me as a student just for the money. And there was absolutely no way that I could take two lessons a week, as Madame suggested.

"Daddy doesn't even want you to come home from school alone. He'll never let you go into Philly by yourself to take singing lessons. How can we be sure you won't just run off to see that boy, instead? I'll be the one who has to drive you back and forth and wait for you, keep an eye on you. I have your sisters to think about, too. I have a lot of work at the office. I have other things to do with my time." All the way home in the car, we argued.

"I'll talk to Daddy, but don't get your hopes up."

Evie saved me, glamorous, single working girl, Aunt Evie. She was my role model, my witness and my ally. She spoke to Mommy. She spoke to Daddy. And she spoke to me. "You're not a bad girl, Joie," Evie told me. "You're just a normal teenager. You're father is overreacting. He's crazy." She didn't tell me how he was crazy or why, but by plainly telling me just that he *was* crazy, she kept me from going crazy, too.

Evie negotiated my future. A deal was struck. Daddy reluctantly agreed to only two lessons a month, and Madame regretfully agreed to try to teach me under those less than ideal circumstances. Mommy agreed to drive me into the city and to be present at all times so that there was no possibility I could sneak off and see the boy. I agreed that if my grades dropped even a little, the lessons were over. Mommy told me "not to get my heart set" on a professional singing career. Daddy said, "She'd just be knocking her head against a brick wall." I had to get good grades so that I could get into a good college and prepare myself for a sensible profession, something I could count on, like practicing law or teaching.

Mommy tried to insist on being in the studio with me during my lessons. Daddy had deputized her as my warden. She was afraid that if she left me alone with Madame, I'd find a way to escape and meet the boy. But Madame firmly, politely, made it clear to Mommy that our lessons must be private. So Mommy, full of resentment, delivered me to Madame's door. "After all, I'm the mother. What can she be doing in there?" she complained to Evie. But she waited, standing sentry in the hall, listening until I came out again. After a couple of lessons, Madame convinced Mommy that it was safe to leave me with her. After that, Mommy went for a walk, met Evie, or shopped for an hour, but she was always back outside Madame's door when my lesson was over.

I kept my promise to Madame. I practiced all the time. Madame allowed me to sing nothing but vocalises and solfeggio exercises, little tunes sung with the names of the pitches—*do, re, mi*—in place of words. During the two weeks between my first and second lessons, I memorized them. Madame clapped her hands. "Oh, child! It's been years since I had a pupil who sang solfeggio from memory." And then she took me in her arms and kissed my cheek. I could hardly wait to tell the boy.

The boy contrived a plan to invite Mommy and me to dinner after one of my lessons. He worried over every detail—finding a restaurant that was suitably impressive but not completely unaffordable, the wording of the letter, the choice of the notepaper. At the post office, he bought a stamp that said "In God We Trust," but he thought that might be "a bit much," so he exchanged it for another one.

The boy was sure that, sooner or later, my parents would relent, and allow me to see him. Mommy and Daddy were sure that, sooner or later, the boy would give up and go away for good. Mommy was nonplussed by the boy's persistence. But she was beginning to soften. I was behaving like a good girl and working hard. I begged her to agree to the dinner. I told her it would be rude and mean to refuse the boy's invitation. I was relentless. I overheard her talking to Evie about it on the telephone. I heard her arguing about it with Daddy. Finally, she agreed.

———

Mommy follows me into the restaurant and he is there, all dressed up in the only tie and jacket he owns, grinning, delighted to see me, leaning toward me, not daring to touch me. The maître d' leads us to a booth. I slide in and the boy starts to slide in next to me but Mommy is quick. "Why don't you sit opposite us," she says, "so we can both see you." No chance for any hanky-panky under the table. I can't bear to look away from him, can't look at the menu, can't eat, can't speak.

Mommy tries to limit the conversation to small talk, but the boy has an agenda. This is his chance to win Mommy over, to make a case for himself. He outlines what he hopes are selling points. He extols his merits. His father is a lawyer. His mother teaches art. He himself has an extraordinarily high IQ. He is very musical. He speaks many languages. He is getting his master's degree. He is getting nowhere with Mommy.

When the check arrives, she snatches it out of his hands, pays for the meal herself, and ushers me out the door. On the way home she tells me he was "blowing his own horn." She tells me that she saw stars fill my eyes when I looked at him, and that I had better wake up.

The bitter taste of bile floods the back of my throat. This dinner should have worked. Mommy should have relented. She should have decided that he was nice and meant me no harm and that it was perfectly okay for me to spend time with him. The boy tried so hard. I am furious with Mommy for stubbornly continuing to support Daddy's position on the boy. "Don't blame me," she says. "I agreed to this dinner, didn't I? You have no idea how opposed to it your father was."

I begin to realize that Mommy doesn't really hate the boy at all, and that Daddy would despise any boy who dared to lay a hand on me. I have committed an unforgivable transgression by wanting to touch this boy so much.

The warm twilight of late summer dissolved into winter's long cold night. Months passed and separation began to wear the boy down, just as Mommy and Daddy had been sure it would. He was meeting new people in graduate school, and some of them were female. Our letters and phone calls were no longer enough to keep my image from floating away. He still wrote to me, but now when I eagerly scanned the pages for loving reassurance, I found painful words, instead.

"Even though I don't have any specific title for it (it certainly is some kind of love), there is no doubt about the feeling I have for you," he wrote.

> *The confusion is how this feeling relates to everything else—especially the fact of our separation. If you hold up a finger in front of your face, you can focus your eyes on that finger and everything else becomes a blur; or you can focus on the background and your finger is now indistinct. In that way, I can look around me and what I'm doing in my daily life, and the fact that you love me seems to have little place or reality. On the other hand, I can read the letter where you wrote me that and everything else seems of minor importance. . . .*
>
> *I'll never forget you, Joie. I can't love you in the same way I did before, but you are my friend and I love you as such.*

What was he saying? How could this be true? We were Helena and Demetrius, Romeo and Juliet. In the blindness of my romantic fantasy, I had enraged my parents and alienated my sisters. Now I would have to make a place for myself in the family again by pretending to be the girl Mommy and Daddy wanted me to be. I studied and practiced. I went to school and came home. I had no social life. I gave them no trouble. I fooled them into leaving me alone just a little. Daddy stopped calling me a whore. He barely spoke to me at all.

There were no more boys. Daddy laid down rules that made dating impossible. I could go out only in groups and only if a parent came along to chaperone. But I didn't have a group of friends to go out with and even if I had, no one in my high school would consider that a date. The Millville boys were getting their father's car keys, and driving girls up to Union Lake to neck. It was a moot point, anyway. I was a teenaged freak, a strange girl with a big purple mark on her face who sang opera—hardly dating material. And there were no boys in Millville whom Daddy would consider suitable dates.

Mommy rewarded my good behavior by buying tickets for the Philadelphia opera season. We saw Renata Tebaldi in *Tosca*, Leontyne Price in *Aïda*, Richard Tucker in *Un Ballo in Maschera*.

I hadn't heard from the boy in weeks. I dragged myself to school every day, cried every night in my bed. Daddy had won. He had taken the boy away from me.

Lucine Amara is singing Mimi in *La Bohème*. Mommy decides to stay in her seat during the second intermission. I tell her I have to find the ladies room. But instead, I find a phone booth.

"Who is it?" the boy asks. *How is it possible that he no longer recognizes my voice?* "Oh, Joie." He sounds disappointed. "We can't go on like this," he says. "It's too hard. Your parents are never going to let us see each other. You have to stop calling me." Something is wrong with my ears. I can't hear what he's saying. I must have misunderstood.

In operas, when the heroine falls down in a dead faint from heartbreak, I never question that it might actually be possible. Now I think it might be happening to me. I clutch the handle of the phone booth door to keep from falling.

"Joie? Are you there? Do you understand what I said?"

My mind is racing back and forth like a trapped mouse. I'm afraid to speak. I can't let him hear me cry. I cover the receiver with my hand, force myself to breathe.

"I won't call you again. I promise."

The last act of the opera has already begun when I sit down next to Mommy. "You were gone a long time," she whispers. "Are you okay? You look sick."

While Mimi lies dying onstage, I am dying with her.

I knew that what I was feeling was an agony so deep it had nothing at all to do with ordinary teenage heartbreak. I had seen girls in the locker room before gym class, sobbing over the boy who no longer cared, giving back his ring, burning his photograph. Two weeks later those girls were walking the school halls hand in hand with somebody new. That would never happen to me. What other boy would want a girl whose face was half purple, a girl who loved Bach and Mozart and *The Magic Mountain*? I had found someone with whom I could share my secrets. How could I ever replace him?

One afternoon, when the house was empty, I stood in the kitchen with the tip of Mommy's butcher knife pressed against my breastbone, wondering if I'd have the courage to plunge it into my heart when the pain became unbearable.

Madame now allowed me to begin learning seventeenth- and eighteenth-century Italian songs. *"O cessate di piagarmi, o lasciate mi morire,"* I sang, Oh cease to hurt me, or let me die.

How well I understood the anguish in Scarlatti's weeping melody.

⁓

Winter crept along, struggling toward spring. Each bleak day was imperceptibly brighter than the last. When at last I woke up to sunshine and the air was warm again, my sorrow lifted.

I began to be in demand on the luncheon and banquet circuit. I sang for all Daddy's clubs. I entertained the Rotary Club, the Kiwanis Club, the Lions Club, the American Legion, and the Veterans of Foreign Wars. I sang the songs Madame taught me at testimonial dinners for retiring judges. At last, I was an asset to Daddy, but his belief in my shameful transgression never went away. It hovered over me, casting its sinister shadow no matter how brightly I shined when I stood up to sing.

I sang for Mommy's clubs, too: the Women's Club and the American Association of University Women. I learned songs in Yiddish for the annual dinner meeting of the Sisterhood at Beth Hillel synagogue.

I decided that if I stopped seeing the birthmark, no one else would see it, either. Mommy always insisted it was no Big Deal. I tried hard to believe that she was right. I twisted my long hair into a chignon, dressed up, and greeted my audience as though there was nothing unusual about my face. That was how I could go on with my life. Instead of hiding, I stood in front of rooms full of strangers. It was my defiance.

When I was on stage, no matter how modest the venue, I was an opera singer. I left the sad purple-faced girl waiting in the wings and walked out into the light, full of poise. The music surrounded me, protected me. I concentrated with all my might on my breath, my tongue, my soft palate, my jaw, on the proper pronunciation of the words, on the dynamic markings, the piano accompaniment. And I escaped into the song, into the poem, into the time and place and person I portrayed. I made beautiful sounds, and the sounds made me beautiful. I was Cinderella, glorious, until my coach turned back into a pumpkin and I was home, again a shy girl with a disfigured face.

Maybe when they were alone Mommy and Daddy asked each other whether appearing in public would be hard for me. But they never asked me that question. They showed up at my performances and accepted the congratulations of colleagues and clients in the audience. We all just went on pretending the birthmark wasn't there.

I was a good girl, allowed to go straight home after school so that I could practice my singing before dinner. The boy was never mentioned in our house. Then one afternoon in May while my parents were still at the office, the phone rang, and I heard his voice again. Six months had passed. I was stronger now. I didn't shriek with joy or weep with relief. I no longer had the unguarded heart of a girl. I had learned to fight like a woman, to defend myself with deception. "Who is it? . . . Oh, how have you been? . . . Yes, I'm well. I've been very well." I had learned to play the game of pretending not to care. "Well, it was nice talking to you. . . . Yes, you can call me again. If you call at this time, my parents won't be here."

I put down the phone and fell back on my bed. I lay there for a long time, trying to sort it all out. I was proud of my performance. But my dreams of Helena and Demetrius, Romeo and Juliet, had vanished. He had dismissed me so coldly, and now I had greeted him so calmly. There could be no more illusion of undying passion. A strange, awful emptiness had taken the place of all the pain. The boy was back, but the romance was gone.

One Thing and One Thing Only

The summer before my senior year, Jackie and I returned to camp at the school in Lenox for the last time. Mommy and Daddy had been assured that the boy would not be teaching there. In a few months, I'd escape from Millville and the confines of my family. I imagined the glorious career that awaited me, singing in Italy, Germany, France. I imagined living in my own apartment, in a building like Madame's with a doorman and a canopy, coming and going as I pleased without having to ask anyone's permission.

Until then, I was going to snatch as much freedom as I could. I was willing to lie, to deceive, to do whatever I needed to do, and I was sure I was smart enough to get away with it.

Daddy had never stopped believing that I had given my virginity to the boy. He still treated me like an anathema. I knew now, after a whole year had gone by, that nothing I could do or say would ever change his mind. It was time to give up on Daddy. I had tried to please him for so long. Now I just wanted to try to get even. I had no reason to repress my adolescent urges and behave like a good girl. I might as well become the slut Daddy believed me to be.

When I got home from Lenox, I called the boy. I told him that I was no longer a virgin. I said that I had had sex with plenty of other boys that summer. "All the kids are doing it now," I said, as though screwing was the latest craze and he just wasn't hip enough to know about it. "So you might as well have sex with me, too." I wanted him to know that I was no longer dying for him, no, not at all. I was having lots of fun, having sex with lots of boys. It was a lie, of course, such an obvious lie that either the boy believed me because he wanted to or he didn't believe me at all, but found it convenient to pretend that he did. He asked me a few times if I was sure. I was very sure. We made a date for the following week.

I practiced copying Mommy's handwriting until I got to be very good at it. I stole a piece of her stationery, and wrote a note to the high school principal explaining that I was ill.

It's the morning of the day I've chosen to lose my virginity. I put on a blue corduroy dress that buttons up the front. It will be easy to take it off in a hurry. I leave the house at the usual time, but instead of walking to school, I walk to the bus station and buy a ticket for Philadelphia. The bus stops in every little town along the way. It's an agonizing two-hour ride. I've brought along a book, *Opera Before Mozart*, chosen partly because I want to read it, mostly because it will impress the boy. But I can't concentrate. I'm much too thrilled—and a little frightened—by thoughts of what I'm about to do. I feel a great tension between my legs, and every time the bus hits a bump, bouncing me on the hard seat, electric shocks fly from my groin to my temples and out to the tips of my fingers and toes.

The boy is waiting for me when I get off the bus. He carries a book bag over his shoulder, and looks at me strangely, half-smiling. We haven't seen each other for months, but he takes my hand and leads me to the subway as though we walk together every day.

He lives in a two-bedroom apartment in a dilapidated building near the university. We stand in the living room, furnished with worn-out secondhand things. There are no curtains, but the grime on the glass softens the harsh sunlight of early September. I have no idea how to behave in this situation. What sort of conversation might be appropriate? We both know I am there for one thing and one thing only. I don't know what to do or say so I look around the room, trying to imagine his life there. He offers me a glass of juice, a cup of tea. I tell him no thank you, so he walks into his bedroom, ready to get down to business, and I follow him.

I sit on the jumble of sheets, watching, as he takes a condom from the top drawer of a scuffed-up dresser and studies the back of the little foil envelope. I feel as though I am about to jump out of an airplane for the first time without knowing anything about parachutes. I have only a vague idea of what it is we are about to do, what it is that I want so desperately.

Without looking at me, he unbuttons his shirt. Then he takes off his pants and I see the bulge between his legs, shrouded in the white jersey of his Jockey shorts. He turns his head to find me, still sitting on the bed, frozen in fear and amazement. "Aren't you going to take off your clothes?" he asks. I unbutton the corduroy dress and let it fall onto the floor. He takes off his underpants, and his erection, big and rosy brown, bounces in front of him. I've never seen a naked penis before. I am horrified. *That thing looks much too big to fit inside me.* He sits on the bed. I put my arms around him. But he doesn't turn toward me. He is too intent on unrolling the condom. Then he pushes me back against the sheets, kisses me, reaches under my back to unhook my bra, covers a bare breast with his hand. "Wait until she gets excited," he mumbles under his breath. *He must be reciting something he memorized from a sex education manual.* But he doesn't wait long. He pulls off my panties. And oh! It hurts! *It hurts so much! I thought it was supposed to feel good. I had no idea that there would be pain.* He keeps moving, pushing into me. *What is he doing? I thought men just put it inside women. Why is he moving it around?* I try to be very quiet. *He must be having trouble getting it in. There must be something wrong with me.* I want to seem so experienced, so confident. I don't want him to know that he is hurting me. I'm too ashamed, too afraid he'll realize that I lied to him, that I'm a virgin, after all.

Then he just stops, lifts himself up, and kneels over me. "I don't think I got it in all the way," he says. Not, "That was so wonderful." Not even "Hey, thanks." I know I can't expect him to tell me that he loves me, or that I'm beautiful. Those aren't things you have to say to a girl who's slept with lots of boys, as I claim I have done. But I long to hear something gentle, something tender, something that acknowledges what we once meant to each other.

He dresses quickly, offers lunch and goes into the kitchen, leaving me alone with the dank sheets, trying to put myself back together, to dress myself, smooth my hair. I don't feel hurt or angry, or even disappointed. I just feel embarrassed, bewildered. Everything seems soiled and in a state of disarray—the bed, my clothes, my body, my hair, my tangled emotions. And I am frantically trying to make it all neat.

Timidly, I leave the bedroom and find him at the stove, boiling hot dogs. I stand beside him and he tosses an arm over my shoulder. *Sweet relief! He's not disgusted with me. Maybe I didn't disappoint him too much, after all.* The hot dog reminds me too much of a penis, but I force myself to eat it. Then he opens a can of peach halves. I look at the fleshy thing in the dish in front of me, sticky with juice, and wonder how I can eat that, too.

I get off the bus in Millville and prance home in the warm afternoon sunshine. On the ride back, I found a way to make it right. I can store the dark feelings where I won't have to see them. I added the pain of that day to all the pain of Daddy's accusations, all the pain of my purple face. In a pot shoved to the back of the stove, I'll leave my pain untended, to simmer and steam, until the ingredients are nothing but unrecognizable burnt bits stuck to the bottom, and it becomes impossible to ever get the pot clean again. But by tightly covering it and forcing myself to look away, I can avoid falling into this putrid stew of humiliation and fear.

I did it! I did it! So there to you, Daddy! Now you are right! The boy wants me for one thing and one thing only—and he's getting it! So there to you, boy, who couldn't love me the way you did before! So there to you, who made me promise to stop calling!

As soon as I walk into the house, Paula appears at the door, spilling questions. She knows why I didn't show up to walk her to school this morning.

"Did you do it?"

"Yes! Yes! I did it!" Now I am one of the cool girls, the tough girls. I feel so proud and powerful. I tell her everything about what I did with the boy, but nothing about how I feel inside.

"I'm worried that I must be a sex maniac because I just got laid and I'm still as horny as ever," I confess. I thought that if a man put his thing in you, you were supposed to be satisfied and that was that.

I go to the bathroom to pee after the long bus ride, and when I stand up to flush, there's a white fuzzy blob floating in the water. *It must be a fetus! I've only had sex once and I'm already having a miscarriage!*

"Paula, come in here!"

"It's a bar of soap that fell in the toilet, you idiot!" She laughs and I laugh, too, grateful for the laughter. I laugh as hard as I can so I won't cry.

Paula and I walk down to High Street to buy green mascara at Woolworth's. I'm celebrating.

―――

After that, I saw the boy from time to time. Our meetings were no longer about discussing J. S. Bach or Thomas Mann. They were about awkward attempts at sex on soiled sheets in shabby student apartments. Weeks or months passed, and then he'd call and I'd sneak away.

One afternoon, driving past Rittenhouse Square with Evie, we saw the boy dash across the street in front of her car, dragging a slim blond woman by the hand. "Oooh, look! There goes what's-his-name!" she said. "You don't care about him anymore, do you, Joie?" But I did care.

I called him. "I saw you yesterday when I was in Philly with Evie," I said. "Where?" he asked. "Why didn't you say hello?" And when I told him, "Oh, with Sophie," he said. There was only chagrin in his voice, no regret. The next time I laid in his bed, I noticed a tag, printed with her name, sewn onto the hem of the blanket. *Her blanket. How often she must lie here, where I am now, naked beside him! How lucky she is!*

So those were the rules. Now I understood that he called me between girlfriends or when a girlfriend was out of town. He called when he was lonely. He kept calling until I was in my second year of college. I had a nice new boyfriend by then, and I told him so. I told him that I was happy. He protested. He argued. He challenged my claim of happiness. "Well, if that's all you want," he said, as though he might have offered more. But he never called again.

The sweet, fragile affection that had connected the boy and me had been shattered, replaced by something sordid. But I didn't allow myself to think about that. All I remembered was the shabbiness of those last encounters. Maybe, in the end, it was I who wanted him for one thing and one thing only. Maybe I had to soil the memory of what might have been, so that I could bear the loss of it.

part two
BEHIND THE MASK

I have invented a mask that makes me look like anybody. People will not even turn round in the streets.

> GASTON LEROUX
> *Phantom of the Opera*

If I had been born in another time, in another place, I would have been ugly. Without benefit of contact lenses, I would have peered at the world through thick-lensed glasses. And without glasses I would have been blind to the world beyond the length of my arm. Without braces, I would have had buckteeth like Bugs Bunny. If I had been born before Max Factor or Elizabeth Arden or Estée Lauder, my face would have been marked with a bloody stain I could never disguise.

The Boyfriend

The lobby of Sargeant Hall is noisy and crowded. Stacks of luggage are piled on all the available floor space, between leather-covered sofas and armchairs. Eighteen-year-old girls and their parents are milling around. Near the staircase, a long folding table holds cardboard boxes full of files.

I have arrived at college disguised as an opera singer, in a blue and white printed silk dress, black patent leather high-heeled pumps, my hair in a neat chignon. I'm surprised that the other girls haven't bothered to dress up for such a big occasion. They are in blue jeans and loafers and ponytails. But I know that wouldn't be good enough for me. I have to look better than everybody else does in order to avoid looking worse. I can't be just another cute freshman, not with my purple-stained face. I wear my silk dress like a suit of armor, hoping these strangers will look at me with respect, instead of alarm.

I am not at Curtis Institute as Madame had promised. Curtis accepted only one singer this year, not one of Madame's students, not me. I am not where I belong. I am at the University of Pennsylvania, the alma mater of Mommy and Evie, Uncle Artie, Aunt Joan, Uncle Leon, Aunt Evelyn, and cousin Judy. I'll get a liberal arts education and study privately with Madame. It's what Mommy and Daddy want for me, a degree from an Ivy League school, something to "fall back on" after the inevitable collapse of my operatic ambitions.

In the confusion of parents and students, filling out forms and getting settled, a man approaches me—brown hair, suntanned skin, a sport shirt and khaki slacks, friendly face, somebody's father. "Where do we go to get room keys?"

"I don't know anymore than you do." I punctuate my reply with a nervous giggle. "I'm a freshman myself." Embarrassment casts a shadow over his eyes. "I thought you were a faculty member," he says. He inspects me more closely, trying to discover the cause of his blunder. Then he turns his head sideways, frowning. "How did you burn your face?" he asks.

———

This morning, the trunk of the family Buick was loaded with my new matched set of Samsonite luggage, brown vinyl embossed to look like crocodile. As Daddy backed the car out of the curved driveway, I turned around in the backseat so I could watch the house disappear in the rear window. It was a defining moment for me. I'd never live in Millville again.

Now afternoon has melted into evening. I'm standing just inside the entrance to Sargeant Hall, on the marble landing two steps up from the plate-glass doors, hugging, saying good-bye. Mommy holds me tight, squeezes me, kisses my cheeks. Daddy gives me a couple of pats on the back. The doors close behind them. I watch as they walk to the corner, as Evie hooks a reassuring hand through Mommy's arm.

Feeling taller and lighter than I have ever felt in my life, I waft up the staircase to my room, to the sound of girls laughing and talking. *I'm free, free, free! No one has to know where I am or what I'm doing. No one knows I'm Pete Davidow's girl. No one knows Pete Davidow. No one cares.* I'm giddy with relief, released from the cramped quarters of Mommy's constant monitoring, of Daddy's constant belittling.

———

From eight every morning until noon I closed myself in a practice room barely big enough to accommodate an upright piano. All my classes were crammed into the afternoons. I saw Madame twice a week. Once a week, I met Evie for lunch.

marked for life

I had room to breathe. I didn't have to be Daddy's bad girl, banging her head against a brick wall anymore. After the suffocation of my life in Millville, my newfound freedom, limited though it was, elated me. Freedom propelled my feet and shot through my body, joyously erupting in a smile that rarely left me from Monday to Friday. But on weekends, I was still the strange girl with the purple-stained face.

Getting engaged was almost as much a part of the curriculum as getting a degree. The game of boy-dates-girl, which was the obsession of nearly everyone on campus, confounded and frightened me. My nascent self-confidence was far too fragile to withstand so rough a sport and I had never dated in high school, didn't know the rules.

Monday and Tuesday nights were for coffee dates, first dates. If those dates were successful, the coffee-date boys would call to upgrade to a Friday-night or a Saturday-night date. In the dorm, banks of phones on each floor accepted incoming calls only. Until they were turned off at curfew, those phones rang constantly. A boy had to persistently, patiently dial and redial in order to get through. And with every ring, hearts stopped beating up and down the halls. We all knew who already had a weekend date, who was still waiting, hoping for a phone call and from whom. The girl who happened to answer the phone announced it to the lucky one. "Barbara, your Friday night came through. He's on the phone!" Every evening I listened to the ringing, the feet stampeding past my door to grab the receiver. But if the call was for me, it was Mommy or Evie, never a date.

On Saturday afternoons there was a fracas of getting ready, of lipsticks and perfumes, of borrowed hair dryers and traded clothes, of parading the halls to ask for opinions, for reassurance. By eight o'clock it was over; the dorm was empty, silent. All the dates had arrived to take the girls by the hand, out into the night. And I was alone in the deserted building, pretending to study.

Hours later, when the bell announced curfew, I was still in my room sitting at the desk. No point in trying to sleep through all the commotion. In the midst of the laughter, someone would stop in. "Hey, you must have come back early? Was your date a dud?" And I would say, "No, I didn't go out tonight. I stayed in to study."

A Jewish guy from Millville saved me. He was a fourth-year oboe student at Curtis, married and already gigging, supporting himself by playing his instrument. Jay and his wife, Carole, invited me to dinner. It was the nice thing to do for a hometown girl. To complete their little table, they invited a boy who lived in their building, a second-year flute student.

Hank was good-looking in an all-American way—dark blond hair and big blue eyes—the kind of guy who wore corduroy pants and Hush Puppies. He was tall and so slim he had to sit on a cushion because there was no natural padding on his behind. But I was short and curvy and I thought his long, lean body was graceful, all angles and lines.

After dinner, he courteously offered to put me in a cab. As I slid onto the seat, he leaned in, kissed me on the lips, and asked if he could call me.

He later told me that when she invited him to dinner, Carole had said, "I might have a girl for you, but she has a big purple birthmark on her face. Do you mind?" Despite my lonely weekends, I had been merrily going about my new college life, trying to ignore the birthmark. I hated being reminded that there was a problem with my face. "Why would Carole say a thing like that?" he asked me in all innocence. "Why would I care that you have a birthmark?"

"I guess she thought it was only fair to warn you," I said. I wondered how many other warnings had been issued, how many other people had been told about my marked face before they met me.

My first date with Hank was almost my first official date with anyone. My clandestine meetings with the boy didn't really count. That Saturday afternoon, I tried on clothes in every imaginable combination, settling on a slim, rose-colored wool tweed skirt and a pink cashmere cardigan that had once belonged to Evie. I brushed my long dark hair and let it flow in waves past my shoulders and down my back. I borrowed my roommate's Revlon Blush-On and dusted it over just my right cheek and eye, trying in vain to balance the colors of my face. Then I ran down the hall to borrow a spritz of Miss Dior perfume.

At precisely the appointed hour, Hank called from the lobby to let me know he was there. I was all dressed, but I told him I'd be ready in a few minutes. I'd noticed that the other girls always made their dates wait for them. I thought I'd better do that, too. It must be part of the game. I'd been on the phone with Evie in preparation for this date. She told me, "You have to give him just enough encouragement, but make sure you don't act too eager, Joie. You have to learn to play hard to get, a little bit."

I start down the steps, holding onto the railing to steady my trembling knees. On the landing, I pause in front of the full-length mirror where generations of girls before me have inspected themselves while their dates waited in the lobby below. I'm satisfied that I've managed to make myself look good. Hank's face, watching me descend the last flight of steps, goes all soft, and I know he thinks so, too.

Hank has no money, but he has a discount coupon for an art film house. Lacking the economic freedom to choose a movie, he can only afford to take me to see whatever is playing at the World Cinema. It's a bleak black-and-white film—Ingmar Bergman's *Winter Light*. I'm very near-sighted but I can't let him know I wear glasses. I can't read the subtitles, can't follow Bergman into his frigid, godforsaken Swedish winter. But it doesn't matter that I can't understand the movie. I'm concentrating on Hank's hand, holding mine. For eighty minutes our hands seduce each other—his thumb stroking my index finger, my fingers lightly brushing his palm.

After the movie, we stand on the sidewalk outside the theater.

"Did you like it?" he asks.

I have no idea what the movie was about. "Yes," I lie. "Did you?"

"I might have if I could have read the subtitles. Actually, I wear glasses but I was embarrassed to put them on in front of you."

"Really? Me, too."

I look up at him, expecting him to tell me what we'll do next, to suggest someplace nice where we can have coffee or ice cream.

He just stands there, shuffling his feet. Then he asks, "Would you like to come over to my place to listen to records? Jay bought a pint of Scotch for me today at the State Store." Hank is only nineteen but Jay just turned twenty-one and can buy booze for the younger guys.

This is not what Evie said was supposed to happen. If I say yes, he'll get the wrong idea. Maybe he just wants one thing and one thing only.

I say, "Oh no. I don't think so. It wouldn't be right to be alone with you in your apartment. This is only our first date."

Hank looks at his feet, so that he seems to be speaking directly to his Hush Puppies. "Yeah, I was afraid you might feel that way, but I figured I'd ask. I'd take you somewhere else, but

I don't have any more money. I guess I should just take you back."

He takes my hand and starts to walk with me toward the corner, looking for a cab. It was a short movie. If he takes me back now, I'll be alone in the dorm. I want to know what it feels like to come in at curfew with all the other girls. It might be a long time before I get another chance. I'm out in the dark air, dressed up and holding hands with a cute guy. He seems so sweet, so honest, so respectful, so polite.

I stop walking. "Wait. I changed my mind. I guess I can trust you."

"You mean you'll come to my place?"

︵

He lives on the top floor of a converted townhouse that has been inhabited by music students for decades. Apartments are handed down from graduating students to freshmen. Jay and Carole live on the first floor. I try to be quiet passing their door. I don't want them to know I'm here. But Hank actually raises his voice. "I'm right behind you, Joie!" Now the whole building knows.

His apartment is a single room, three long flights up a narrow staircase. It's much nicer than I expected it to be—very tidy and well decorated—though it's not much bigger than my dorm room. There's a single bed, made to look passably couchlike with a black twill cover and colorful throw pillows; a black canvas butterfly chair; a small, round wooden table with two matching bistro chairs; a long, low black dresser; a Japanese white paper lantern lamp; and a state-of-the-art stereo system. The tiny bathroom and kitchen occupy what must have been closets. I'm alone with a man I've just met. I don't dare sit down. Needing to escape for a minute, I move to the narrow windows and pull aside the black muslin curtains to find the shadow of a fire escape garnished with the branches of a scrawny tree trapped in the alley below, reaching up in a desperate quest for sunlight.

Hank is putting ice in glasses. The surging harmonies of the love duet from Wagner's *Tristan und Isolde* gush from big speakers on either side of the dresser. *This must be his idea of make-out music.* He sits down on the bed, hands me a glass. *Maybe I should sit on the butterfly chair.* He arranges a couple of throw pillows, to make a comfortable spot for me beside him. "Sit here," he says. I sit on the bed. I want him to like me enough to keep calling, to keep me out of the lonely dorm on Saturday nights.

We tell each other the basic facts about ourselves, about our hometowns and our families, as though we were filling in a form. He is an only child from a little town in Missouri where his father is a meat cutter at the local supermarket and his mother is a secretary at the local bank. Back in Missouri he was an Eagle Scout. I know what it means to be an Eagle Scout. I was once a Girl Scout. Eagle Scouts are trustworthy—physically strong, mentally awake, and morally straight.

I feel safer knowing I'm alone with an Eagle Scout. When he kisses me, I let him. But I keep his hands from wandering below the waist. I want him to respect me.

Our taxi pulls up at the dorm just before curfew. The sidewalk is crowded with couples saying goodnight, kissing and holding each other until the last minute. Hank puts his arms around me and gives me a long kiss.

"Would it be all right if I called you again?"

Yes! Yes! Call me! Please call me! But I can't say that. Instead I use one of the phrases Evie taught me: "Sure. I'd like that."

A bell rings, and the girls stream inside, some of them making no effort to hide the fact that they've thrown their clothes back on in a hurry. They are catching each other's eyes, smirk-

marked for life

ing, feeling cool. And I am one of them. I can stay up late and swap date stories. I've been seen outside the doors at curfew with a cute guy. I have something to laugh about, too.

As I follow the throng into the dorm, I turn around to watch Hank, standing alone on the other side of the street, his hands in his pockets. He's blown his last dollar on the taxi that brought me back. Now he's waiting for the bus that will take him home.

───⌒───

Two dates later, he invites me to dinner at his apartment. I sit on the bed, trying to get comfortable in my pantyhose and skirt, and let my high-heeled pumps clatter onto the floor so that I can curl up as I read a sheaf of typewritten pages. Hank is pacing the small room, shaking a brown paper bag with veal chops and flour inside, pretending not to be watching my face.

He has been shyly offering to show me his poems, waiting until he trusts my affection for him, and I, expecting embarrassing, sentimental rhymed verses, have been preparing my platitudinous response to them in advance. What sort of poetry would an Eagle Scout from a little town in Missouri write? I'm only eighteen years old but I've read so much all my life, I think I can tell a good poem from a bad one.

The first poem is a revelation. I read it over and over again, making sure I really get the meaning of every word, every phrase. I read the second one slowly, carefully. It takes me a long time to fully digest all eight poems. When I finish the last page, he is standing beside me, still holding the bag of veal chops. But he looks different to me now. The poems are beautiful, full of emotion expressed through unexpected imagery—weeds hanging in water, spiders spinning in puddles, rivers of roots, brute moons, moaning birds, and stars that scatter like gnats.

During dinner, I stare at him across the little table, trying to find the poet, searching for some clue I must have missed. His surface is shy, boyish humor, Midwestern reserve. He has never shown me what's underneath. Nothing I know about him suggests that he can conjure those images, can see what he sees and write it down.

He is looking for a girlfriend and he thinks I might do. I am looking for a steady date to keep me out of the terrifying game of boys calling girls, boys not calling. He could be my ticket to the social life at Curtis Institute, my invitation to the parties. He is the sort of boy who would be safe, and I can't risk being hurt again. But now I know he's not just a blue-collar guy who plays the flute. Something much more complicated is going on inside his head.

There were rivals to be dispensed with. He told me of his high school sweetheart, Elizabeth, of her beautiful red hair and creamy skin. I knew my dark brown hair and olive skin couldn't compete with that. I actually considered dying my hair red (again), but there was nothing I could do about my complexion. And Elizabeth, who had broken his heart, was safely back in Missouri.

He spoke admiringly of Joan, whom he'd met during the summer when they were both counselors at a music camp in the Adirondacks. Joan, he said, was a certified genius. I thought I was a bright girl, but I didn't feel I could compete with a genius. Joan was the more formidable opponent. A girl can't dye her IQ. And Joan was in New York, only a short train ride away.

She invited him to spend Thanksgiving with her family. I couldn't match the offer. He could have a pleasant holiday weekend with Joan's family, but not with mine. Mommy and Daddy had sent me to the university to meet a nice Jewish boy.

The university was crawling with nice Jewish boys, but I never dated even one of them, despite Mommy's pleas. She said that I was "jumping the gun." She wanted to know if we were "getting serious," "making a mistake." She said I was "closing the door," when I should be giving myself "the opportunity to meet people."

Daddy would not be pleased to meet any boy I was dating, certainly; he would not be at all pleased to meet a *goyishe* boy from Missouri. I was afraid that Daddy would win again. He'd take this boy away from me, too. I'd never have a boyfriend. I'd end up old and alone because Daddy would never accept any boy who touched me, and no boy would be able to withstand Daddy's hostility for long.

So Hank went off to Joan in New York and I went home to Millville. All weekend I forced myself to seem cheerful, while I imagined him having a lovely time with Joan's warm, accepting parents, imagined him realizing that what he really wanted after all was a girl with a stellar IQ and a well-adjusted, friendly family. I knew I didn't have a chance.

Sunday afternoon, it began to rain. On the bus ride back to Philadelphia, I prepared myself for the worst. I told myself not to expect to go on seeing him. He'd try to let me down gently. He'd say he hoped we'd still be friends. I'd smile bravely, and make him think that was just fine with me. I told myself that we'd had six very nice weeks of dating and I could be grateful for that. I was stronger now. I could face the lonely dorm. At least I'd had a boyfriend for a little while.

I dragged my suitcase down the hall toward my dorm room. Most of the girls were still away and the building was quiet. We used the nameplate holders on our doors to stash messages scrawled on bits of paper. My holder was crammed. Hank had been calling for the past three hours, not knowing when I'd be back. He called from the train station in New York. He called from the train station in Philly. As soon as he got back to his apartment, he started timing his calls at fifteen-minute intervals.

I left my suitcase in the hall and ran downstairs to the lobby where I could make an outgoing call from a pay phone. He answered on the first ring. He said, "I wonder if you could come over. I have something important to tell you."

"Yes, I guess so." I couldn't let him think I would hop into the next cab. I remembered Evie's admonition against seeming too eager. "Give me an hour or so to unpack and get settled," I said.

I opened my suitcase and spilled the contents onto my bed, took a hanger from the closet, and began to put things away. But I couldn't wait to hear the important thing he wanted to tell me. I threw on a new red dress, fluffed my hair, and raced out of the dorm into the cold, wet November evening, searching frantically for a taxi, as I turned up the collar on my coat and pulled on my gloves.

Hank is on his tiny fourth-floor landing, watching for me as I climb the stairs. He hugs me and kisses me and now that I'm with him everything feels different. Inside the little apartment we lie side by side on the bed, talking of nothing much. He asks about my weekend, tells me about New York, about Joan's family, and I am bursting because he's not talking about the important thing. "You said you had something important to tell me?"

"Well," he rolls away from me, onto his back, licks his lips, hesitates. "Just to put it very simply, I love you." *He loves me! He loves me! Now I'm really a woman, a woman loved by a man.* And now it's my turn to react. I give him my very best kiss, a reward kiss, a gift kiss. I look at him and smile without speaking. And I see that he's waiting for me to say something. But I can't say anything and I don't know why I can't.

marked for life

He says that he realized it was me he loved, that he had to rush back to Philly, rush back to me. He says that Joan walked him to the subway station and that's where he left her, crying in the rain, standing at the top of the steps holding her umbrella.

And then there's nothing else to talk about, because I'm not saying anything. I don't know what to say. I really care for Hank. I'm thrilled to have a boyfriend. But this doesn't feel anything like the great romantic yearning I had for the boy.

We walk down the street to the Harvey House, which offers forty-eight different kinds of hamburgers. I decide on my usual—topped with avocado and melted Gruyere. And when I look up from the oversized menu where all the kinds of hamburgers are listed and described, the defeat in Hank's face hurts me. He chose me. He left a genius in tears in New York, rushed back to declare his love for me. But all I can do is reach across the table and give his hand a squeeze.

On the first floor of Sargeant Hall, behind the lobby and lounge area, a warren of private "date rooms" is used exclusively for necking, the very activity they were designed to discourage. Each little room is just big enough to contain a couple of chairs and a small table. There are no doors. There are no light switches. The overhead lights are always on, blazing until curfew when the rooms have to be vacated and the dates ushered out of the building.

On weeknights, Hank often comes to visit me at the dorm. I meet him in the lobby, and we look for a vacant date room where we can push the two chairs close together, lean across the wooden armrests, and make out. From time to time, one of the dorm monitors patrolling the rooms peers in to enforce the rule of four feet on the floor at all times.

We spend two or three hours at a stretch in those little rooms, barely speaking, kissing and touching from the waist up. Hank's gentle yet urgent embraces arouse me in a way I never experienced with the boy. I discover that if I cross my legs and keep my thighs squeezed together tightly, I can climax, just from prolonged kissing. I'm much too embarrassed to tell Hank what's happening. When I have to stop and catch my breath, he thinks it's my signal that he's "going too far." He sits back and takes a break, then resumes making out with me until I have to stop and catch my breath again. In this way, I can manage to behave like a good girl while enjoying multiple orgasms.

He knows I'm not a virgin. I told him about the boy. But I'm not going to "go all the way" so fast. I'm not a cheap slut, no matter what Daddy says. Hank is a nice boy. He expects to be made to wait. I'm waiting too, waiting for him to ask me nicely so that I can say yes.

⁓

On a Saturday night, alone in his apartment, after hours of rolling around on his couch-bed fully clothed, bodies pressed together, loins grinding, he pulls away and looks at me.

"I want you," he whispers through half a shy smile, half a wry giggle. "But if you think it's a Big Deal."

"No. It's not a Big Deal. I don't think it is." He leaps up and finds a condom in a drawer, hidden among his neatly folded socks and underwear.

⁓

College girls were kept under lock and key. While the boys, being biologically incapable of bearing children, were consoled with the freedom to come and go as they pleased, we child bearers had curfews. The doors to the dorm were locked at midnight sharp from Sunday to Thursday, at one A.M. on Friday and at two A.M. on Saturday. From time to time, there were unannounced post-curfew bed checks. Bodies were counted and accounted for. I didn't dare miss a curfew. The consequences were too grave. Mommy and Daddy would be informed, and I would be made to appear before a student court, a panel of upper classmen who would mete out my punishment. If a girl missed more than one curfew, she could be expelled from school. The boys who kept her out too late had no such problem.

Parents were given some control of the liberties their daughters were granted. They were asked to choose among a range of varying degrees of permission. If parents granted "A" status, a girl could simply sign herself out of the dorm to go and stay overnight wherever she pleased. All she had to do was to give an address where she planned to be and a time and date when she planned to be back. Most of the girls had parents who trusted them enough for that. But Mommy, and especially Daddy, thought "A" status was a scandalous idea. They chose the strictest possible option for me, "C" status, which meant I could only sign myself out to a limited number of preapproved destinations.

So I had no choice but to sign myself out as though I was spending every Saturday night with an unsuspecting Evie. I felt a little guilty because Evie was my ally, my defender. But I justified my behavior by condemning Mommy and Daddy for being so unreasonable, for not trusting me, for suspecting that I might do exactly what I was, in fact, doing.

On Saturday afternoon, I pack up and sign out of the dorm, timing my departure so that my arrival at Hank's apartment will coincide with the end of the football game I know he's watching. I let myself in with my key and find him lying on the bed, his eyes fixed on the small television set, which occupies one of the bistro chairs, antennae askew, elevated on a stack of books so he won't have to lift his head from the pillow in order to see it comfortably. He barely moves when he hears me come in. I put down my bag filled with homework, opera scores, a change of clothes, and sit beside him, as he knows I will. I lean over to take off his glasses and kiss his eyes. He kisses the corners of my smile. His cat, who is less coy in welcoming me, gives up her sentry post on the fire escape, where she has spent the day patrolling for sparrows, stalks in through the half-open window, and announces herself with a gurgle as she leaps onto the jumble of our limbs.

In the gray light of a cat-cozy afternoon, Hank studies my face. "You're so pretty," he says. "I just can't believe it." *Pretty. Me, pretty! Maybe it's true. Maybe I'm really pretty. Maybe the birthmark really is no Big Deal!*

"Well," I ask, "what shall we do about dinner?"

I knit him a mohair sweater for Christmas. If a Jewish girl was really interested in a boy, she knit him a sweater. Our grandmothers, mothers, and aunts had taught us to knit, and we knit incessantly. We knit everywhere. We carried our knitting around in our tote bags with our books. We sat in the old ivy-covered College Hall, in the back rows of lecture rooms as grand and gothic as the sanctuary of the Presbyterian Church, knitting during class. We sat on the steps leading down to the women's dining hall, waiting for the doors to open for the six-thirty seating, knitting for our boyfriends. After dinner we sat on our beds, knitting and gossiping, trading stitch holders and needles, and inspecting each other's work.

I made a mohair cardigan, beige with green and brown cabled stripes down the front. Hank was almost a foot taller than I was. I had no idea what size he wore. I just knew that he was big. I made a sweater for a giant. When he tried it on, the sleeves came down to his knees. That sweater would have been too big for Wilt Chamberlain. But Hank was thrilled with it, so

marked for life

proud he insisted on taking it to Missouri to show his mother. After Christmas, I had to take it to a knitting shop and have it cut down so he could wear it.

We came back to Philly in time to spend New Year's Eve together. Since the dorms wouldn't reopen for another week, I stayed with Evie in suburban Elkins Park. Nearly all the families on her street were Jewish, the affluent sons and daughters of poor immigrants from Eastern Europe. And nearly all the women, even Evie, made an enormous effort to look as much like Grace Kelly as possible. They tortured wavy dark hair into sleek frosted blond pageboys, had their noses surgically diminished, and wore cashmere sweaters and cultured pearls with their tweed suits. They loved saying they lived in Elkins Park. It sounded so genteel, so English manor house. Looking like a Protestant, even passing for a Protestant, was very desirable. But for a son or daughter to date an actual Protestant, or, God forbid, to marry one, was horrible, unthinkable, tragic. Evie was tolerant of Protestant Hank because she liked him, because she thought he was cute, and because she was sure our romance wouldn't last.

It's the night before New Year's Eve. Tomorrow we'll be at a party in town with music students from Curtis Institute. But tonight Hank has taken the train to Elkins Park so that he can escort me to a dessert and sherry party, just down the street from Evie's house, hosted by the parents of one of the nice Jewish girls in my dorm.

Hank is the only gentile in the room, the only Missouri boy. I am nearly as uncomfortable among all the cut glass and engraved silver as he is, working too hard to make small talk with frosted blond, pruned-nosed Jewish girls, clones of their mothers, whose lives have been so different from mine, and who all seem to have known each other for years. Frantically filling in the awkward silences, looking around for Hank, worrying what he can find to talk about with the rich Jewish boys, I keep checking my watch, wondering how much longer we have to stay before we can leave without seeming rude. I make excuses, claim that Evie is waiting up for us.

But Evie has gone to bed early, discreetly leaving out a bottle of Scotch. Sitting on the couch in her darkened living room, we keep our voices low. "Everything seems so nice," Hank says. "But you never say anything, and sometimes I feel empty inside." I look away, slide my glass around on the mahogany tray table, fold and unfold a paper cocktail napkin embossed with Evie's initials. *I don't want to hurt him. I can't afford to lose him. But I can't lie to him. If love means the desperate passion I once felt for the boy, I don't love him. But maybe I'll never feel that passion again. Maybe what I'm feeling now is a better kind of love. Maybe this is "mature" love.* I can only manage to say it in a whisper. "I love you."

Ticket to Aspen

We spent that summer at the Aspen Music School and Festival. I was a student in the opera department. Hank played in the orchestra. Mommy and Daddy, not knowing that Hank would be at the festival, bought me a plane ticket to Denver. The festival van would pick me up from there. Hank didn't have airfare; he didn't even have bus fare. He was stranded in Missouri with no way to get to the festival, so I cashed in my plane ticket and bought a Greyhound bus ticket from Philadelphia to Missouri plus two tickets from Missouri to Denver. I used Evie as an accomplice so that Mommy and Daddy wouldn't know where I was for a few days. I spent only one night at her place instead of four, then she drove me to the bus station instead of the airport and told me I owed her. She said, "Just be sure you never tell your mother, Joie. No kidding. She'd kill me."

This would be my introduction to Hank's parents. I'd visit them in Missouri for a couple of days, and then Hank and I would go on to Denver together. I thought of meeting his mother as a crucial test, like an audition. I reasoned that since Hank was an only child, she wouldn't surrender him easily. Before I left Philadelphia, I prepared myself, spending hours at Bonwit Teller in search of the perfect first-impression outfit. Finally, I found a wrinkle-proof black jersey shirtdress and, for my hair, a big black satin bow attached to a barrette.

For three days I rode Greyhound buses, trying to curl up on two seats, so that I could sleep for three and four hours at a stretch, waking up cramped and bleary, brushing my teeth, repairing my makeup, and changing my clothes in dirty bus station bathrooms. Mommy and Daddy would have been horrified if they had known where I was or what I was doing.

I expected each state to look different, a constantly changing landscape, but they all looked the same. Ohio looked just like Pennsylvania, Indiana looked just like Ohio. Illinois looked just like Indiana—the same trees, the same houses, the same billboards, the same gas stations. I changed buses in St. Louis, and, at three in the morning, I was in Hank's hometown. He was waiting for me at the bus station with his father's secondhand but still spiffy Lincoln Continental.

Overjoyed to see me and insanely horny, he said he had been driving around Missouri for two weeks in that big car with the air-conditioner blasting his crotch, trying to get a little relief. We didn't dare do anything in his parents' house, not even while they were both sound asleep, not even while they were both at work. I couldn't risk another trauma like the one with Daddy and the boy. There could be no getting caught.

When I woke up late the next morning, Hank's parents were long gone, and he had been awake and dressed for hours. He told me that his mother was expecting me to meet her for lunch. I spent an hour lining my eyes with black pencil, brushing blush onto my good cheek, twisting my long hair into a chignon, and positioning the big satin bow at the back of my head. Hank walked me out to the main street. He had his own lunch date with his father, so he pointed me in the right direction and went on his way.

Feeling grown-up and sophisticated in my new black dress and my high-heeled patent leather pumps, I parade down the length of the street, from the town's only supermarket, where Hank's father works, to its only bank, where I'm scheduled to meet his mother at noon, sharp.

marked for life

Men in overalls come out of the shops to get a better look as I pass by. *Is it the sight of a new girl in town that intrigues them or my purple face, brazenly displayed with my hair pulled back?* I don't like these strange men, their eyes crawling over my skin. I cross the street so that my birthmark side is to the traffic. I keep my eyes focused straight ahead, passing in profile, showing only my good cheek. I walk fast, trying to go too fast for anyone else to notice me. In the space of only four blocks, I've walked from one end of the main street to the other. *Is it possible that I've spent three days on a bus only to find myself in a town even smaller and more provincial than Millville, New Jersey? Where are we going for lunch? There must be another, nicer part of town farther on.*

The church clock strikes twelve just as I enter the revolving doors of the bank, right on time, the clatter of my high heels echoing off the marble floor. I have no idea how to find Hank's mother, so I wait in line for the first teller. I lean into the window, as though I'm about to tell a secret. "Excuse me," I whisper, "I'm looking for . . . I mean, actually, I'm supposed to have lunch with—" "Oh yes! She's been expecting you!" Heads lift from the row of desks at the back of the lobby, as if everyone in the bank has been expecting me.

Hank's mother is a tiny woman, not five feet tall, and as slender as her son. She looks me up and down, but she's smiling and offering her hand. She's wearing a pastel blouse, a printed cotton skirt, and flat shoes. *I'm an idiot, all dressed up like a city slicker. Where did I think I was going?* I smile back. *Maybe I can still make a good first impression.* She takes me around to all the desks, introduces me as "Hank's friend." *Hank must have warned her and she must have warned everybody else.* No one asks questions about my face.

"We'll walk over to Woolworth's and get a sandwich," she says, "if that's all right with you." Woolworth's is not what I think "going to lunch" means. I'm dressed for a nice restaurant. *It's fine. I don't have to be embarrassed. Mommy and Daddy often eat at Woolworth's lunch counter in Millville.*

It turns out to be a pretty big Woolworth's, as they go. There are wooden booths, so we don't have to eat at the counter, and a waitress comes to take our order. Hank's mother doesn't waste much time with small talk or polite questions about my family. Ignoring the sandwich and potato chips on her plate, she lights a cigarette and gets to the point. She says that Hank has to finish school and that nothing is going to interfere with that, especially not me, and do I know what she means. I say I know. She says that he is not ready to get married, and that he is certainly not ready to have a family—maybe a few years down the road, but that remains to be seen. She says that if he gets tied down, that will be the end of his education. She says that all the money she makes working as a secretary at the bank goes toward Hank's school expenses and she wants to make sure that her sacrifice pays off, and do I understand where she's going with this. I say, "Well yes, I most certainly do." I say, "I would never want Hank to drop out of school." She says, "And I suppose you're planning to finish school yourself."

I can't believe she is saying all this! I say, "Hank and I haven't talked about getting married at all." *No matter what I say, I sound ridiculous. She must be afraid that I'm putting out, that I'll get knocked up and trap her son. What kind of a girl does she think I am?* I'd like to reassure her, but I'm not about to tell her that Hank always uses rubbers so she shouldn't be too concerned.

I try to set her straight by telling her about my hopes for a career as an opera singer. I say that I'm certainly in no hurry to get married myself. She says, "Uh huh. Well, that may be. I just want to be sure that we understand each other." Satisfied that she has done her maternal duty, she turns her attention to tuna salad and sliced tomato on white toast and I change the subject.

When I got back after lunch, I took off the black dress, threw on a pair of Bermuda shorts, and let my hair down. Then I went through the house, from room to room, tidying up, fluffing sofa cushions. I washed the breakfast dishes I found in the kitchen sink. I ironed all the shirts Hank planned to take to Aspen and folded them in a neat pile.

That night, Hank's parents threw a barbecue so that the relatives and neighbors could say good-bye to him and have a look at his new girlfriend. The turnout was impressive. I was the first Jewish person any of them had ever met and they weren't at all embarrassed about telling me so. My Jewishness was easily as exotic as my birthmark.

The women lifted handfuls of my hair and held it up to the light. "Look how black it is!" they marveled. "Well, I guess it's kind of dark brown," I mumbled, "I never thought of it as black." "You don't think that's black? Why, that's the blackest hair I've ever seen. Does everybody in your family have black hair like that?" I began to suspect they were looking for those little horns Jewish people are supposed to have hidden under their hair.

There was also a lot of concern about my dietary habits. "Now, you won't eat a hot dog, though, will you? I don't b'lieve your religion allows that." I stumbled around, trying to find polite ways to explain that not all Jews kept kosher, although, of course, I did have great respect for my religion.

The next day before we caught the afternoon bus to Denver, Hank was summoned to meet his mother at the bank. It was his turn for a private lunch meeting at Woolworth's. She told him that if he wanted to marry me, that would be just fine, so long as he finished school first. She said, "You'll have to look a long time to find another one like her. She's a worker." The cleaning and ironing had paid off.

⌒

I'm knitting for Hank again. He wants an afghan—an ashcan, he calls it. It's a summer-long project. On the bus from Missouri to Denver, I keep an ever-lengthening strip of knitting across our laps. Hank uses it to conceal the erection that rarely leaves him. At night, while the other passengers doze, we grope and dry-hump in desperation.

I wake up in Kansas on a road that is the only interruption in an otherwise infinite cornfield. The land is flat, perfectly flat. For hours we pass through miles and miles of identical rows of corn. The view never changes. It's as though the bus has stopped moving, as though we've been parked in front of the same cornfield all morning. *At last, a state that doesn't look just like the rest of them.*

We arrive in Denver two hours ahead of the van that will take us on to Aspen. Hank has been planning on using the time well. He hurries me into a cab and asks the driver to recommend a cheap hotel. I avoid the driver's eyes in the rearview mirror. There is disgust in his voice when he answers, but it isn't because he disapproves of our moral standards. The bus station is surrounded by cheap hotels. We are a crummy fare. He drives around the block and drops us off a few feet away from the spot where he picked us up.

I have never seen the inside of a building like this hotel and I am in no hurry to see it now. "You go in," I tell Hank. "I'll stay outside and guard the luggage while you get a room."

I watch through the glass door as Hank speaks to the skinny clerk behind the ancient desk in the tiny lobby.

He comes out with a key. "Are you sure you want to do this?" he asks.

"I'm sure that I *don't* want to do this."

marked for life

"I'm sorry. I'm sorry. We can just walk back to the bus station and wait there. You don't have to go through with it."

"No, I said I would do it and I'm not going to back out now."

I follow Hank up a narrow, dark staircase. The bed takes up most of the room, leaving space for only an old dresser with a mirror above it. The only window is in the bathroom. I can see that Hank is miserable and ashamed, that he knows just how appalling the situation is, but I feel the need to tell him, anyway. "I don't want to sit down on that bed with all my clothes on, let alone get naked and lie on it."

Hank tears off the bedspread. The sheets, which must once have been white, are almost the same gray as the spread, which must once have been blue. But I have my period, and as tired as those sheets are, I don't want to leave a bloodstain on them for the maid to find when she comes to clean up after us.

I take the single white towel from the bathroom and spread it on the bed. Then I undress and carefully position myself on top of it. Five minutes later, it's all over.

There's no hot water in the bathroom, and we've already soiled the towel. I try to dry off between my legs with toilet paper. Then I grab the stained towel from the bed and begin scrubbing it, trying to get it clean.

Hank comes into the bathroom, already dressed. He has changed into a clean shirt—one of the shirts I ironed for him.

"What are you doing? Let's just get out of here."

He hurls the towel out the bathroom window. I lean into the afternoon sun and watch it float in the breeze for a few seconds, like a bloody white flag, signaling surrender, before it tumbles onto the roof below.

Then I throw on a fresh dress and we run down the stairs and out of the hotel. I'm afraid the hotel manager might come after us and make us pay for the towel.

I lived all summer with three other girls in the luxury of a ski resort room meant for two. Hank found cheap lodgings for himself in a tourist camp two miles from the center of town. His tiny log cabin was dark and cold at night, offering neither amenities nor rustic charm. But it was private. Hank insisted on privacy. He was a private person, an only child who wouldn't suffer roommates gladly. And he needed a place where he could be alone with me.

We met for meals at the Roaring Fork Café, and hung on each other, necking shamelessly while we waited in the cafeteria line. Sometimes someone would comment loudly that it was disgusting to watch us locked in a passionate embrace before lunch, but the other diners—most of them fellow students—just ignored us.

I spent hours in the opera classes, learning stage movement and repertoire, intently scribbling in my notebook, meeting other young singers from all over the world, all of whom intimidated me. And I watched the famous and soon-to-be famous from a shy distance. James Levine was a coach with the opera department. He would become the artistic director of the Metropolitan Opera, but that summer he was just an incredibly enthusiastic young man who adored singers. Benjamin Britten arrived for a celebration of his work. Peter Schickele took over the old Opera House for a week, creating his comedic character, P.D.Q. Bach, to our amazement.

Under the big festival tent, I listened to the orchestra rehearse while Hank played on stage. In the evenings we sat at outdoor cafes eating pizza and drinking watery 3.2 beer, which could be served legally to eighteen-year-olds in Colorado. I knew I should be happy. I was with my nice boyfriend, at a music festival surrounded by the summer glory of the Rocky Mountains.

But my brilliant opera career was going nowhere. I was one of the youngest singers there. When the opera department gave its recital of scenes, I was assigned to the unglamorous role of *marked for life* 163

the sandman in an excerpt from Humperdink's *Hansel and Gretel*. I had to tiptoe out on stage and sing, "I shut the children's peepers." With Madame, I had been studying the romantic heroines—Violetta in *La Traviata*, Mimi in *La Bohème*, Nedda in *I Pagliacci*—and here I was making my operatic debut in a pointy hat with a sandbag over my shoulder.

Hank wouldn't stop teasing me about it. On the night of the concert he sat in the audience with his orchestra buddies, laughing his head off.

It's August, and I have bought all the new fashion magazines, thick, heavy, back-to-college issues of *Glamour* and *Mademoiselle*, fall fashion issues of *Vogue* and *Harper's Bazaar*. Between rehearsals and dinner, as the slopes of Aspen mountain modulate from shimmering green to shadowy blue, I sprawl on my bed, ignoring the spectacle outside my window, concentrating on the pages of those magazines. They contain maps that will guide me out of a labyrinth. I need direction, instruction on how to choose the right shoes, the perfect blouse, the latest skirt length. I need to make a list of must-buy items to update my wardrobe for fall. It's important, very important, that I dress stylishly, appropriately. I have seen the way some fat women compensate for their weight, by making sure they are always beautifully, perfectly groomed. I can compensate for my birthmark in the same way.

A girl with a purple face can't afford to be seen in messy clothes and with unkempt hair. I know that. I know how terrifying I would look—like the crazy women with open sores on their legs, who beg for change in bus stations.

I turn hundreds of pages, paying special attention to the cosmetic advertisements, reading the fine print, searching for the words *flawless coverage*. I have to find a way to disguise my face. Hank often tells me he is lucky to have such a pretty girlfriend. But in Aspen there have been too many strangers, too many questions, too many stares. Each time I catch someone looking at me and then quickly looking away, I want to run into a dark room and hide.

There must be something better than the thick stuff Mommy bought nineteen years ago when I was born. Something new must have been invented since then. Mommy says nothing else is available because there just aren't enough people with birthmarks to make it profitable for the cosmetic companies. That might be true. Except for the scary-looking man on the subway when I was little, I've never seen anyone else with a face like mine.

I want to wear the latest cosmetics, not something sold in doctor's offices. "Corrective makeup" sounds horrible—like a prosthetic device, like a truss, like orthopedic shoes. I don't want to be corrected. I want to be beautified. I want to wear makeup that smells nice and comes in pretty packages like the fragrant bottles and jars in Grandmom's bedroom.

I dream of obliterating my birthmark with a mist sprayed on from a can. I dream of a filmy mask the color of the right side of my face that will conceal the purple on the wrong side. I dream of a pigment light as a veil but dense as a cloak, of an opaque but weightless chiffon that will shield my face, hide the shame of my birthmark, the way my clothing hides the shame of my nakedness.

I turn the page and a gorgeous brunette wrapped in fur says, "The most luxurious cover-up of all isn't mink, darling . . . It's Pan-Stick makeup!" Max Factor Pan-Stick covers "every flaw, every uneven skin tone with subtle color. It applies just as lightly as your fingertips . . ." I turn the next page and find a picture that looks like a lipstick. It says, "Max Factor's Erace Secret Cover Up hides blemishes, conceals flaws." *Erase!* I can erase my birthmark with a lipstick-shaped stick. I can erase it, like a mistake. I can correct my face, cover up my birthmark, make it secret.

I Could Fool Everybody

Back in Millville at the end of the summer, I wait for school to start again. At Miller's Pharmacy on High Street, I find the woman Daddy called *Faygeleh* presiding over her turf as always. Faye Miller, a little woman with big features—big dark eyes, big nose, big mouth—isn't pretty, but she carries herself as though she were, with girlish flirtatiousness. Her husband, Lou, balding, bespectacled, not much taller than she, has filled our family's prescriptions for as long as I can remember.

I'm shy about asking for what I want, afraid she'll guess that I'm buying it to hide my birthmark. I'm supposed to pretend the mark isn't there. I can't stand to mention it to anyone, let alone Faye Miller, one of Mommy's friends from the synagogue. She might say something like, "Of course, you want to cover it up, honey. You're in college now. You're meeting people. You want to find yourself a boyfriend. Why shouldn't you want to cover up that big birthmark?" What if someone comes into the store midlecture and overhears her?

But in that little store, in that little town, Faye Miller is a makeup expert. She just nods at my request, and slides behind her cosmetics counter with the calm authority of a doctor preparing for surgery.

She rummages through the boxes stacked on shelves behind her and pulls out the items, checking the colors, matching them to the right side of my face without ever referring to the stain on the left side. From the ringed and manicured hands that traded my childhood quarters for candy bars and chewing gum, I receive the promise of Pan-Stick and Erace in a shade called Natural. Then Faye, ever the saleswoman, suggests, "Why don't you pick up a little something to make yourself pretty?" She rummages through the shelves again and brings out a tube of Max Factor Petal Frost lipstick, pale and luminous. Waving her hands on either side of her face, fingers splayed, bracelets jangling, she says, "I just got it in. It's the new shade—for that all-eyes look."

In my room, in front of the mirror, amid the black and gold butterfly decals, I practice, following the instructions printed on the boxes, improvising to cover the stain. With the stick of Erace, I draw circles around my eyes. I draw lines of "natural" color along my cheek, across the birthmark. I pat the makeup onto my skin, until the purple fades to pink. Then with the wider Pan-Stick crayon, I draw lines over it again, adding another layer of makeup. I draw Pan-Stick stripes across my forehead, down my nose and along the good, clear cheek, and I blend lightly with my fingertips, according to the instructions, until my face wears a smooth, even mask. Under the narrow window, I check carefully with a hand mirror, scrutinizing my left cheek and eye inch by inch. Wherever I find persistent tinges, I pat on more layers of makeup as meticulously as if I were hiding the evidence of a bloody crime, and then I check at the window again, to be sure not a trace of red is left. Finally, I press loose powder over my face to set the mask.

The heavy foundation obliterates all of my complexion's natural shading and gradation of color. My face is a blank canvas, demanding to be painted with blush, eye shadow, eyeliner, and mascara.

For days, I practice, learning to paint my face like an artist. It isn't the face I've dreamed about. The makeup is heavier than I hoped it would be, not really "natural" at all. But at least it's ordinary makeup, meant for ordinary people with ordinary imperfections to hide.

When Evie comes to visit, I'm ready to show off my new face. I turn up my marked cheek so that she can inspect my work. "You did a good job, Joie," she says, "I just think you used a heavy hand." *A heavy hand! Does she know how hard it is to cover bright purple with "natural" beige?* Evie's handkerchief is on my cheek. She rubs, blends. "Don't, Evie! It won't move now. You can't fix it once the powder dries!" "Yes, you can. Go look in the mirror," she says. "That looks better. You just need a lighter touch." But pink shows through where she has rubbed my cheek.

Jackie looks me over. "Ooh!" She grimaces. "Your makeup is all cakey. You look like you're wearing a mask." *I am wearing a mask. I'm hiding behind a mask.*

"I don't know why you want to wear such heavy makeup," Mommy says. "You have such beautiful skin; it's a shame to cover it all up like that. You're a pretty girl. You have nothing to worry about. You shouldn't make a Big Deal about the birthmark."

But she surprised me with the gift of a makeup mirror to take back to school, a magnifying mirror encircled by light bulbs.

I installed the mirror on top of the metal dresser in my dorm room. Every morning I woke up early, flicked on the lighted mirror, and stood there for an hour, perfecting the mask before I left my room. Hank wasn't particularly impressed with my new face. At first he wanted to watch me put it on. He sat in the tiny bathroom of his apartment one Saturday night, asking questions while I made myself up. After that he got bored with the whole thing and was annoyed that he had to wait so long for me to get ready whenever we went out.

The girls I knew in the dorm had gotten used to my birthmark. Now they had to get used to my makeup ritual.

Every morning, my friend Kathy waits for me so that we can go to breakfast. I am always late. She knocks on my door and I beg for ten more minutes, then ten more. "I'm almost finished. Go without me. I'll meet you there." Impatient, she comes in, sits on my bed, and watches me work. I bend toward her, turning my head, bringing my cheek close to her eyes. "How does it look? Can you still see the birthmark? Does it still show?" There can be no traces to make a stranger suspect I'm hiding something under all that makeup, nothing to give me away.

Kathy squints up at my face. "It's just a shadow. You'd really have to be looking for it. Come on. Let's go." But I can't go. I have to be sure no one could ever see it. Not even if they were really looking for it. I have a secret identity now. I wear a disguise. I don't dare to let the mask slip, not ever.

We walk down the street to a rundown convenience store and coffee shop we call the Dirty Drug. We sit on cracked red vinyl upholstery and order our usual—coffee light, small orange juice, and rye toast—always the same breakfast, always eaten from behind the open pages of the *New York Times*.

This morning Kathy has something funny to tell me. "You know my friend George? He must have seen you in the Student Union because he said that there was a girl at school last year who was really pretty except that she had this big purple birthmark on her face. Yesterday he saw another girl who looked almost exactly like her, except that she didn't have a birthmark and he thought it was really strange!" We both fall apart laughing, but I am more thrilled than amused. *The mask worked! I fooled George! I can fool everybody.*

There was a new conductor in the music department that year. He was the first person I'd ever met who didn't see my birthmark. I introduced myself early in my sophomore year, fully made up, mask firmly in place. When he shook my hand and looked me full in the face, there was something profoundly different about the experience. He seemed so at ease. *What a nice man,* I thought.

This happened over and over again with each new person I met, until I realized they were reacting not to me, but to the mask. There was nothing unusual or strange about my face to surprise them, nothing to make them uncomfortable. No one stared. My face certainly didn't look fresh and natural, but I never had to explain what was wrong with it. Slowly, I began to stand differently, face forward, head up.

Just as Grandmom had chosen to believe that by destroying unflattering photographs of herself, she could avoid ever looking like that, I tried to believe that the mask of makeup was the real me. I could hide behind the mask forever and never show my face again.

When I finished applying my makeup, I saw a beautiful young woman in the mirror. Everyone who saw me saw only her, the creature I created. My deception was my freedom, but it was also a threat that hung over me like a lie. Monster Girl, Bride of Frankenstein, Purple Face always lurked beneath the paint, threatening to reveal themselves if the mask slipped. I learned to be very careful.

Indian summer's hot, sticky air descends on Philadelphia, smothering the glory of October. Skin damp under my too warm back-to-school sweater and skirt, face damp under my too heavy makeup, I hurry along Thirty-fourth Street, where not a single tree shields me from the midmorning sun. I keep patting my face with tissues, stuffing the makeup-soiled wads into my tote bag, hiding the evidence.

I rush into College Hall, cool and dark, thick stone, ivy-covered walls, into the ladies room on the first floor, drop my book bag, peer into the mirror. Foundation and powder mixed with sweat, like flour mixed with water, has formed little doughy balls, which are rolling off my face. I pull a rough paper towel from the dispenser, dampen it with cold water, blot my cheek, pick off the balls of makeup.

The ladies room door opens and closes again and again. Girls come in to use the toilets, fix their lipstick, smoke cigarettes. *Nobody I know.* A girl glances at me. Stares for a moment, looks away, looks back, says nothing. I find an empty toilet cubicle, close the door, hide.

A bell rings. Cigarettes fizzle under water taps. The ladies room empties out. I come out of the cubicle, take out the makeup I've learned to carry with me always. When the mask is back in place I rush up the stairs, slide into the back row of the lecture hall late, very late.

The next morning, I roll underarm antiperspirant over my face before I apply the makeup. My face is suffocating in the heat and my body feels hotter than ever. My skin can't breathe, but it can't sweat either. The makeup won't melt.

At the library, I sit in a cubicle, trying to study, writing Hank's name over and over in my notebook, his last name with my first name, his name with Mrs. in front of it. I sit there for hours, my left cheek resting in the palm of my left hand, while I scribble with my right. Then, in the ladies room mirror, under the cold fluorescent lights, my birthmark blazes purple. My makeup has rubbed off where I rested my cheek in my hand. I brush my hair with my fingers, pulling it over the side of my face, hiding. Head down, I hurry back to my cubicle, collect my books, and dash off before anyone can see me.

Safe in my dorm room, the door closed so no one can come in without knocking, I sit at my desk and practice resting my head with my thumb under my chin, fingers tapping my lips to remind me to keep my hands away from the marked cheek.

marked for life

To celebrate his first paying gig, Hank takes me out on the town—dinner at Bookbinder's, martinis, shad roe wrapped in bacon. I'm all dressed up in one of Evie's black cashmere sweaters and a black wool skirt, a strand of pearls, and my real gold graduation-from-high-school-present earrings. I've spent a lot of time making myself pretty. I know I look good. I'm in a famous restaurant with a cute guy who adores me. I'm feeling martini fuzzy and happy.

But in the ladies room mirror I discover a wide smudge of powder along the neckline of my sweater. *How did it get there? I was so careful pulling the sweater over my head. How long was I sitting in the restaurant with makeup on my clothes, feeling beautiful but looking like a fool?* I try to scrub it off with a wet paper towel, frantic that I've left Hank sitting alone at the table for so long. The paper towel crumbles, leaving white lint all over the sweater. I brush it off like mad with the palm of my hand. Then I come back to the table smiling, hoping the wet spot won't show in the restaurant's dim lighting.

From now on, I have to remember to keep my chin up.

The makeup rubs off on Hank's clothing, too. Pulling away from a goodnight hug, I spot a big smudge of powder on the lapel of his tweed jacket. Pretending to stroke him fondly there, I try desperately to wipe it off before he discovers it for himself.

I learn to carefully turn my head so that only my hair rests on his shoulder.

After we make love, there is makeup all over his face, all over his bed.

Just as I finish applying my mask one morning, a speck of powder lodges under the contact lens in my left eye. Tears pour down my cheek, ruining all my painstaking work. The skin around my eye is bright red, livid as a sty where the birthmark shows through. Frustrated, enraged, impossibly late now, I have to remove all my makeup, clean the lens, and start over again, sending Kathy off to have breakfast without me.

If my eyes water in the wind or after a sneeze, I learn to blot quickly, gingerly, before my cheek becomes streaked with rivulets of red. Crying is out of the question. The first time I look in the mirror after a hard cry, I start crying all over again at what I see—swathes of red and purple, streaks of black mascara.

I train myself to suck in tears as I would suck in breath. Nothing can ruin the mask, the pretty face I paint on to fool the world.

Each morning I ask myself, "What sort of pathetic freak am I, standing in front of the mirror for an hour or more, patting on layers of heavy makeup trying to make myself look like everybody else?"

Mine! All Mine!

Hank moved into another fourth-floor walkup, another single room, but a much larger one, with larger windows overlooking a larger alley. He joined the musician's union and began to get gigs, playing in pickup orchestras all over town. He played in the pit during the opera season and when Broadway musicals came through town. He played in big churches at Christmas and Easter when their choirs performed Handel's *Messiah* or Bach's *Magnificat*.

He was convinced that all of his buddies wanted to sleep with me. He was both proud and insanely jealous. One afternoon, as I sat studying on his bed, he leapt delightedly on top of me crying, "Everybody wants you, but you're mine, all mine!"

If my skirt accidentally rode up when I sat with our friends, Hank gave me the look that told me to pull it down. If I didn't catch his look right away, he pulled my skirt down over my knees himself. My thighs were for his eyes only.

He didn't much care whether I wore makeup or not. The birthmark was not an issue to him. I wasn't spending my mornings with Max Factor for his benefit. I was doing it to avoid the stares, the questions. I was doing it for myself, so I could live in peace.

On a sunny Sunday afternoon, we take a long walk along the Schuykill River, past the university boathouses, past the Rodin Museum. Hank walks with his arm over my shoulder, trying to slow his pace so that my short legs can keep up with his long ones. I put my arm around his waist and hook a finger into the belt loop of his corduroy slacks, holding on. We wander into the park and through the zoo.

He is intrigued by the lizards. He waits, watching, for them to roll out their long tongues. I am in love with the lemurs. I want to stay with them for hours, peering into the big cage where they cling to the leafless branches of a tree with long black fingers—not claws, but tiny hands like a newborn baby's. The lemurs stare back at me without blinking, as though they really are looking at me, as though they are trying to tell me something.

Hank kisses me and laughs. He thinks my love of lemurs is adorable. And I feel adorable. I see myself as he sees me—cute, silly Joie, cute like the lemurs. "I'm going to call the zoo tomorrow," he promises. "I'm going to get you a pet lemur for Christmas." From the promise of a lemur, we begin to build our future together. We build the dream house where we'll live with my pet lemur. I want to decorate the lawns with peacocks. Hank wants pink plaster flamingos. We'll have screeching peacocks in the backyard, voiceless pink plaster flamingos in the front.

Vietnam and the draft are a threat too terrifying to be mentioned out loud. Hank is a poet, not a fighter. He is sure he wouldn't survive combat, and I know he is right. We both pretend the draft will somehow go away, and drift right past it, drift past the aviaries and monkey cages, making other plans. Hank hopes to find a job as principal flutist in an orchestra somewhere. Better to play first chair in a small city than second or third chair in a bigger one, he says.

I love the dream-house game. But I can't imagine myself inside the house, living my life as his wife in Omaha or Springfield or Terre Haute or Tulsa, frying up pork chops for dinner, throwing potluck suppers with the other orchestra wives on Saturday nights, giving singing lessons in the living room, raising kids. *Even with a pet lemur and a backyard full of peacocks, I wouldn't survive it.*

Hank wears velour cardigans. He calls them his "cozies." *He is a cozy person with cozy clothes and cozy dreams. I'm afraid of his cozy velour life. I left Millville behind and I have to keep going. Hank knows I have to be a singer. He knows I have to live in New York or Milan or Paris. I can't go back to singing for the Lion's Club, the American Legion, and the PTA.*

Hank assumes a wife will follow him from orchestra to orchestra bearing his children. *It's a perfectly reasonable expectation. That's what nice girls do with their lives. They give up their own dreams for the better dream of being with the man they love. That's what Mommy did when she married Daddy. Sometimes I think Mommy is gasping for air in Millville. I'm afraid I'll suffocate if I follow Hank.*

At the peacock pavilion, I begin choosing birds for our dream-house backyard. *I know I'm not playing fair.* "Look, Hank," I say, "I can't think about getting married and raising a family. I just have to think about my singing now." I imagine Madame nodding her head approvingly. "That's right, child. The voice must always come first."

Hank defends his dream house. He can't understand why I'm so hesitant about marriage. "We can always get a divorce if it doesn't work out," he says. He says he needs to know that things are settled between us. He wants me to promise that we'll get engaged by the time he graduates. Just that we'll get engaged. That way, wherever he ends up, even if we're apart for a year or two, he'll know I'm there. He says that if I really love him, I can at least promise him that much. *I don't know why I can't.*

So I get angry, puff myself up and blow great clouds of rage over my fear and confusion. "I'm not coming home with you. Go without me. Go away!" And he is gone, walking very fast now, no longer slowing his pace to accommodate mine.

I wander around the zoo alone, dabbing at the tears that might ruin my makeup. *I don't have the voice; the voice has me. And this is the price I'll have to pay for it—no dream house, no loving husband, no children. Now it's real, not just a promise, not just nodding to Madame.*

I visit the flamingos, stare wet-faced at them as they prance in their pool on spindly legs. *How can I marry a man who prefers the plaster version to such natural grace?* Then slowly, I follow him home. I don't know what else to do.

The door is open when I get to the top of the stairs. He isn't surprised to see me. He's waiting in his black canvas butterfly chair as the afternoon light dims in the windows behind him. I fall onto his lap, crying, "What's going to become of us?"

"I guess we're good for another fifty or sixty years," he says.

In the afternoons, I take the bus from campus to Hank's apartment. I spread out on the bed, watching soap operas and studying until he comes home. When I hear his footsteps on the stairs, I get up and go to the refrigerator, ready to hand him a Coke or a beer as he comes through the door carrying his flute and his scores in a black leather briefcase. In the electric frying pan Hank's mother gave him for Christmas, I cook pork chops or hamburgers according to her instructions. We eat on tray tables, sitting on the edge of the bed. Then he practices his flute and I go back to studying. At eleven-thirty, we watch *The Tonight Show*. The minute Johnny Carson finishes his monologue, Hank puts me in a cab so that I can slide into the dorm just before curfew.

Hank is practicing, preparing for a concert at school. He has the TV positioned so that he can keep one eye on his music stand and the other on a baseball game, which is being played soundlessly, in black and white. I'm cross-legged on the bed in a heap of books and papers and Pepperidge Farm cookies, trying

marked for life

to force myself to concentrate on my homework. At one end of the room, the cat is curled on the low windowsill, staring at the pathetic city trees in the alley, imagining she sees a forest.

Hank stops playing midphrase, suspending Mozart's exuberant allegro in the air between us, where it hovers for an instant before plummeting into stillness. Surprised by the sudden silence, I lift my head from my book and turn toward him. He has taken the flute away from his mouth and holds it upright, like a staff. He is looking at neither the music nor the ballgame, but at me. And, in his face, I see how he loves me. Beyond anything he could tell me with words, it's there. In that moment, I am beautiful. And I am something better than cozy. I am safe.

Two flights below Hank's apartment lived a middle-aged lady named Bella Kaminski. Hank and I giggled over her old-fashioned name on the doorbell when he first moved into the building. "Can't be a real person," we said.

As I waited on the sidewalk while Hank turned his key in the outside lock, Bella Kaminski came up behind us, portly under her dark wool coat, her gray-streaked hair neatly curled. "You must be the new tenant on the fourth floor," she said. "Is this your wife?"

"Not yet. This is Joie."

After that, she had a smile for us whenever we ran into her. "Here come the lovebirds," she teased. When we found Bella on the landing, struggling with her groceries, Hank offered to help, picked up her bags, and bounded up the stairs, strong, long legged. I followed behind him with Bella who moved slowly, holding on to the railing, pulling herself along. She leaned her head toward my ear and whispered, "Oh, you are so lucky, you two! You don't know what it's like to be alone at my age. Believe me, you don't want to find out."

Bella told us that she worked as a secretary at an insurance agency. She had kept the same job and the same apartment for thirty years. She said that eating all her meals in coffee shops had ruined her digestive system, so she had decided to try cooking for herself. She planned to retire soon. Cooking would help fill her days.

A couple of weeks later, she invited Hank to come downstairs. She wanted to give him some of her homemade chicken soup. When he came back with the glass jar, he laughingly described the décor of Bella's apartment as a blend of "late Salvation Army and early filing cabinet." The chicken soup had no discernible flavor.

If I don't marry Hank, I'll end up like Bella Kaminski. I'll need to make a better chicken soup.

What Kind of Fish Is a Gafaltuh?

Hank and I never entertained at his apartment. His buddies showed up from time to time, but none of them was ever formally invited. Few of them lived in a place comfortable enough to have friends over, so they didn't invite us, either.

Because he was married, Tom, the bassoon player, had a nice home. He lived with his wife and their pet skunk in a comfortably decorated townhouse. Tom and Martha invited us for dinner often, so it embarrassed me that we never invited them back. I thought that Hank and I could invite them to his big one-room apartment. But the place was a mess.

The tiny bathroom at the back had never been cleaned. The kitchen had received only the barest hygienic maintenance. We postponed washing the dishes until every plate and fork and coffee mug was dirty, and the stack in the sink was so high, nothing else would fit.

We'd long since given up eating at the round bistro table, which was piled with books, scores, poems in progress, Hank's portable typewriter, and assorted parts of a disassembled wooden flute he tinkered with from time to time. I told him that if he agreed to invite Tom and Martha for dinner, I'd clean up the apartment and cook. All he had to do was clear off the table. I was willing to do that too, but he wouldn't allow me to touch his piled-up things.

I'd never given a dinner party before and I wanted everything to be perfect for Tom and especially for Martha, who had served us many nice meals. I wanted to impress Hank, too.

But apart from my recently acquired skill with the electric frying pan, I didn't really know how to cook. Mommy didn't care much for cooking. She had better uses for her time. She just plopped a frozen chicken into a Pyrex dish, poured frozen vegetables over it, put the whole thing in the oven, set the timer, and went to the office. But the table was always properly set with cloth napkins and a tablecloth, and we had to sit up straight and make polite dinner conversation.

Once in a while, on a Sunday morning, Mommy woke up in the mood for Grandmom's specialties. Then she made sponge cake, blintzes, kugel, eggplant and peppers, stuffed cabbage. Mommy never taught me to cook those dishes, but at least they were familiar.

I couldn't ask Mommy for help, anyway. She was not thrilled about my continuing romance with Hank, who was hardly the son-in-law she had in mind. I didn't dare admit that I'd ever seen the inside of his apartment. I could hardly tell her I planned to entertain there. Evie was no help, either. She relied on Schrafft's frozen entrees for her dinners at home.

So I prepared myself. I went to the bookstore and studied all the cookbooks on the shelves until I found *Simple Jewish Cookery*. It was only sixty-two pages long, but it had recipes for the dishes Mommy and Grandmom made, just as I remembered them.

Two days in advance, on a Thursday afternoon while Hank is at a rehearsal, I start cleaning the bathroom. I figure I'll work my way forward through the kitchen to the main room.

I'm down on my hands and knees, going over the tiny hexagonal-shaped white tiles with a sponge, emptying the bucket when the water gets murky, refilling it, getting back down on my hands and knees.

I have been down on this floor for two hours. It can't be more than six or eight feet square and I still have the whole apartment to clean. I've never done anything like this before in my life. I can tidy up. I had chores at home. But Mommy always had a cleaning lady to do the real work. I had no idea this would be so hard. Cleaning must be a skill I don't have.

My jeans are wet and caked with scouring powder. My knees are stiff and my shins are getting sore. Right now I could be having dinner with Evie at the Warwick Hotel, both of us dressed up in cashmere sweaters and skirts and pantyhose. Evie, in her alligator pumps and scarab bracelets, will order Dry Sack on the rocks with a twist. Then she'll lean across the table and tell me, "You look stunning. Your makeup is flawless." What am I doing on this filthy floor in this crummy apartment?

Hank comes through the door. He's expecting to find his apartment nice and clean. "I guess you're just getting started," he calls. "What time did you get here?" I stagger out of the bathroom. "I've been here since four o'clock this afternoon. I've spent the whole time trying to clean up this piss pot back here."

Hank inspects the bathroom. He says he doesn't really see a big difference.

The next morning I'm back. I struggle up the steep steps to the fourth floor carrying two heavy bags full of groceries. Hank goes down to bring up the other two. I put things away, sweep and mop the floor in the main room. I go through a whole roll of paper towels, wiping years of soot from the windowsills. When I'm finished, his place is clean enough to look presentable in the dim lighting of a dinner party.

That's what girlfriends do. They clean. They fix themselves up so that their boyfriends are proud to be seen with them in public. They "put out" for them in bed. I want to be a good girlfriend. I know the rules.

I have my doubts about our future, but I do love Hank. I love his facility with words, the way we can use language as a game of wits. In his eyes, I am pretty, sexy, adorable. His Midwestern, Eagle Scout values make me feel safe. I have become so attached to him that I am terrified of losing him. I'm hoping to find a way to keep him without losing myself. In daydreams, I plan our wedding, design my wedding dress. I can't quite picture Daddy at this wedding.

Saturday morning and I'm in the kitchen again. I start the stuffing for the cabbage, frying onions and ground beef in the electric frying pan. I boil water, make rice, mix it all together with raisins and spices. Then I dunk a big cabbage headfirst into a pot of boiling water until the leaves get soft enough to shape into neat little envelopes, just the way Mommy does, just the way Grandmom did.

I rush back to my dorm room so I'll have the two hours it takes me to make myself pretty. I have to look good, really good, like a confident hostess, nothing at all like a pathetic girl with a purple-stained face. I wash and set my long hair in enormous rollers, then I pull the big plastic bonnet over my head and turn on the hair dryer. I stretch the electric cord so that I can stand up in front of the lighted mirror and I start to paint. The face in the mirror is awful, blotchy purple-red cheek and eye, freckled nose, dark circles under my eyes. But I'm not worried because I know I can create a beautiful mask. I'm good at this now. Makeup is my art form. I'm an expert. And I'm an addict. I can't go outside without makeup, can't let anyone see me barefaced. I'm terrified of running out of concealing makeup so I stockpile it. I always have enough to last me at least six months. *What if they stop making it? What if I can't find it? What if I don't have the money to buy it?* I can't go back to living with a purple face.

The heat from the hair dryer makes my face perspire, melts the full coverage foundation. I have to keep blotting and touching up, going over the birthmark.

When Tom and Martha arrive at Hank's place, carrying a

bottle of wine, the little bistro table is set with candles and flowers. Martha, who has never been to the apartment, says she is "pleasantly surprised." Tom, who has been here many times, says he is shocked. Tom is in a sports jacket; Martha, in a simple black dress. They are attractive people who look remarkably alike: short, small boned, delicate, like a matched pair of porcelain figurines.

Hank is good at mixing one cocktail, the grasshopper, a sticky concoction of crème de menthe, crème de cacao, and heavy cream. He brings out his cocktail set, a black leatherette case that holds a shaker, a stirrer, a strainer, and a shot glass for measuring. I think it's very sophisticated to offer guests a drink before dinner. Hank refills our glasses. After our second drink, I suggest that we sit down at the table.

My idea of hospitality comes from Grandmom, who always served much, much more food than anyone could possibly eat. I'm worried that there may not be enough food. Too much food is not a possibility. There can never be too much. I don't know that Tom and Martha were brought up to believe that it's rude not to eat everything that's offered them.

I start the meal with canned gefilte fish served on a lettuce leaf and nicely garnished with a dab of purple horseradish and a carrot slice. Tom and Martha look at the little gray log on their plates. "What's this?" Tom asks. "It's gefilte fish. It's fish." "Gafaltuh? What kind of fish is a gafaltuh?" I took it out of a jar. I don't even know what's actually *in* gefilte fish. "It's not raw, is it?" Hank pokes at the rubbery log with his fork as if to make sure it's really dead. "No, no, it's cooked." Martha says she'll try it, takes the tiniest bit on her fork, and delicately places it just between her teeth. *What was I thinking? These people want roast beef and mashed potatoes.* "Mmm . . ." Martha says. "It's really different."

"Try it with a little of the horseradish," I coax Tom. He spreads horseradish over his gefilte fish with the back of his fork and takes a big bite. His eyes water, he coughs, keeping his mouth closed, trying to be polite. "I'm okay," he insists. "No, I'm fine." I offer him a chunk of challah bread to cool off his burning mouth. "Great bread!" he says. At least he can eat the bread. "Don't tell me you baked this yourself!" Well, no.

I'm pinning my hopes on the stuffed cabbage and rice kugel. But they are mystery foods to Tom and Martha and Hank. Martha thinks the kugel reminds her of rice pudding. They all like the stuffed cabbage, but by that time I'm feeling Hank's grasshoppers and Tom's wine and I'm too far gone to care.

My coup de grâce is the dessert: baked Alaska. I think it's a very elegant touch. I made it once before on Mother's Day, surprising Mommy with a melting ice cream cake breakfast in bed, as my sisters and I serenaded her with our rendition of "My Yiddish Mama." But it's a tricky dish and I'm in no condition to get it right. I have to stay in the kitchen and stand by the oven to make sure the ice cream doesn't melt while the meringue browns. It comes out a little messy, but I camouflage the runny bits by squirting whipped cream over each plate.

No one is hungry for dessert. No one can move. But everyone gallantly goes on eating, forking down the baked Alaska, too polite to refuse.

Then the cabbage begins to work it's wicked magic. Martha excuses herself and goes into the bathroom. Tom and Hank are too drunk to be embarrassed. They begin blaming each other for their farts, loudly accusing Martha of hiding out so she can fart privately. At least everybody's laughing. My first dinner party is a resounding success.

Malformed

I'm in the waiting room at the University of Pennsylvania Hospital, Student Health Department. I've chosen a seat near the door that leads to the elevators so that I can get away if I change my mind. My long hair falls over the left side of my face, a curtain hiding my birthmark. I'm embroidering a pillow cover for Evie's new apartment, which gives me an excuse to keep my head lowered over my work. Chin down, I shift my eyes, looking to my right, to my left. Only one other person sits on the row of chairs, a freckled boy, pudgy, with sandy hair. I've never seen him before. I hope I never see him again. I catch him looking at me, shake my head to be sure that my hair curtain stays lowered.

Today, for the first time in more than a year, I am in public without makeup. I feel as though I am out on the street stark naked. And I am terrified to face the doctor, terrified of what he will tell me. So I keep working the needle in and out of the fabric stretched tightly between the rings of my embroidery hoop. I concentrate on the satin stitch, make it neat, wipe the palms of my hands against my skirt when they become so sweaty they leave round spots of moisture on the cloth.

This afternoon, in the dull light of winter, I walked out of the dorm without a mask to hide my purple shame. I walked four blocks down Walnut Street, turned the corner, and walked toward the university hospital, praying no one would see me, cursing the wind for blowing my hair around, for lifting the curtain.

It has taken me more than two years to find the courage to come to this place—one year of living barefaced in a big school full of strangers, living with stares, with double takes; and one year of living behind a mask, living with makeup that melts when I cry, melts when my eyes water in the wind, melts when the heat of summer makes me sweat. For more than two years I've known that I could come to Student Health, ask a doctor, get an opinion for free. And for more than two years I've been getting up the nerve to do it.

On a day when I hated the birthmark, hated the makeup so much that I couldn't imagine living the rest of my life with that cursed purple stain on my face, I sat in the dorm, dialed Student Health, and asked for an appointment to see a plastic surgeon. "What seems to be the problem?" the woman's voice on the other end asked me. Silence. I wasn't expecting her question, didn't think I'd have to explain it to anyone but the doctor. I'll have to say "port wine stain" out loud. I'll have to say "birthmark." I hate those words. They stay stuck in my mouth, too bitter to swallow, but I can't spit them out. I find it very hard to say these words when someone asks me what's wrong with my face.

She gave me an appointment two weeks away. "After all, it's not urgent," she said. "No, I was born with it." And a laugh came from somewhere deep in my belly, a strangled, barking laugh that tasted bitter, like the hateful words I just had to say.

For two weeks I decided not to keep the appointment, decided to keep the appointment, then decided not to keep it. Even this afternoon, when I came back to the dorm after class to take off my makeup so the doctor could see my face, I was still deciding. I stood in front of the lighted round mirror on my dresser, opened the jar of cold cream, held a tissue in my hand, then put my hand down and put the lid back on the cold cream jar.

I can't do it. I can't take off the mask. I can't go outside and face the world without makeup. What if I run into someone who doesn't know I have a birthmark, someone who has only

marked for life

seen me with makeup? They'll stop, take me by the arm, stare at my face, and ask me what happened. And what will I say then? Will I say that I've been lying all this time, hiding behind a mask?

I can't do it, I can't go into the hospital, can't look at the nurse in the reception area, can't watch her look at me, look at my birthmark. I can't sit in the waiting area. What if someone I know shows up there? What will I say when they ask me why I'm seeing the doctor? What will I say when they ask me how I got that big ugly bruise on my face? I can't do it. I can't go into the examining room and let the doctor look at me, look at my birthmark, shake his head.

Mommy told me not to do this. "I made an appointment to see a doctor at Student Health. I want him to look at my birthmark. Maybe they've invented something new since I was a baby. That was a long time ago." I took long deep breaths, pressing the phone hard to my ear.

"Oh, no, Joie." Mommy spoke, deliberately, as though the word "no" should be enough to stop me, like a wall, the impenetrable Wall of No. "Why do you want to put yourself through that? Why do you need that aggravation? You do a good job with the makeup. You shouldn't monkey around. It's not worth it. You'll monkey around and you'll be left with something worse, like a scar that you can never cover up. Just leave it alone. You shouldn't make such a Big Deal."

"I just want to find out what he says, Mommy, that's all."

The doctor comes into the examining room. He's tall, with thinning hair, a white coat covering a paunchy belly. I smile my hello, try to be charming, try to make him like me, to make him be kind. He looks down at his clipboard, looks back at me. He says the words "port wine stain, yes." He says "hemangioma." *Hemangioma.* I repeat it to him, try to memorize it so

I can look it up later. He says, "malformation." *Malformed.* *I'm malformed.*

He asks me to come over to the window, and sit on the narrow shelf that covers the sill. He wants to get a better look, but the dusky winter sun isn't strong enough. So he moves a lamp closer, adjusts it until it blasts my face with bright white light and I have to squint my eyes shut. With two fingers he stretches the skin over my birthmark, looks and looks. "Hmm. Umhmm," is all he says.

Then he hands me a mirror, as if to show me something I haven't noticed before. "I don't see too many of these hemangiomas," he says. "The color is caused by veins that are very deep under the skin. It's not a pigmentation. It's blood vessels, veins. That's why we can't do anything about it. If the veins were closer to the surface..." His voice trails off and he's stretching my skin again. I watch him do what I have done myself so many times, pulling at my face, trying to make the birthmark go away. "It fades when you stretch the skin," I point out, hopefully. "Umm... But no, your hemangioma is quite extensive."

He looks straight at me. I put down the mirror and look up at him, scared, more scared that I might cry than scared of what he might tell me. "You have to forget all about getting treatment for this," he says.

"Well, I... I just... I just thought there might be something new. Maybe something had been invented...." I'm making creaky sounds. I can see that the doctor doesn't want to waste more time with me, that he doesn't think I should make a Big Deal.

"We will never be able to invent anything to treat this," he says. He looks me squarely in the eyes now, not smiling. "There's no way we can excise veins so far below the surface of the skin. You need to resign yourself. You're just going to have to learn to live with this. Just cover it with makeup. There are corrective cosmetics designed for these sorts of problems. Is there anything else?"

No, there is nothing else. Nothing at all. I am in the hall, punching the elevator button without saying thank you and good-bye, without stopping to see the nurse at the reception desk. Out the revolving doors, onto the darkening streets, hurrying, head down so no one will see me, scurrying like a mouse back to its nest, rushing back to my dorm room as the streetlamps come on.

Maybe Next Time It Will Be My Face

I'm sitting on the bed in Hank's apartment with the black cat, a pad of staff paper, and lots of pencils with worn-down erasers, struggling over my counterpoint homework. All music students must master the rudiments of composition. In counterpoint class, we learn to make pleasing tonal combinations from horizontal lines of music, melodies moving along together in harmony. I hate and fear counterpoint. Sometimes, when I have counterpoint class the next morning, I wake up in the middle of the night and run to the bathroom to vomit. It's part of my major, so I have to get at least a grade of B and I don't know how I'm going to do it. This semester I have to write a fugue. Johann Sebastian Bach could write fugues. I'm not Johann Sebastian Bach. I know my fugue is full of mistakes. Tomorrow morning, I'll be sitting around the piano with all the other students. The professor will take my manuscript, begin to play it, and he'll hit clunker after clunker, dissonance after dissonance. None of the other students are as dumb as I am. The professor will make exasperated, disparaging remarks. I'll be humiliated in front of the class. This is hard for me, too hard.

Hank is good at counterpoint. He is sitting on his straight-backed chair, playing his flute, his heavy white ceramic coffee mug on a tray table at his side. I keep the mug filled with coffee just the way he likes it, milk and sugar precisely measured. He has one-eye on his music, one eye on the TV. He's dividing his attention between Bach and the ballgame and he doesn't want to be distracted from either, but every time he puts his flute up to take a break, I ask him a question. He answers, I still don't get it, I argue, ask again. I beg him to come over and show me.

marked for life

He puts down his flute, takes my pencil, writes the correct notes on the page worn thin from being erased over and over, goes back to his chair and his flute, his TV. I struggle along, get hopelessly confused and panicked, and ask again. And again. And again. And Hank says the unthinkable. He calls me a dumb cunt.

Then he erupts; throws the heavy mug all the way across the room. It strikes the wall; coffee splashes everywhere, milky brown puddles, white ceramic shards. He's on his feet and at the round table where the portable typewriter is smothered under piles of papers and flute parts. He turns it over, typewriter crashing to the floor, poems soaking up spilt coffee, tiny screws and metal keys and bits of wooden flute flying across the room. He's screaming, screaming. His fist pounds a hole in the wall.

I'm off the bed and racing past him into the kitchen, grabbing the roll of paper towels, rescuing the drowning poems, mopping up the milky brown puddles, picking up the bits of flute.

And it's over. The storm has passed and he stands quiet now, head hanging, arms at his side, fists clenching and unclenching.

Is it my fault, my fault he went off like a volcano? Did I drive him to such rage? Did I deserve it? Did I deserve it when Daddy blew up at me? "Shall I make you another cup of coffee? I'm sorry, I'm sorry." And he's sorry, too. "I hit the wall so I wouldn't hit you," he says. *Maybe next time it will be me. Maybe he'll punch my face instead of the wall.*

I clean up, carefully lift the typewriter, keys tangled like gnashed teeth, set them right, see if they still work. The period key, stubborn, stays stuck, refusing to end another sentence. I lay the poems sheet by soggy sheet on the windowsill to dry, coax the terrified cat out from under the bed, hold her, stroke her, comfort her, longing to be stroked and comforted myself.

Hank curses the tiny screws lost somewhere in a corner

where only the cat will find them. And how will he manage to put that old wooden flute back together without them? He turns the table upright, piles the papers back on top of the typewriter, collects bits and pieces of the splintered flute, sits back down on his chair.

I bring him a mug of fresh coffee. He takes me on his lap. "I am not a dumb cunt," I say quietly. He says he knows. He knows.

I try to scramble back into the cozy nest of his love. I've seen rage before. I've been called bad names. I've seen Daddy, heard Daddy. I don't think Hank is crazy for going off like a bomb, not Hank the Eagle Scout, not Hank the sensitive poet. I couldn't believe Daddy was crazy, either, not my daddy, the respected attorney, not my daddy, the magistrate. *This must be how men behave. You have to be careful not to upset them, the way Mommy is always careful not to upset Daddy.*

I'm thinking of Bella Kaminski, two floors down, listening to the screaming and the smashing. *Next time she sees us, maybe she won't say, "Here come the lovebirds." Maybe she won't whisper how lucky we are.*

Tanglewood

Sixteen plates. I can carry eight dinner plates and eight vegetable plates on one tray. I know how to arrange the plates so they all fit, how to bend my knees and lift the tray onto my shoulder. I can serve a table of eight with only one trip to the kitchen, and that's what I have to do. I have to remember who ordered the *kasha varnishkes*, who wants extra applesauce, who wants the vegetable plate. I have to remember who is on a restricted diet, and I have to be patient when I'm asked over and over if I'm sure there's no salt in the fish dish.

Nice people have been assigned to my tables. Plump Mrs. Rosenfeld treats me like a granddaughter, pats my hand. She is delighted with anything I serve her, never complains. Her husband has a crush on me, but she doesn't mind. We joke about it, look at each other and roll our eyes when he tells me what a *shayne madel* I am.

My back is killing me and I'm exhausted. My hair is pinned up in a messy French twist, and I haven't had time to paint my full mask. I'm just wearing makeup to hide my birthmark, so my face is pasty, pale against my white nylon uniform. Mr. Rosenfeld is disappointed when I come to take his order. "You don't look so good," he tells me. "Put on at least a little lipstick." "Leave her alone," says Mrs. Rosenfeld. "She works hard."

When Mrs. Rosenfeld wears short sleeves, I see the numbers tattooed on her arm. I've never seen that before. I'm ashamed that I asked her what they were. I know what it's like to be asked embarrassing questions. "Dahlink," she said, never letting the smile fade from her face. "You've heard of Auschwitz?"

I serve not so nice people, too. Mr. and Mrs. Stern insist on sitting at a table all by themselves, because they don't like any of the other guests. They always sit up very straight in their chairs, never smiling. Mr. Stern wears a blazer when he comes in to dinner, even though the evening air is still and hot. Mrs. Stern wears a perfectly plain, perfectly pressed blouse and skirt with stockings and flat shoes, her short gray hair neatly slicked back behind her ears. The Sterns are haughty and nasty and complain about everything. I cringe when I put down their plates.

This morning I had to bring Mr. Stern his boiled egg three times before he was satisfied that the chef had cooked it for exactly two minutes. He tapped the shell open with his spoon, then put it down, and looked up at me with sheer disgust. Twice I waited for the chef to boil the egg again, then again, watching the timer myself to be sure.

When I set the Sterns' table in the mornings I have to remember that there must be no little bottles of jelly, no butter. I have to remember to bring their own special cereal, prunes, and bread, without being asked, the minute they sit down. If I forget any of these things, Mr. Stern clucks and sighs as though I've done him some irreparable harm.

The VIP table is next to my station. I try not to stare at the people who sit there, but I can't help myself. Leonard Bernstein is at that table, and the composer Aaron Copeland, and the young Japanese conductor Seiji Ozawa and his wife. When they are performing at the Tanglewood Music Festival they stay at this resort. The VIP table is presided over by Hannah, the wife of the owner, and Al, who is piano player–in–residence and also fixes Hannah's unruly frosted blond helmet when she's between hairdresser appointments.

I serve three meals a day, seven days a week. My salary is only fifteen dollars a week plus tips, but I get room and board. Board is not the regular food that the guests eat, but whatever

marked for life

cheap stuff Hannah's husband, Jerry, decides to feed us: cornflakes for breakfast, spaghetti for dinner, no fresh fruits or vegetables.

My room is in a ramshackle building behind the main house. There are six cots in the room, with just enough space between them to get in and out of bed. My roommates are all waitresses like me, or busgirls. Next door there's another room, almost as big as the room where I sleep, with windows that look out over the croquet lawn. Two nice Jewish ladies share that room. They're working in the office as secretary and bookkeeper, so they won't have to spend the summer in Brooklyn. All of us share one bathroom.

It's almost impossible to find the privacy to put on my makeup. I go to sleep with the makeup still on, and get up before anybody else so I can wash off what's left of the old mask and paint on a new one. No one here knows about the birthmark, and I want to be sure no one finds out. I don't want to answer anyone's questions. I don't want anyone's sympathy.

As I stood in the dining room, kibitzing with nice Mrs. Rosenfeld one morning, waiting for the other guests to drift in for breakfast, she gave me some unsolicited advice. "You such a putty girl," she said. "Why you cover youself up with makeup? You bootiful enough, dahlink." "I just like it. I really like makeup," I said. "Oy, feh!" said Mrs. Rosenfeld.

On Tuesday and Thursday nights, we entertain guests in the music room with Al at the piano. After I finish serving dinner, I have to rush out the kitchen door, across the path and up the steps to my room, tear off my soiled apron and uniform, fix my makeup and hair, throw on a long gown, scramble to find my earrings, and dash back through the kitchen, transformed from a waitress into an opera singer, humming as I go to warm up my voice.

My part of the program is scenes from *Rigoletto*, which I sing with Sam, a sweet, gay black baritone with a rich, full voice, who likes to call me Signorina Coloratura. Between our arias and duets, Al, at the piano, tells the story of the opera, mixing it up with his corny Yiddish humor. I'm relieved that Leonard Bernstein, Aaron Copeland, and Seiji Ozawa are never around for these evening musicales. This is no way to sing an audition.

Hank plays in the Tanglewood student orchestra but tonight he's free, so he's come to hear me. After the concert, it's part of my job to mingle and be charming. Helmet-hair Hannah isn't thrilled to see that I have a visitor, a freeloader drinking her tea and eating her cookies. She can't make a scene in front of the paying guests so she just looks at me with narrowed eyes, then looks at Hank, then looks at me again to be sure I get her meaning. Mrs. Rosenfeld calls me over, smiling, to tell me she approves of my boyfriend, even though she knows he isn't Jewish. She takes my hand, pats it. "Det's him? Very nice, dahlink. He looks very intellectual, very sensitive." I look over at Hank in his cozy beige velour cardigan. Now that he is a poet, a professional musician, now that he no longer lives in Missouri, he has given up his Eagle Scout grooming. His hair covers his collar, and he buries the stem of a meerschaum pipe beneath a bushy mustache.

Engaged-to-Be-Engaged

The following spring, Hank's parents came to Philadelphia for his graduation ceremony. We joked that they'd find my underwear hanging up to dry in his bathroom, but we made sure that didn't happen. I helped him clean the apartment and got all my stuff out of the way.

His mother and father had saved up their money and used all their vacation days to make the trip, so Hank made a real effort to show them a good time. They visited Independence Hall and the Liberty Bell. We all went out to dinner and to see the film *Dr. Zhivago*. Afterward, we went back to the apartment and I made coffee. His mother sat back against the pillows on the bed, took off her shoes, and offered a foot to his father, seated nearby in the canvas butterfly chair. "Massage it for me. It's all cramped up," she said. He willingly complied. I was amazed. I'd never thought of asking Hank or any other guy to do anything like that for me. I'd never heard my mother ask my father to rub her or scratch her.

For the ceremony, I wore a pink bouclé suit and a pink straw hat. I watched Hank sitting on the stage with the rest of the small class as his eyes scanned the audience, till they rested on me, beside his mother. That night he said, "You were the prettiest girl in the room. I couldn't believe you were mine." I was so proud that I'd managed to look pretty for him, me, Miss Grape Juice Face, the Bride of Frankenstein.

In two weeks, we'd go our separate ways, and I didn't know when we'd be together again. I dreaded it. I was used to him now, used to having a boyfriend, a hand to hold. And I trusted his love for me.

After his parents went back to Missouri, I spent every possible minute with him. We agreed to be engaged-to-be-engaged. It was a commitment I could make. No formal engagement, no wedding date. We bought rings to make it official, to bind us together while we were apart.

Walking down Chestnut Street we found gold-lined jade bands in the window of a small jewelry shop. The Chinese man behind the counter, short and round, beamed at us. "Ow! Wedding ling! Wedding ling! You wan' wedding ling! Shuh, shuh! Why nah? Nice young couple." I looked away. "No," I said. "Not exactly, not yet." We asked the round man to engrave both sets of our initials in the gold lining of each ring.

Hank had gotten a bad number in the draft lottery and passed the physical. He had a set of X rays and letters from doctors attesting to the pleurisy that had plagued him all winter with chest pain and coughing, but Uncle Sam wanted him anyway.

He'd have to play his way out of Vietnam. It was his last hope. The Army, the Navy, and the Air Force maintained bands, choruses, orchestras. The competition to get in was fierce. The auditions were virtually a matter of life or death. But acceptance into a band was no guarantee you'd survive the war. Eight Army bands were stationed in Vietnam, sometimes in combat zones. The Navy's Fleet Bands could get shipped off anywhere.

Ironically, the safest gig was with the Marine Corps. The band John Philip Sousa led for a dozen years still wears white gloves and red jackets with lots of shiny gold buttons and braid. Named "The President's Own" by Thomas Jefferson, the Marine Band is always at the disposal of the commander-in-chief. Marine violinists line the White House staircases, serenading guests during state dinners. Marine trumpeters stand in White House doorways, blowing fanfares to announce the arrival of world leaders. During the war, the band was busy playing funerals at Arlington National Cemetery, and regaling Lyndon Johnson with "Hail to the Chief," but they never, ever went to Vietnam.

marked for life

Marine Band members didn't go to boot camp, either, or live in barracks. The band that represented America's toughest warriors didn't have to endure Marine training. Their hardships were relatively minor: a salary too small to live on, a terrible haircut, and a four-year enlistment.

Hank couldn't stand the thought of four years in the Marines, but the thought of boot camp was worse. Every graduating musician in America wanted to get into the Marine Band. Hank had to hope that there would be an opening in the flute section and that he could play better than any other flutist who got drafted that year.

When the letter came, I wanted to celebrate. No more nightmares of him dying in a jungle far away. He'd be in Washington next year. I'd still be in Philly, not so far by train. We could see each other on weekends. We were okay for now. Hank knew he had no right to complain when so many young men were dying every day in Vietnam. But he felt as if he'd been sentenced to four years in prison.

In June, he was back at his parents' house in Missouri, getting ready to report for duty with the Marines. I was back in New Jersey at my parents' house, getting ready for another summer music festival and school, this one on Cape Anne in Massachusetts at Castle Hill, an estate bequeathed to the New England Conservatory of Music. Daddy had forbidden me to go. He thought it was time I gave up on this singing nonsense. He wanted me to spend the summer in Millville, working in his office, "helping out." But I was determined to get there because Sarah Caldwell, the legendary director of the Boston Opera, would be a guest artist. I passed the audition and was given a work scholarship. I'd spend another summer waiting tables, serving the other students, then I'd go back to Philly for my last year of college.

Castle Hill

My alarm goes off at six-thirty A.M. I pull a chair up to the window and lift my Samsonite train case full of cosmetics onto the sill. I don't have much time. I have to report to the kitchen in forty minutes and it will take at least that long to apply my makeup. I take out a magnifying mirror and get to work. My room is small, four flights up, on the floor that was once the servants' quarters. The estate, modeled after the great villas and gardens of Italy, was built by an American who made his fortune in plumbing fixtures. On the lower floors, where the faculty lives, the bathrooms are extraordinary.

The shadows of my attic room are too forgiving. I lean into the open window. It's early, so early that the summer sun lazes low in the sky, gathering its forces, but the left side of my face, lashed by the morning light, flames blood red. I have to be prepared for noon, when the sun will strike my skin at full strength, like an X ray, when the heat will burn through my makeup and sweat will threaten to wash away my mask. With my fingertips, I pat foundation over the birthmark, layer over layer, angry, angry. *Why, why do I have to do this? Why, why do I have this stained face?*

Past my mirror, past my makeup-caked cheek, I look out over the grassy *grande allée*, flanked by half-naked marble ladies, a long parade of creamy muses and blue-green trees halted by a wall of blue-gray sky. And at the end of the *allée*, at the bottom of the cliff, the languid morning sun glances off the waves, announcing the sea. I look away from the mirror, look out. Look out.

At night, I call Hank from the pay phone on the mansion's

first floor. I call him more out of guilt than longing. Our conversations aren't cozy anymore. They're not about loving and missing and wishing we could touch. They're about demands and excuses, accusations and defenses. Hank wants to know why I no longer have time to write him every day. I don't even have time to miss him. I'm busier than I've ever been in my life and Hank's not busy at all. He's bored at his parents' house. He says I've abandoned him. He says, "That wonderful sense of security I had is gone." I don't know how to answer.

One night when he was out drinking in St. Louis, he slammed his hand on the bar and his jade ring broke in two. He's trying not to think it's an omen. I think maybe it is. He wants to drive up to Massachusetts to visit me before he reports for duty with the Marine Band in Washington. I don't want him to come. I don't want to hurt him. I just want him to leave me alone, so that I can do what I have to do here. I tell him it's a really bad time for me. When I'm not rehearsing, I have to work in the dining room. I say, "I won't even have time to see you." I'm twenty years old, making new friends, finding myself in their reactions to me. I'm on my own, learning, changing without him. Scared and lonely in Missouri, Hank needs me to stay the same.

Sarah Caldwell and her entourage have arrived at the estate and it's as though the circus has come to town. The seaside casino at the end of the *allée* has been transformed into an outdoor theater. An acoustic shell has been built; a set is going up; there are vintage cars, horses, a rain machine. We are told to expect photographers from *Life* magazine. Sarah is directing Benjamin Britten's *Albert Herring*, and although I have only been given the tiny role of a little girl called Cissy, I'm part of the cast, a member of the club.

Sarah Caldwell is an enormous, disheveled woman—unwashed gray-streaked hair, baggy, rumpled dresses, brilliant mind, gruff manner. On the first day of rehearsals she tells us to call her Sarah, never Miss Caldwell. She is strict and relentless. She makes us work very hard, and she makes us laugh. We begin rehearsing in the morning, right after breakfast, and keep going until eleven o'clock at night.

When Sarah finally tells us "I think that's all for today," too excited to sleep, I walk down to the beach. Someone has built a bonfire. Someone has brought a case of beer. Someone has a transistor radio. We sit by the fire telling stupid dirty jokes, getting up to dance in the sand.

The next morning, I wake up on my cot, on top of the blanket, still wearing my shorts and T-shirt, my bare feet still caked with sand. It's barely dawn. My alarm hasn't gone off yet. Someone's knocking, knocking.

"Joie, Joie, wake up! I just went out for my morning walk and I found a man sleeping in a parked car. He asked me to get you. He said the doors were locked when he arrived and no one answered the bell. He said he's been waiting all night."

"I'm not expecting anybody. Are you sure he meant me?"

"He said 'Joie.' Who else could it be? You'd better go down there."

This is a bad, bad surprise. We are two days away from the first performance, rehearsing nonstop. I told Hank not to come. Why is he here?

I check in the mirror. I fell asleep without washing my face, so my makeup is still partly intact. I run downstairs, sandy bare feet on cold marble steps, sticky, sandy eyes, sour, muddy mouth, hoping it will turn out to be a mistake. It won't be Hank. It can't be Hank.

Out through the heavy door into the gray light, into the damp breeze, into the aroma of grass and sea, into the squawking gulls. The mist begins to awaken me, begins to wash away the sandy, muddy hangover, and the sensual joy of a morning by the beach overcomes me, so that when I focus on Hank, standing in front of his car, his arms folded, his face shut tight, I'm beginning to smile. But the smile is not for him. I'm not happy to see him. And he's not smiling at me.

Rough gravel claws my bare soles. Slowly, painfully, I hobble toward him. The party is over.

I send Hank off to the Sunnyside Motel. I tell him to get some rest. I tell him I'll find him there after my morning rehearsal. I tell him he can't stay with me in my room, that I can't even invite him in for breakfast without getting into trouble. He doesn't understand any of that and goes under protest.

Hank wants me to prove to him that he's more important to me than anything in the world. He thinks that if I really loved him, I would understand how much he needs me at this moment and I'd be with him at the Sunnyside Motel right now. I resent him for showing up when I asked him not to come and I feel guilty for resenting him. I try to tell myself that if Hank really loved me, he'd leave me in peace to do what I have to do for a couple of weeks.

Back in the kitchen, I retrieve my apron from the hook. For a few hours, my life can return to normal. In the dining room, I put bread baskets out on the tables, take orders for eggs or French toast, patrol the room with a coffee pot, refill cups, wait for a friend, any friend, to come in so I can talk.

By the time I get to rehearsal, the entire cast and crew has heard about the dramatic arrival of Joie's boyfriend. I won't have any trouble getting a ride to the Sunnyside Motel. Everyone wants to have a look at Hank.

Hank is waiting for me at the open aluminum screen door. Rust streaks the white stucco wall, as though the metal room number has been leaking.

He says, "Here you are looking more beautiful than I ever remembered you. And you don't even want to see me."

"It's not that I don't want to see you," I say. "It's that I want to see you next week, when the opera is over."

But if Hank's orders come through, next week he'll have to report to the Marines. And I'm not really sure I'd want to see him next week, either. I feel as though he's dragging me down, demanding something from me that I can't afford to give him.

I don't want to talk about anything. We've been through it all on the phone, over and over again. I don't want to abandon him but I can't abandon myself, either. And I feel as though he's making me choose between his life and my own.

I have only an hour before my afternoon rehearsal—just enough time to make love. No time for accusations, no time for arguments, no time to make promises I can't keep. He follows me into the room as I pull my shirt over my head, unhook my bra, unbutton my jeans.

Hank drives me back to the estate, but he won't leave. "Please, just go into town and look around," I beg him. "I have a rehearsal now. I'll meet you later on."

I need to concentrate on my music, on my blocking, on the entrances and exits that Sarah changes every time we go through my scenes. I want to do a good job, and I want to relax with the rest of the cast. I don't want to be ripped away from all of that. I don't want to have to think about appeasing Hank.

Sarah comes into the rehearsal room, flanked by Ray, her stage manager, and by Roland, her assistant conductor. A special chair has to be brought in to accommodate her excessive girth. She lowers herself slowly onto the seat and looks around. Hank is sitting on the floor, leaning against the wall. I'm sitting on a folding metal chair on the other side of the room, ignoring him. Sarah runs her fingers through her hair, whispers to Ray, then she beckons to me.

I walk over to her chair, bend down to hear her. She leans in to speak to me, a chubby elbow cushioned on an enormous thigh. Her voice resonates from the depths of her massive flesh. It's deep and very focused, like the sound of an English horn. Even though she speaks softly, every word reaches into the corners of the room.

"Joie, I don't think I know that man. Is he a friend of yours?"

"Yes, Sarah."

"Please ask him to leave. We don't allow visitors at our rehearsals."

Everyone is watching as I approach Hank.

"Sarah says you can't stay here."

"It's okay. I'll just sit quietly."

Maybe he didn't hear. "No, Hank, she told me to ask you to leave."

"Then you come with me."

"I can't. I can't miss rehearsal. Please."

"Then walk me to the car."

"I can't. I can't just walk out. Sarah's starting right now."

For two days I race between rehearsals and Hank, calming him down, keeping him happy. On opening night, he is in the audience, and I am backstage, trying to pretend he isn't there.

A makeup artist has come up from Boston. I have a moment of panic, wondering what to do about my birthmark, wondering if the makeup artist will know what to do about it. I can't show up barefaced in front of the rest of the cast. I decide to wear concealing foundation to the dressing room tent. Maybe I'll get away with it. Maybe she won't tell me to go clean my face. There's a long line of cast members waiting to be made up. She won't have time to fuss with me. When it's my turn in the chair she says, "Oh, you've got foundation on already." I lower my head, mumbling, apologetic. "Just a little concealer." She shrugs and sponges on another layer of pancake makeup, then uses a pencil to draw freckles on my nose and across my cheeks.

It's easy for me to act the part of little Cissy Woodger. Most of the time, I just prance around the stage like a rambunctious child. In my brief solo turn, Cissy sings a song celebrating Albert, the May Day king. But she's so nervous she has to be pushed forward and makes one false start after the other. I lived that scene in the choir loft of the Presbyterian Church in Millville. I understand Cissy perfectly.

The next morning, there is a post-performance meeting for the cast and crew. Before Sarah begins to give us her notes, she calls me aside. "Last night your acting was really very good. You're very talented in that way." I try hard not to grin. Sarah doesn't pause. "But you sang a few wrong notes, so I've decided to replace you for the rest of the performances. You don't need to stay for this meeting." I don't move. She has to tell me, "You can go now."

I find Hank just outside, sitting on a stone ledge, black-rimmed sunglasses protecting his blue eyes from the glare of the sand and sea below. I put my arms over his shoulders and he holds me while I tell him, looking out at the ocean so he won't see my face if I start to cry. I'm not so angry with him anymore. I should have been more professional. I should have been able to separate my work from my private life. I should have been able to concentrate better.

I have to find a way to turn things around in my head so I can survive the shame of having failed so terribly. It was just a tiny role, and I screwed it up. What hope do I have for a career as an opera singer? I hurt Hank, betrayed him, let him down—and for what? If I try to make it up to him, maybe I'll be able to forgive myself. I'll find a way to send him off to the Marines feeling reassured and loved. He has received orders to report to

marked for life

Parris Island boot camp. He has been promised that it's just a technicality. His revised orders should arrive any day. But he's terrified. What if they don't?

Hank says he couldn't bear it if I left him now. I know I'm not living up to his Eagle Scout code. I have abandoned my duty to stand by my man and he feels ashamed of me for it. I'm ashamed of me, too. I hope that once he gets settled in his new life, he'll be able to let me go, but I don't dare to tell him that. I know he doesn't have the strength to hear it now. So I say goodbye with a compromise. We'll see each other as much as possible for the next year. I'll come down to Washington on the weekends. He'll come up to Philadelphia whenever he can get away from the Marines. No promised marriage. No threatened breakup.

The Bargain

After Hank left, the festival didn't seem so exciting anymore. The opera was over. All the production people from New York and Boston, the assistants and stage managers, set builders and costumers, were gone. I spent a lot of time by myself trying to figure it all out. I wanted to think that I was a good person, but I was afraid that I'd ruined Hank's life. My guilt was a heavy bundle I couldn't put down.

Hank sent his anguish to me in letters. His orders came through just in time to spare him from boot camp. He was living in a studio apartment in Arlington, Virginia, sleeping on a foam mat on the floor, waiting for his furniture to arrive from Philadelphia. His only companion, Bill, a French horn player he'd known at school, lived with his wife, Marilyn, a nurse, in a one-bedroom apartment a floor above Hank's. They lent him a kitchen chair, which he used as a desk, balancing his portable typewriter on the seat, while he sat facing it on a stack of telephone directories. It was hot and sticky in August, and he had neither air-conditioner nor fan for relief. Broke and lonely, he spent hours sitting on the floor without even a TV set for comfort. Driving the Volkswagen bug in Washington traffic completely unstrung him. The morning commute to the Marine barracks for roll call left him shaking with nerves.

When he had off three days in row, he wrote a long, plaintive letter. "I'm alone in a strange city. I can hardly cope with the basic necessities of life. I can't even remember how to cook. I'm terrified of driving that car in this traffic. And I have lost you."

I called him. I promised to visit. He pressed me to commit to a firm date. He said he needed to count the days until he could see me again.

I had gone off to the festival full of confidence and optimism, ready to have a good time. Now I was chastened, sad. The realization that my behavior could have a profound effect on another person had sobered me. I had always leaned on Hank. Now that he was falling apart, I'd have to keep myself together.

I stood up to Daddy. I told him I wouldn't return to school if I had to live in the dorm. I was a senior now and I wanted my own apartment. I hadn't really been living in the dorm anyway. I had spent most of my time at Hank's. I couldn't go back to the charade of curfews.

Daddy said, "Under no circumstances." I persisted. He yelled. I yelled. He had "episodes" of stomach pain. He reminded me that I was killing him with my obstinate behavior. Mommy had "episodes," too. She had a rapid heartbeat that lasted all afternoon and into the night. Daddy kept repeating, "I wonder if you realize what you're doing to your mother." I didn't want to upset Mommy, but I had to win this time.

Evie said, "You're just turning out to be your mother's daughter, Joie. I don't know why she's so surprised by your behavior. You're no tougher than she is." Once more, Evie negotiated a compromise. Mommy and Daddy agreed that I could live in an apartment only if I spent no more money than the cost of a dorm room. And I had to live in a respectable, secure building with a doorman. Daddy thought he had handed me an impossible equation, but I was determined to make it work.

I lined up a roommate, Christy, a mezzo-soprano. She didn't have much money for rent, either, but she liked the idea of a doorman building. I spent a few days in Philadelphia, staying with Evie while we looked at apartments. Christy and I found something we could afford. It was just a single room with a dressing area, a bathroom, a kitchen, and a dining alcove. But it was two blocks from fashionable Rittenhouse Square, where Madame lived, and our ninth-floor windows looked out over rooftops and trees. Evie inspected it and told Mommy she approved. Christy and I bought two rollaway cots, two bedspreads, and a set of turquoise Melamac dishes. Mommy gave up the fight. She contributed utensils and kitchen supplies, a folding table and four chairs.

I didn't have enough money left from the rent to afford bus fare, so five or six days a week I walked a mile and a half to campus and back. Every time I turned into the canopied entrance of the building and crossed the lobby to the elevators, I felt like an elegant, grown-up lady.

Although Christy and I could barely manage the rent, that didn't stop us from entertaining. When I came home after classes, I'd usually find at least one music student sitting at the table or sprawled on the floor, doing homework, practicing, gossiping. They brought whatever they could—Coke, chips. If somebody had just gotten paid for playing a gig, there might be a few bottles of beer, a pizza, a pint of Scotch. The regulars were almost all guys. Neither Christy nor I were interested in dating any of them. We just liked the company.

We both studied singing with Madame. Sometimes at night we'd sit on one of the cots, sharing a copy of Rossini's *Serate Musicali* and read through the duets, delighting each other and ourselves with the lovely blend of our voices, her viola to my violin.

I had my first apartment. I was surrounded by fellow musicians. I was a senior at the university. I'd been with Madame long enough to be one of her favorites. I was happy.

A week after I moved in, I kept my promise and took the train to Washington for my first visit with Hank. If Mommy called while I was gone, Christy knew to call me at Hank's, so that I could call back, pretending I was still in Philly.

Three nervous hours on the train, three hours, wondering what it will be like to see him again. I make my way to the smelly bathroom on board, check my face in the mirror, fluff up my hair. As the train pulls into Washington's Union Station I'm standing on the platform, ready to step off, balancing my suitcase between my legs, trying to look casual, looking for Hank. He is waiting for me, grinning. In his Marine greens, his bushy mustache gone, his head nearly shaved except for an incongruous shock of blond bangs, he is not the Hank I remember.

The station feels like a furnace after the air-conditioned train. When he hugs me, the back of his shirt is damp under my hands. His face is moist against mine. He has come straight from morning roll call. He says he worried that they'd keep him too long, that he'd have to race through the dreaded traffic. But he made it, he says, he's here, I'm here, and he says he can tell that I think he looks ridiculous, no matter how I try to hide it from him with teasing words and smiles.

He takes my little suitcase and my tote bag, and we find the Volkswagen. Gripping the wheel, he timidly negotiates Columbus Circle, cursing at the oncoming cars that seem bent on smashing into us. I have never seen Hank so afraid. In Philly, he was confident. He was working, making money, a fine musician in demand, a prize-winning poet. Now he's afraid to drive his own car.

When we're out of town and on the bridge over the Potomac, he relaxes enough to take his eyes off the road and looks at me. "I can't believe you're really here," he says. I've been watching him all along, trying to get used to the way he is now, telling myself this scrawny Marine is the shaggy poet I once knew. I want to be a good sport, cheerful, comforting. I turn away from him, look out my window, down at the boats, the sails like tiny white squares floating on the river. We drive into a shimmering sky that spills into the water below us. I tell myself it's only three days. I can do this for him.

We pull into a brick apartment complex, two stories high, probably only ten years old but already run down. Drooping box hedges flank doors lined up in a row on the ground floor. The building is set back from the street by a wide lawn, but there are no trees to shield the grass from the merciless September sun, so only the odd patch of green survives, and the bleached yellow expanse reflects the heat like desert sand.

Hank's particular door opens onto a narrow room with windows at either end. Venetian blinds conceal a view of the parched lawn in front and an alley full of trashcans in back. His furniture still hasn't arrived. A foam mat is neatly made up as a bed on the cracked linoleum floor. A stack of telephone directories doubles as a chair. The one actual chair is piled with scores and papers. Hank's white coffee mug is balanced on the ledge of a folding music stand.

He shows me the kitchen, which is not large enough to contain us both. He has bought a mop, a bucket, and a sponge, as well as a box of Spic and Span and a can of Bon Ami scouring powder, my preferred brands, the brands we used at home in Millville. He also has a couple of bowls, another mug, two spoons, two forks, one knife, and a single saucepan, which I will use to boil water for instant coffee or hot dogs and to heat up a can of baked beans. I tell myself that this is an adventure. I'm in Washington. But I wonder how I will keep the bargain I made.

I find Cokes and ice in the refrigerator. Then Hank pulls me down on the foam mat and we make sweaty love until he has to go back to the barracks for band rehearsal. Alone in the room, naked, I wrap myself in the sheet, adjust the Venetian blinds to

marked for life

let in the afternoon shadows. Then I sit down again on the mat and lean my back against the wall. For company, I have a tote bag full of fashion magazines and opera scores, and a head full of sorrow and remorse, which needs sorting out.

Hank's key clicks in the lock. The door squeals when it opens. He switches on the overhead light. "Why are you sitting in the dark?" he asks. "I was afraid you weren't here." I smile at him. "How do you like finding a naked lady in your bed when you get home?"

The next morning, Hank is up early, getting ready for roll call. He shows me how he's learned to spit-polish his heavy black Marine boots. When he leaves, I shower, make up my face in the medicine cabinet mirror. I dress and busy myself with the bucket and the Spic and Span, wiping grime from the windowsills. I need to prove to myself that I'm still a good girl, and to reassure Hank that I'm still here for him, still cleaning.

He's home two hours later. He wants me to help him pick out a rag rug at Sears. I have never been inside a Sears store. I have no interest in Sears. But I'm grateful for any excuse to get out.

At the store, the rugs are displayed hanging on swinging metal arms. Hank flips through them like the pages of a catalog. He is counting on my superior sense of style to help him in his selection. But I have a problem with the very concept of a rag rug. I think of my father's collection of Persian rugs, the deep red carpet in my bedroom that once covered a floor in Grandmom's house. The rag rug is more proof that Hank and I can never be a married couple. I have to force myself to concentrate on the color choices and sizes. Hank is taking much too long to make up his mind. I try to offer opinions, reasons the beige and green rug would look better in his apartment than the blue and gray one. What difference can it possibly make on that cracked linoleum floor?

On the way home, the rug rolled up in the backseat, I ask

him to stop for pizza. I'm stalling. I don't want to go back to his hot, bare little apartment. I can't believe it when he tells me he doesn't know where to find a pizza parlor. I'm feeling so cranky now, so crowded and alienated; it takes all my strength to keep smiling. I remind myself that I'm here to comfort him.

~~~

Once Hank's furniture arrived, he began to adjust to life in the Marine Band. He settled into the routine of playing rehearsals, parades, state dinners at the White House, funerals at Arlington Cemetery. His letters were less pained. When we could afford it, we talked on the phone. And I kept my promise. Every other Saturday after my singing lesson with Madame, I took the train to Washington and spent a night or two with him. Sometimes I thought about all the fun I was missing back in Philly. I knew that I could never marry Hank, but I also knew that I loved him, and I spent hours puzzling over the disparity, trying to find a way to resolve it. Love and marriage were supposed to go together. Why couldn't I make this work?

I envied the nice Jewish girls I knew at school. Most of them weren't especially pretty, but they all seemed so easy with themselves, so comfortable in their own, clear skin, their faces clean, shining. They were perfectly presentable with no more than just a dash of lipstick. Everything about their lives seemed so uncomplicated.

By senior year, nearly all of them had progressed from wearing their boyfriend's lavalieres around their necks, to wearing fraternity pins on their sweaters, to accepting substantial engagement rings. It seemed to me that those girls had not chosen their future husbands, but had been chosen by them. They seemed content to be doing what their mothers expected of them, marrying nice young men who, in turn, were doing what their own mothers expected of them. I could see that those girls were emotionally attached to their guys, but they never spoke about them passionately.

One night during my sophomore year, I sat cross-legged on my bed in the dorm, with a room full of girls, all of us dressed in long flannel nightgowns. Hank had written a love poem for me. Long after I had memorized it, I kept it tucked in my wallet. Now the girls were demanding to hear it, so I carefully unfolded the worn page and read it to them. "You're so lucky," someone said. "It makes me feel good just to know that somewhere in the world some guy is writing poetry like that." I am lucky, I thought, I am.

So why couldn't I marry Hank now? I wondered how many of those girls in their flannel nightgowns would have turned their lives over to a guy who wrote love poems, even if he wasn't Jewish, even if it would nearly kill their parents. I just knew that I wasn't a good girl. I wasn't a nice girl. Nice girls didn't get almost engaged and then break it off to find their own destinies. Nice girls didn't try to make it through life on their own. And nice girls saved themselves for their husbands. They did everything but actual intercourse. They knew they had to hold out on that one thing. I'd been sleeping with Hank since my first semester.

This Can't Be My Boyfriend

When I got back to school after Christmas break, there were flyers posted on all the buildings and trees. The Penn Players were holding auditions for a production of *The Mikado*, fully staged with orchestra. I thought if I could sing Bellini and Puccini, surely I could manage Gilbert and Sullivan. I went to the audition convinced that I could sing better than anyone else at school. I had a classically trained voice, summers at music festivals. I walked onto the stage at Irvine Auditorium full of confidence and sang my standard audition aria, *"Una voce poco fa,"* from Rossini's *The Barber of Seville*. And I got cast in a leading role. I'd play fair Yum-Yum, the young ward of Ko-Ko, Lord High Executioner of Titipu.

We had six weeks to prepare before opening night. I was back in rehearsal, bonding with another cast. This time I had an important part. Nothing was going to distract me. No more wrong notes. Hank would have to understand that I couldn't visit him for a while.

At first, he was supportive. But he was spending a lot of time talking to my roommate, Christy, because I was never home when he called. We rehearsed every evening, sometimes late into the night.

I had a new social life now, new friends from the cast and crew. Hank used to tell me I was the straightest chick in the world. My body was my instrument and I took good care of it. I never smoked. I rarely drank. When Hank started smoking pot, I told him he'd get arrested.

Now I was falling in with theater people, hippies. I wanted to be like them. I made friends with the guy who played the leading role of Ko-Ko. Trent was something of a heartthrob, a minor celebrity on campus. He was one of those guys who prided himself on his scruffiness. He wore Frye boots without socks, Levis without underwear. He let his hair grow long and he shaved only when it was absolutely necessary. It was his rebellion against the strict blazer-and-tie dress code of his prep school years at Choate.

I began spending a lot of time with Trent and his girlfriend, Fran. He took it upon himself to coax me out of the cloisters of classical music. One weekend he scored a nickel bag of pot and taught me to inhale fast and deep, and to hold my breath as long as I could. We walked around campus with Andrea, who was doing makeup for the show. They kept watching me, grinning. "Notice anything?" Andrea asked. "No, nothing. I don't think I'm stoned at all. It didn't work." But when we got back to Trent's apartment I was dying to taste the kibble he fed his dog. After I started getting stoned, Trent found it easier to turn me on to Bob Dylan and Judy Collins, J.R.R. Tolkien and Carlos Castañeda. My mind was blown.

One afternoon I walked into our apartment and regaled Christy with my newly acquired hippie-speak.

"Score?" she asked. "Score? As in a page or pages inscribed with musical notation? What do you mean by 'He scored'? What's happened to you? I wanted a roommate so I'd have company, but you're never here anymore. I might as well be living alone. And I'm tired of running interference with poor old Hank!" She slid off her bed, pulled on her boots, reached for her coat. "I'm going to the library," she said.

I stood there alone, wondering whether I should be annoyed or contrite. I didn't want Christy to be angry with me. I was afraid that I had ruined the tranquillity of our little nest. But I wasn't sorry that I sounded like a hippie chick.

I was given the key to my dressing room. I had my own address at the theater. My wig and costume were waiting for me there. I freaked out when I saw the name "Tebaldi" written inside the kimono I'd wear as Yum-Yum. The great soprano Renata Tebaldi must have once worn it when she sang *Madama Butterfly*. I pulled it over my shoulders, trying to feel her presence in the layers of heavy fabric. Andrea told us we'd be made up to look like geishas, so I wasn't worried about the birthmark. I could easily hide it under thick white pancake makeup.

Mommy and Daddy bought a whole block of seats for opening night and filled it with friends and clients from Millville. For one brief, shining moment, I was Daddy's good girl.

Hank came to Philly for the second performance. His train arrived at eleven o'clock that morning. I told him to meet me in my dressing room. I put on the lavender silk robe I'd bought especially for lounging and receiving guests backstage, then carefully arranged my body in a graceful diva-in-repose posture, my long hair dripping off the edge of the couch. I was enacting my leading lady glamour fantasy, finding one more way to escape the frightened girl with the purple face. I turned my head to check in the mirror, and satisfied that Hank's first glimpse of me would be breathtaking, I closed my eyes, exhausted from the night before.

When he arrived, I pretended to be asleep, partly so that he'd have to wake me up like Sleeping Beauty, and partly because I was uneasy about seeing him again. He had traveled in his Marine uniform to get the military fare. I sat up and sleepily put my arms around him, leaned into his body, thanked him for coming, but then I closed my eyes again. Compared to the disheveled, pot-smoking college boys I'd met in the theater, Hank looked super straight. In his short hair and Marine greens, he was the opposite of sexy. *This can't be my boyfriend.*

He asked me to follow him into the mens room while he changed back into his usual corduroy slacks and velour cardigan. He didn't want to let me out of his sight. It wasn't his fault that he didn't look sexy to me anymore. He'd been garrisoned in the straight camp, while I'd been joyfully discovering the counterculture. I knew I was fickle, shallow.

In the empty auditorium, I went through my solo scene. "Ah, pray make no mistake; we are not shy," I sang. "We're very wide awake, the moon and I." And Hank helped me. He gave me suggestions on how to improve the phrasing, the dynamic shading. That night I sang better, not worse, because of him.

But after the last performance, I found it hard to go back to our old routine. There was always something I'd be missing in Philly if I went down to Washington for the weekend. I negotiated, rescheduled, made excuses, but I wasn't ready to let him go.

Blind Love

> From the neck over the left shoulder down to the breast and below, and spreading like a red tongue to the back was this ugly blob—dark as blood, like a ragged liver on a butcher's window, or some obscene island with ragged edges. It was as if a bucket of paint had been thrown over her.
> "You didn't tell me," he said.
> If only she had told him, but how could she have done!
> She knew she had been cursed.
>
> V. S. PRITCHETT
Blind Love

He made me beautiful, me, Purple Face, marred with an enormous imperfection. He made me perfect. He made me so pretty he just loved to look at me, the prettiest girl in the room, the girl everybody wanted, and I was his, all his.

Now I would have to worry about many things, solve problems he had already solved for me. What would happen with the next one? (And surely there would be a next one.) On that first morning, would he be indignant? Would he feel betrayed when he found out that I had tricked him, fooled him into believing I was beautiful? Would he say that he had gone to bed with a beautiful woman, only to wake up beside the Purple People Eater, Bride of Frankenstein?

What if I slept alone until someone invented an indelible makeup that wouldn't wear off through the most passionate rubbing of skin against skin?

marked for life

    What if I kept the curtains drawn, the room so dark that my morning face was no more than a shadow?
    What if I trained myself not to sleep while he slept? What if I crept out of bed in the darkness of dawn, silently closed the bathroom door behind me before I dared turn on the light? What if I painted myself there and crept back, carefully lay down again beside him, so that when he opened his eyes he would find my naked body, but not my naked face?
    What if I trained myself to sleep always with my good cheek against the pillow so that my makeup wouldn't rub off in the night?
    What if I trained myself to sleep always on my bad cheek, so that when he opened his eyes in the morning he'd find me good side up?
    What if he opened his eyes to find my makeup smeared across the white pillowcase, beige powder streaked with black mascara?
    What if the next one was a man with such artistic vision, when he opened his eyes in the morning, he found my purple-stained face beautiful? At least, he might find it interesting.
    What if the next one was a man with such little vision, when he opened his eyes in the morning he didn't even notice the purple stain on my face?
    What if the next one was blind?
    What if I just held on to this one? What if I married him, after all?

I tried to protect Hank from my own ambivalence with lies and evasion, the same tools I used to protect Mommy and Daddy from finding out what they didn't want to know about me. They were the only tools I had, but they weren't working. I was just hurting him more and more. I felt like an inept Houdini, twisted and tied with ropes and locks, but not skillful enough to bow out gracefully. I wasn't sticking to our bargain. I was afraid to be honest. He seemed so fragile, ready to fall apart. I didn't have the courage to tell him it was over. I didn't know how.

Hank did it for me. He gave me an ultimatum. He said I had to promise to marry him, or he wouldn't see me again. I wasn't ready to lose him, but I knew I couldn't marry anybody, not now. I blamed him for being so needy, for trying to smother me just when I was learning to breathe freely.

And I blamed myself. If only I could have loved him more, maybe I would have stayed with him, married him after graduation, found some sort of job in Washington, just to be true to him, just to be near him. I worried that I was inadequate, even cruel for having loved him almost enough, as though I had thrown a drowning man a rope that fell just short of reaching him.

"Just now I'm mad, and I have a right to be," he wrote.

> It may be this past winter has been a perverse arrangement, but we agreed on it and it seemed to work. Anyway, it was okay until you started an independent social life. . . . I believe we could probably have married, been happy and stayed that way if you had wanted it. I have always expected us to come to a parting of ways. But I also have expected that you and your ambitions might come to a like parting. Frankly, I don't think your aspirations are going to lead to personal happiness and you may be clinging to them out of sentimentality or just confusion. . . .

Before I left, I told Christy and Trent that I was going to Washington to break up with Hank. I said it to bolster my resolve, the way people tell friends they're going to go on a diet or quit smoking. I told them so it would be harder for me to

marked for life

come back to Philly having chickened out, having mollified Hank, unable to hurt him, hurting him more by stringing him along for a few more months.

"Are you sure?" Trent kept pressing me. "You're really ready to do this? You won't regret it?" I had begun to realize that I wasn't making a choice at all. I was simply steering away from the road I couldn't take. I didn't feel acquitted, but merely resolved to accept my own shortcomings. Christy took Hank's side. She had watched me squirming away from him, then reeling him back in. She didn't think I deserved him.

⁓

Hank wants to make love all Saturday afternoon, all Saturday night, over and over again. I suppose that he's trying to get what little he still can, squeezing the last drop of love out of me, and I feel I owe it to him. It's the least I can do. He doesn't know when he'll ever get laid again, so he's making sure his tank is full before that long lonely ride into the desert.

I wake up to find Hank propped up on one arm, watching me with a murderous expression on his face. It's a dark morning. Rain pelts the trashcans behind the apartment, drumming a merciless martial rhythm. Hank says there is no point in dragging it out anymore. He wants me to pack up all my belongings, everything I've left there during the past few months, and all the things I've left with him over the past four years, stuff he moved from Philly to Arlington. He says he wants me to be sure to take everything, that he's afraid of being ambushed, of unexpectedly running across something of mine lost in the back of a drawer somewhere. So I get up and dress quickly. The apartment is chilly and the rain seems to seep in under the door.

I make instant coffee as I have always done—just the way Hank likes it, the right measure of milk and sugar, of dark crystals and hot water. Then I begin taking my books from his shelves, my clothes from his closet, double-checking the bathroom cabinet. I haven't really thought of this moment, haven't brought empty suitcases to pack things in. So I find some paper shopping bags in the kitchen and begin to fill them. Hank is going through the record albums lined up neatly on the floor by the stereo, sorting mine from his. I sit beside him. "You don't have to do that. Just keep them. At least keep all the ones you want. I can't carry them, anyway." *How can this be the end? My body feels so comfortable against his, my head on his bony shoulder where I've rested it so often.* I say, "I love you." He turns to me, "Then *why*?" He's falling apart and my arms are too weak to hold him together, but I hold him as tightly as I can, all the same.

In the middle of the afternoon, everything is packed and waiting by the door; all that remains is the torture of staring at each other, waiting for the hours to pass, listening to the rain. "I'd just as soon put you on the next train," he says. And now it's really happening. We begin to carry bags to the Volkswagen, filling up the backseat, running back and forth, getting wet.

On the way to the station, Hank starts to cry, and I can't bear to watch him taking off his glasses to wipe his eyes, and the windshield wipers are going like mad, too, so that he can barely see to drive. "Wouldn't it be just so poetic," he says, "if I crashed the car and we both died right now?" *He might actually do it on purpose, he is that distraught.*

He double-parks and helps me carry the bags inside the station, then he says, "You're on your own from here. I'll be damned if I'm going to help you leave me." It's the first time he's made me fend for myself—his last good-bye. I throw my tote bag over my shoulder, arrange the handles of the shopping bags, three in each hand, and begin to struggle across the station, stopping every few feet to reorganize the load.

marked for life

We had been living in that awful place between breaking up and staying together, but for a time, I could still find a tiny patch where I felt safe and I had stored stuff there, as a way of holding the space. Now the remains of our love are tearing through the bottoms of soggy, crumpled paper bags. I don't turn back to look at him. I've seen too much of his sorrow.

At the platform, a handsome man with brown hair and a brown suit leans over to help me. He carries my bags inside the car, stows them by my seat. *How nice that strange men are always around to oblige a young woman, that I don't have to fend for myself, after all.*

⌒

I'm bouncing around in the dilapidated train car. The seats are hard and shabby, and on a Sunday afternoon, they're all full. My shoes are wet and my long hair lies soggy on my neck and shoulders. I'm shivering and sobbing, my hands covering my face, and when I can open my eyes a little, I notice that the rain is drawing patterns in the soot on the windows. In the seats opposite mine, an elderly couple has been watching me. The woman, in her gray wool suit and tan raincoat, looks concerned. Her husband looks uncomfortable. When they see that I see them, they look away. They are the couple Hank and I might have become, should have become. Hank used to say that whenever he saw an older couple walking hand in hand, he thought of us.

I don't know how I will ever be able to stop crying. I see Hank driving home in the rain alone, walking into the empty apartment. I tear through the disintegrating shopping bags looking for notepaper. I have to convince him to take me back.

I've made a terrible mistake. No one will ever love me so resolutely; no one will ever need me so badly. No one else will ever think I'm beautiful.

I write fast, racing to get the words down, telling him how

much I love him, begging him to forgive me, promising to marry him, forsaking all others, forsaking the person I might become. I write illegibly, barely able to see through the tears, smearing the ink. Then I copy the pages over again, cleaning up the prose, trying to say it neatly.

At Penn Station in Philly, I stagger up the steep staircase into the cavernous great hall, drag my bags across the marble floor, muddied with the tracks of hundreds of pairs of damp shoes. I load my burdensome cargo into the revolving glass door piece by piece, the paper bottoms beginning to tear now. And I emerge into the clear, gray light of an April evening. I wait on the curb, surrounded by crumbling shopping bags, looking like a homeless person, my cheek streaked black with mascara and striped purple where crying washed away the makeup. The storm has passed and a clean breeze, blowing off the Schuykill River, dries my face. The sun, in a valiant, final effort, is straining to break through the clouds, leaving a red glow lingering low in the sky like a last kiss. The letter I wrote on the train is in my pocket. I stand in front of the trashcan for a long time before I gently bury it among the discarded newspapers, hot dog wrappers, and empty soda cans.

part three
THE MASK SLIPS

". . . what will be my triumph when I shall have corrected what Nature left imperfect in her fairest work!"

NATHANIEL HAWTHORNE
"The Birthmark"

Another Look in the Mirror

My operatic career never took off, although I studied and auditioned and sang here and there. Instead I fell in love and, like Mommy, turned away from my own path to follow a man down his. I did for him what I had been unable to do for Hank, sharing his dreams instead of striving toward dreams of my own.

I lived in New York with this man, an artist who thought my purple-stained face was beautiful. He hated the makeup mask. "It's a fear leftover from childhood," he said. "Now it's time to put childish fears away."

One night to please him, I went out for a pint of chocolate fudge ice cream without wearing makeup. I crossed First Avenue in the dark, avoiding street lamps, but inside the little deli the cruel blue fluorescent light cast no shadows. The woman behind the cash register had seen me dozens of times. She put the ice cream in a bag, looked at me, frowned, handed me my change, leaned over the counter to get a closer look at my face.

"What happened to you?"

I wanted to tell her that my boyfriend had beaten me. Surely that was what she was thinking, so why not say so? But instead I said, "It's nothing. It's a birthmark."

"How come I never saw it before?"

"I always wear makeup."

"Humph. You sure, honey? You sure you're okay? Your eye looks awful red."

"I'm fine, really."

I shook my head so that my hair covered the stained cheek, the red eye. After that night, I walked an extra three blocks to buy ice cream at a different store. I never went out without makeup again.

———

Six years later, our long affair came to a crashing close. The man for whom I had forsaken my dreams had forsaken me, moved out of my life and in with a new girlfriend. I sold the loft I'd shared with him and followed my sisters to California. Julie said it was as far as we could get from Millville without having to learn Chinese. And I needed to move far away from my New York life, far away from him.

I went on trying to do as Mommy taught me, I didn't make a Big Deal, I pretended the birthmark was nothing, but it was always there, coloring my life. Every time the makeup mask slipped, prompting someone to ask about my face, I was miserable—not only because I was embarrassed by the question, but because the questioner had forced me out of my denial.

In spite of my fears that no one would ever love my purple-stained face, I found boyfriends. Some lasted a few months, some nearly a decade. It was always the man who left me. I held on and kept trying as long as there was a shred of love left.

Many of my friends weren't doing any better than I was. I watched relationships fall apart all around me. I thought that they failed because the woman expected too much. My women friends always blamed the men for having disappointed them, for not living up to their expectations, for refusing to make the compromises they felt entitled to demand. I was determined that this would not happen to me. I was wiser than that. I was grateful for any attention, any affection a man offered me. I expected little. I settled for less and got less and less and less until there was nothing left and the relationship was over.

I chose carefully, but my criteria did not include sanity, honesty, reliability. I was looking for a man whose vision was so acute that he might find my stain interesting or so dull that he might not notice it. And I learned to wait until these men were safely smitten before I let them see me without makeup. If there were men who didn't call again because they decided they couldn't bear my stained face, I never knew it. I told myself that once I had gained a man's affection, the birthmark would cease to be an issue. And I could hide the stain. I thought that men wanted to be seen with a woman who looked pretty in public. What my face looked like when I was undressed wouldn't matter much as long as my body looked good. Some men might have felt uncomfortable if they were asked, "Why does she wear so much makeup?" but at least they never needed an answer for "What's wrong with her face?" I never even considered that I might have lost lovers because of the birthmark. There are too many other reasons for a man to leave a woman.

Sometime in my early thirties I stopped trying to sing and began trying to write. It was the perfect job for me. Always living on the periphery, looking in from the outside, hiding behind a mask, harboring a secret, I had never felt as though I could fully participate. Writing gave me an excuse to merely observe, to hang around the edges of life taking notes.

For years I wrote a newspaper column I called "Style," in which I chronicled and commented on the Los Angeles fashion scene. I turned my need to look better than anybody else into a profession. When I couldn't find anything better to cover, I wrote funny, self-deprecating stories about my endless makeovers, diets, and wardrobe adjustments. When I lost my contact lenses the same week that a big cold sore blossomed on my lip and my body bloated up from PMS, I wrote merrily, "This has been the ugliest period of my life." But I never mentioned that a purple stain covered half my face. I was willing to tell any humiliating story about myself except that one, the story that set me apart from the rest of the human race. I found my contact lenses; the cold sore healed; the PMS went away. I had good hair days, successful weight-loss plans, but the birthmark was always there; no course of self-improvement could alter it.

I sometimes wondered if the makeup artists who made me over gossiped among themselves, if they whispered, "You'll have your work cut out for you if you have to do her makeup. She's got a big purple birthmark on her face and it's a bitch to cover." But I couldn't afford to think about that. I couldn't make a Big Deal.

Eventually, I grew my "Style" column into a magazine, *L.A. Style*, an oversized publication that chronicled the aesthetics of the 1980s and early 1990s. I published hundreds of pages of superstar models shot by superstar photographers. I tried to promote models with unusual faces. The magazine's covers often featured exotic women of mixed races, who defied the blond-blue-eyed ideal.

Twice a year, I covered the runway shows, following the fashion caravan from Milan to London to Paris to New York. No matter how beautiful the skies had been before I arrived, for those weeks in October or March, it rained.

On my last trip to Paris, it rained all week. I hurried along the covered walkways of the Rue de Rivoli on my way to the Louvre where the shows were held. I sat for hours in damp shoes and panty hose. Crushed by the black-clad hordes, pushing and shoving impatiently at the entrance to every show, I used my umbrella as both sword and shield to protect my head from the rain and my face from the dense cloud generated by hundreds of chain-smoking photographers and editors.

The final show of the European season was that of Yves Saint Laurent, a hot ticket even then, when *le maître*, in poor health, still personally designed the ready-to-wear line. It was my final show as editor in chief of *L.A. Style*. I had chosen to give up the magazine and I was determined not to allow myself to become sentimental about it. My life as editor and publisher had been exciting but exhausting, and the sale of the magazine to American Express Publishing two years earlier had only made the job harder and more stressful. Still, I couldn't help feeling conflicted. It had taken years of luck and hard work to get my fifth-floor suite at the Hotel Regina, my seat just behind the editors from *Vogue*, and now I had decided to quit the game, leaving my chips on the table.

As I walked out of the YSL show, I knew I was walking away from the exclusive club I'd fought to join, away from the world where trends mattered, where the right silhouette, the latest handbag were important considerations.

It was windy and the sky slowly opened up as though big gray flats were being wheeled offstage for a change of scene. Pigeons fluttered about the sidewalks drying their wings. I wondered if I'd ever be in that place again, in Paris, in a designer suit, a car and driver waiting for me. And I wondered how I'd ever gotten there at all.

When I was a teenager with no hope of achieving the current standard of beauty, I tried, for a time, to look "interesting" instead. If I couldn't look pretty, I'd look odd. When the other girls wore loafers and bobby socks, I wore the thick cotton stockings and heavy shoes issued to nuns. When the other girls wore matching sweaters and skirts in pastel colors, I dressed in black.

At fifteen, in desperation, I embellished the birthmark I couldn't hide. Drawing over it with green and blue eye pencils, I tried to plant flowers on the dark red stain. Who was to say that a decorated face was less beautiful than a clear complexion?

In seventeenth-century Salem, a stained-faced woman would have been burned at the stake as a witch, the blotch on her skin proof that she had been marked by the devil. Who would have dared to say that she might have been marked by an angel instead? Who decided what was beautiful and what wasn't?

How did it happen that I had become one of those arbiters of beauty, hiding my secret devil's mark, promoting the very notions that had imprisoned me behind a mask? It had been the ultimate denial, the perfect disguise.

When I relinquished my place in the spotlight, I considered for a moment that I might find the courage to go barefaced. I might move to another country where no one knew my masked face, where everyone I met would see me only as I am. I could become an interesting character in long skirts and flowing hair, like a gypsy marked by a curse. I could celebrate my oddness, flaunt my birthmark instead of hiding it, accessorize it with shawls and unusual jewelry. I was walking away from the masked woman I had invented. Now I would have to reinvent myself as someone else.

As my fortieth birthday approached, throwing its shadow over the fading sunlight of my youth, the birthmark began to darken. The elastic fibers around the vessels, which had been swollen with blood for so long, had weakened with the years, becoming flaccid. It took more and more time, thicker and heavier makeup, to camouflage the stain, and the purple skin was no longer smooth, but pebbled with tiny bumps. I tried to tell myself that it didn't make a difference since no one saw me without makeup anyway. Not even my closest friends knew about the birthmark. But despite all the makeovers, the celebrity hairdressers, the personal trainer, and the designer clothes, when I woke up in the morning and looked in the mirror, what I saw was not the glamorous Brenda Starr image I'd worked so hard to create, but my stained, strange face. And I was single. I didn't dare to show my naked face to yet another man. The mark had grown dark purple, coarse and scattered with black flecks, like seeds in boysenberry jam.

One evening as I finished dressing for dinner, I absently brushed my hand across my cheek and a bump in the birthmark spurted blood. I ran to the kitchen for a wet paper towel, pulled ice cubes out of the freezer. Blood covered my face, ran down my chin, spotted the front of my dress, spattered the kitchen floor. The bleeding didn't stop for nearly an hour. I called the restaurant where my friends were waiting, made excuses. "Order without me. I'll get there as soon as I can."

The next day I was in my dermatologist's office having the bump cauterized with an electric needle. It was a small blood vessel that had risen to the surface of the skin, its walls weakened by decades of pooling blood. Port wine stains do that as one ages, the doctor told me. He said I could expect to start noticing more of these bleeding bumps. I was afraid to ask him, afraid to be disappointed again, afraid of being reminded that my face was a hopeless case. "Can't we just cauterize the rest of my birthmark?"

"No," he said, "You'd be left with pitted scars and it would take forever. There are too many blood vessels and most of them are too deep."

"Well, I was just wondering . . . I thought something new might have been invented, some new treatment for port wine stains."

As a matter of fact, he said, he knew a doctor in Pasadena who had been experimenting with a ruby laser to treat port wine stains like mine.

The Douro River winds through the mountain passes of northern Portugal, flowing downhill to meet the sea at Porto. On narrow terraces, carved into steep slopes that rise above the river's path, vineyards have been cultivated since the days of

Caesar's Empire. During the harvest, pickers still spend the last hours of the day treading on the fruit of these vines, extracting the juice, staining their feet and legs a deep dark red, the color of my face. Barrels from these vineyards still float downriver to the city of Porto, where the wine is bottled and aged. At the turn of the seventeenth century, British merchants came to Porto. Their supply of Bordeaux threatened by frequent wars with France, and reluctant to become overly dependent on the Spanish sherries of Jerez de la Frontera, they turned to the hearty grapes of the Douro valley. They added brandy to the vinho, *fortifying it for the rough sea voyage across the Atlantic. The brandy created a complex wine they called port and deepened the ruby red liquid to a shade the color of a blood stain.*

The Blood-Seeking Missile

My first treatments were part of an FDA trial. There was no guarantee that the treatments would work and no promise that I wouldn't end up scarred. But I was so tired of hiding behind the mask of makeup, of keeping vigil over my secret. And now that I had begun to understand how it would mushroom with age, I thought I couldn't bear to go on living with the mark. I had always wondered what I'd do when my skin became so wrinkled that the heavy concealing makeup caked up in the folds. I had never realized that the birthmark itself would get so much worse. But now it had begun its metamorphosis from a flat wine-colored stain to an eggplant-black growth. I was terrified of what I might look like by the time I was fifty. I wanted to get the wretched thing off my face, to burn it off, rip it out, dig it out with my nails.

I drive myself to the doctor's office. No one can know about the birthmark, so no one can go with me. The doctor threads a long needle under the skin of my cheek, my forehead, my eyebrow, the corner of my eye, stabbing me over and over again, flooding my face with lidocaine, burning, stinging. My cheek swells, my eye swells shut. "I hate to do this to you," he says. "I know I'm torturing you." He tries to distract me with talk of local restaurants and travels abroad. He keeps talking through the smell of burnt hair as the laser's heat speeds through the surface of my skin, a blood-seeking missile, singeing the down on my cheek, burning off bits of eyelash and eyebrow. Deeply buried vessels melt, collapse, and shrivel. The blood congeals; the red turns black.

When the treatment is over, relieved but dazed from all the lidocaine shots and from the laser's assault on my face, I drive myself home. One hand on the wheel, one hand holding an ice pack to my cheek and eye, I navigate the treacherous on-ramp of the Pasadena Freeway like a blind drunk.

At home alone, wounded, I comfort myself with a coddled egg, an *eggila*, just the way Grandmom used to make it, bits of buttered toast soaking up the runny yolk, a little salt, a little pepper.

The next morning I wake up with neatly spaced round black spots, bruises, circles of dried blood under the skin. It looks exactly as though someone had dipped the end of a pencil eraser in black ink and stamped my face in a polka-dot pattern. At first the skin is so tender that a terrycloth towel feels like broken glass slicing my cheek. For days I hide in the house watching videos, cradling a bag of frozen peas against my face to bring down the swelling. My skin blisters in places, scabs over. Then slowly, slowly, my body disposes of the debris under the stained skin, washes away the dried blood, the dead vessels. Week after week I watch the black fade to deep purple, then to red.

One night I have difficulty taking off my makeup, it seems to resist the washcloth. And then I realize that the makeup really is off. In the hours since I covered it that morning, patches of birthmark have vanished. Each tiny patch of clear skin is a conquest, reclaimed territory. The ruby laser is a magical weapon. Two months later, I have the courage to do it all again, to reclaim another bit of my face.

I get lost driving to the doctor's office, partly in fear of the pain, partly in fear of confronting my birthmark, of admitting it's there, of making a Big Deal about it. After half a lifetime of believing I was marked for life, trying to accept it, to live with it, I'm finally able to do something about it. The thought is so shocking, it disorients me. I grip the wheel, lean forward toward the dashboard. I take the wrong street, make U-turns, stop, and consult the map again and again.

When I arrive for my third treatment, the doctor looks grim. He tells me that the FDA has decided that the trial is over. His magical ruby laser will be taken away in a few days. He says he wants to do as much as he can to help me this time, since this may be our last chance. He says if its okay with me, he's going to really turn up the juice. I tell him to go ahead and blast the damned thing.

When the swelling goes down and the black spots fade away, the edges of my birthmark are gone. It's smaller, lighter; the bleeding bumps have disappeared. But my skin looks like a relief map. The patches where the birthmark faded are white and scarred. Thick scabs that formed on my cheek and forehead have left deep dents in my face, the way glaciers leave canyons in their wake.

Five years after the FDA took away the ruby laser, I heard of a doctor in Orange County with a new FDA-approved machine. One more time I got lost on my way to the doctor's office. One more time I bared my face to a stranger in a white coat. I'd spent so much energy hiding the birthmark, worked so hard at pretending it wasn't there. I didn't want to think about it, to talk about. Admitting I had a stained face, a malformation, a birth defect, was horrible. Even in a doctor's office, it took courage to say the words "port wine stain." I tucked my hair behind my ear so the doctor could get a better look at my cheek. I explained my history with the ruby laser, pointed out the scars.

"Do you think you can do anything to improve on this?"

"Oh, I think so," he said dryly. "We'll try it." Then he shook my hand and was gone.

His nurse ushered me into a little room draped on all sides

with heavy curtains. A box of tissues had been placed beside the plump couch. It might have been a psychiatrist's office, a room decorated in the expectation that those who spent time there would inevitably cry. The nurse opened a cabinet to reveal a small television set. She pushed the start button on the VCR and left me alone.

Even in the offices of the doctors I'd consulted, I had never met anyone else with a port wine stain. Until Mikhail Gorbachev came along very few people had ever seen one. The news magazines had to run stories explaining that red blotch on his head.

I'd met a couple of women who covered their faces with heavy makeup, but I didn't dare to ask if they were hiding a birthmark. Except for the sad man on the subway long ago, I'd never seen anyone with a stained face like mine.

Watching the video in the doctor's curtained room, I saw men and women, boys and girls with stained faces, stained hands, stained arms and legs. I saw them before and after treatment, purple stains faded to pink. They talked about their birthmarks. The adults who had grown up with stained faces made a Big Deal about it. The parents of children with birthmarks talked about how hard it was for their little girl or boy. The little girls and boys talked about not wanting to go to school, about being teased and tormented.

In the parking lot, I had trouble finding my car. I didn't think I could drive back to L.A. I was afraid I couldn't manage the freeways. All that I had felt about the stain, all that Mommy told me I wasn't supposed to feel, overwhelmed me. The stained people on the videotape had said they felt it all, too.

I had left the magazine, taken myself out of the public eye. I had time to hide while my face healed. Over the next year, I was treated six times with the pulse-dye laser. This doctor didn't bother with numbing injections. It was better that way, he said. He said that the laser just feels like you're being stung with a rubber band and that the pain isn't bad enough to require numbing, but I thought it felt like I was being burned with the business end of a lit cigarette. Twice the doctor talked me into allowing him to insert a metal shield over my left eyeball so that he could zap my eyelid, which was completely purple. His nurse had to hold my head tightly to prevent me from jerking when the blinding light blasted me.

I learned to bring my own painkillers, extra strength over-the-counter medicines or prescription pills I'd hoarded after I had a wisdom tooth pulled. I learned to pack a cooler with ice for the drive home. My friend Eileen came with me. It meant having to tell her about the birthmark. We had been close friends and colleagues, totally trusting and confiding everything. She was amazed that I'd kept this one big secret for so long, but she wasn't angry or hurt. She saw my naked face and she understood. Necessity had forced me out of my fear and shame. I couldn't drive myself all the way back to L.A. half blind.

The new laser softened the scars left by the old one. More tiny patches of my face were reclaimed. The birthmark faded, but it was still there. The doctor said I would require three treatments. After six I decided not to subject myself to any more.

I was happy enough that the growth of the birthmark had been interrupted, the lesion shrunk and flattened, at least temporarily. The laser treatments could set the clock back, but they couldn't stop it. The spreading stain had not been halted in its path, but merely slowed. I'd have to have "touch up" treatments for the rest of my life. But I could paint a mask over the lightened stain in only five or ten minutes.

And I had new and better tools in my paint box. The science of cosmetic camouflage had made strides since I first began to cover the stain with Pan-Stick. Many of the big cosmetic companies designed special products for people with something serious to hide: birthmarks, tattoos, scars. Even Covermark, which had disappointed me so much when I was a little girl, had been reformulated. I told myself that I should be happy with the results and learn to live with this paler birthmark. I told myself it was no longer a Big Deal.

A couple of years later, I saw an advertisement for a new machine—not a laser but an intense pulsed light source, which was used for removing unwanted hair and spider veins. In the small print I read that it could also remove port wine stains. I found a doctor whose office was not far from my home. I made the appointment very early in the morning, hoping that his waiting room would be empty at that hour, that no one would notice me sitting there barefaced.

This new treatment was much less painful, no blisters or scabs, no swelling, no black dots the morning after. Every month or two I showed up at the doctor's office. Every month or two more tiny bits of the birthmark faded, as though someone had randomly sprinkled bleach on a blood stain.

The receptionists and nurses got used to me. One day, while she was zapping my skin, a nurse told me that she used to date a guy with a birthmark like mine. She said that the man not only had a port wine stain covering half his face, but he also had severe scarring from failed treatments. This man had a twin to whom he was identical except that his brother didn't have a birthmark. The "normal" brother grew into a confident and outgoing man, a trial attorney. The stained brother grew up shy and reclusive, an engineer who worked at home. He refused to submit to any more painful and ineffective treatments. Nothing the nurse said convinced him that he should try to get help again.

When I was a little girl, I stared at myself in the mirror for hours, trying to see my face without the awful stain. But this man, as a little boy, would have constantly confronted his corrected reflection in the face of his twin. How desperate his parents must have been to fix his face so that it would match his brother's. How devastating it must have been when none of the treatments worked.

I no longer found the stain hideous. It looked more like a severe rash than a rare deformity that needed to be explained. It was still a part of me, an intruder, disrupting my life. I still wouldn't leave the house without makeup. But I didn't worry so much about opening the door to the FedEx guy. Once a deliveryman asked me if I had a rash on my face and I said that yes, it was an allergy, but that it was getting better. A port wine stain would have taken too much explanation.

I had loathed the stain for so long, dreamed of removing it, knowing it was hopeless. Now I began to wonder how I would feel if it continued to fade until it was totally gone. Could I give up thinking of myself as someone different, someone apart? And how ironic that this should be happening at an age when my whole face was changing anyway, when the first thing I saw in the mirror was not my old familiar stain, but my newly sagging jawline.

Evie died of ovarian cancer just one year before she would have been able to retire from her job as home and school counselor. Mommy was devastated by the loss of her little sister and best friend. As we packed up Evie's Philadelphia apartment one cold, snowy December day, Mommy noticed that my makeup was streaked with tears. "Why are *you* crying?" she asked angrily. For the first time, she was unable to hide the jealousy she must have always felt for the closeness Evie and I had shared.

Mommy and I began a ritual of having long talks every Saturday morning. Sometimes Daddy picked up the phone in another room. Having founded a magazine, I had finally proved myself worthy of his attention by succeeding as a businesswoman, and he liked to hear about my dealings with the board of directors, my efforts at fund raising. If Mommy or I changed the subject, he got off the line. As soon as he hung up, Mommy began a litany of complaints about him. He may once have been the love of her life, but he seemed to have become nothing but an endless source of aggravation.

One Saturday morning I called Mommy as usual, but she didn't answer the phone; Daddy did. And for the first time, he stayed on the line and talked to me, just me, without Mommy listening in. Before he hung up he said, "Bye, bye, honey bunny." *Honey bunny! He called me honey bunny!* Daddy had never used sweet names with me. "Bye, bye, sweetie pie," I sang back. And for the rest of the day, I was happy. Mommy and Daddy were coming to visit me at Christmas. They'd be in L.A. in less than a month. I'd have a chance to really get through to Daddy. A limb that had been torn off my body so many years ago could still be reattached.

Before the dawn of the next day, Mommy called. She said that she had woken up to find Daddy sitting on the couch, as she so often did. But this time, he hadn't fallen asleep in front of the TV—this time, Daddy was dead.

I thought Mommy's grief would be short-lived. I couldn't imagine that she'd feel anything but relief. In their last decades together, my sisters and I were tense whenever we were with them. They were not pleasant company. Mommy criticized Daddy constantly. And he constantly repeated, "I'm getting sick and tired of your deprecating remarks, Florence. I guess I'll just keep my mouth shut." He pressed his thin lips together so hard, they disappeared. He claimed to be the subject of endless ridicule and, in turn, he ridiculed his daughters.

But after he was gone, Mommy seemed to forget all her complaints about him. I thought she'd realize she was free at last, leave Millville, and move into the Manhattan hotel suite of her dreams. Instead, she stayed in the family house. For the rest of her life she claimed to be closing up their law offices, but she went on working there.

My sisters and I tried to fill the void in her life by taking vacations with her. Julie took her to Canyon Ranch. Jackie took her to Hawaii. When it was my turn, Mommy and I went to Ensenada, just an hour's drive south of the border in Mexico. We had a big suite on the top floor of a little hotel, with terraces overlooking the sea.

I rarely mentioned the birthmark to her. It had always been a taboo subject. If she noticed that it had faded, she didn't say anything. But in the warmth of the moment, I confessed to her that my birthmark developed bleeding bumps, that I had been treated with laser surgery, and that I planned to continue treatments so long as I got results.

Mommy sat down on her bed. "I feel terrible. I want to pay for the treatments," she said. "Why should you pay?" I asked her. "The insurance covers it, and besides, I have my own money now." Mommy was quiet. "Why should you pay?" I asked again.

"Because all these years, I've felt so guilty."

"Why, Mommy? Did you ask for a child with a stained face? Did you have a choice? Did you say, 'No, not that one, give me the *birthmarked* baby'?"

Mommy shook her head.

"When you were born, the doctor told me that your birthmark would grow and get darker. He told me it might start to bleed. I never told you. I never warned you. Now everything the doctor said has happened."

She looked so morose sitting there, slumped over, her hands clasped together tightly.

"I'm sure it was for the best that you didn't say anything, Mommy. There was nothing we could have done about it then, anyway."

After that, I told her whenever I got a treatment, but we

didn't talk about it much. I knew that it was too painful for her to hear it. Maybe she thought she'd damaged me in her belly by crying so hard when she found out she was pregnant. Maybe she'd drunk vile teas or thrown herself down the stairs trying to abort me.

Eight years later, we lost Mommy. She'd gone to the office on Friday, gone to a luncheon on Saturday, and on Sunday she was gone forever. She floated away lying in her own bed. When my sisters and I came back to Millville to close up the office and the house, we found Daddy's briefcase on the floor by his desk, exactly where he left it the day he died. For eight years, nobody had touched it. Mommy had left it there like a shrine.

Under Mommy's desk, I found a box full of the letters Daddy wrote her before they were married. In a filing cabinet, I found the notebook in which she'd kept all the songs and poems she'd written for my sisters and me when we were very little. She had kept every letter, every greeting card, every postcard my sisters and I had ever sent her. In my old room, where butterfly decals still danced across the mirror, I found the locked box where I'd hidden letters from the boy, written so long ago, and a manila envelope with Hank's letters, and the poems he'd sent me.

She Looks Just Like I Did

Alone at home, tired and bored, curled in front of the TV set, flipping through the channels, I happened upon a show featuring the story of a woman who compulsively pulled out her hair. Every night in her sleep she pulled out bits until she was nearly bald. She wore a wig whenever she left the house so that no one would know her secret. Doctors were unable to cure her of this obsessive behavior, but she found solace in an Internet support group of people who shared her problem.

This woman had a secret like mine. She couldn't leave the house without a wig, just as I couldn't leave the house without makeup. But I didn't see that our stories were in any way similar. I thought the woman was bizarre, nothing at all like me.

I was more impressed with her support group. If there was an Internet group for compulsive hair-pullers, there must be something for people with port wine stains. It's not that I felt the need for support myself—not at all. I was fine. I was just curious. I often wondered why I had never met anyone who looked like me. Were they hiding in their houses like the man who dated my doctor's nurse? Were they hiding behind makeup, like I was?

There was nothing interesting on television, anyway, so I moved from the couch to my desk, logged onto the Internet, and ran a search for "port wine stain," then "birthmarks." It took only a few clicks to find the Port Wine Stains Website Home Page. It had been there for years, but it had never occurred to me to look for it. I didn't like to think about the birthmark, didn't like to make a Big Deal.

The site contained information about the physiology of vascular malformations, laser treatments, insurance coverage, related medical problems, a bibliography, and useful links. And it gave instructions on how to join the port wine stain private newsgroup.

I was not a joiner. I belonged to no clubs, no professional organizations, no committees, no teams. I was so used to thinking of myself as different, I'd never felt comfortable belonging to any group. If this was a club for people with disfiguring birthmarks, I didn't want to join. That wasn't me. I was a successful businessperson, a journalist, and with makeup, I was still considered attractive. I didn't have anything in common with a bunch of freaks.

But I wanted to get into the private archives, which contained dozens of personal stories contributed by stained people from all over the world. So I signed up. It was safe. I didn't have to see anyone, speak to anyone. I didn't even have to send e-mail to other members of the group. I could just sit alone in my house and read about them, still standing in the shadows on the playground, just beyond the circle of kids jumping rope.

I read about a little girl who told her teacher she was part Indian when her first-grade class learned that Native Americans were once called "redskins." I read about a boy who tried to sand the stain off his face with a file from his father's tool chest. I read about a girl whose parents began applying makeup to her stained face when she was only a year old. No one outside her immediate family had ever seen her without it. I read about a woman who was so clever with makeup, her own husband had never seen her birthmark, although they'd been married for ten years. I read about a man who wouldn't go down a supermarket aisle if he saw children there, for fear that his face would frighten them.

When I was a little girl, I couldn't cry because it upset Daddy and I'd be locked in the dark on the cellar landing. When I was older, I couldn't cry because my makeup would run and I'd look like a monster. Finally, I couldn't cry at all, even when I really wished I could, even when something really sad happened. But as I read these stories, I was sobbing, doubled over in my chair.

All my life I tried to ignore the birthmark. Now I was reminded of it every time I checked my e-mail. Every day I read postings from people with stains like mine, and from the parents of stained children. When women posted questions about concealing makeup, I began to write back. After all those makeovers, all those years of painting a mask on my face, I considered myself an expert. It was a safe topic. Most women wear makeup. I didn't even have to admit I had a problem.

I read a posting from a little girl in South Africa who was scared of going to a new school where no one knew her. I wrote to her. That happened to me, too, maybe I could help. I wrote to a young woman in Malaysia whose heavy makeup melted in the tropical heat. I knew what she was talking about.

A woman in Paris wrote to me privately. "I have been lurking for a while but didn't dare to write to the group. If I remember, we are the same age and you always seemed to me like an empathetic person." She wrote that her whole face was stained—her ears, her lips, her gums, her neck, her scalp. Both eyes were involved, and as a result, she suffered from glaucoma. As a child, she was subjected to all sorts of painful, ineffective treatments. In her early forties she met a man who loved her and tried to help her accept her birthmark. He told her that as long as she refused to even answer the door without makeup, she would never accept herself. They had been married for seven and a half years. He had recently died, and then her father had died and she was alone.

How could I compare my life to hers?

"Thank you so much for writing to me. It helps me, too, to

share life stories with you," I wrote. "I have never met anyone in the world who looks like me. I also wear makeup all the time and I don't blame myself for it. Only someone who has lived with a birthmark can understand this. After my last treatment, I had to stop in a pharmacy on my way home. Walking through the store without makeup, I felt the eyes of the other customers and wondered how I had survived all the stares when I was growing up. So I don't go out without makeup. Not ever."

Sharing my secrets with the only people who could truly understand them taught me that the pain I had experienced from living with a stained face could be a source of comfort for others. The birthmark was good for something. I didn't have to go on hating my own face. And I didn't have to go on hating myself for making a Big Deal about the birthmark, for being too sensitive, self-pitying, weak. My new friends were just words on a computer screen, mute voices, telling me that I was not crazy, not alone, that everyone with a marked face feels those things.

I began trading e-mail with Margie, a teacher, in New York State. When the Vascular Malformations Foundation announced the First International Port Wine Stain Conference in Charleston, South Carolina, we both signed up. I was interested in the scholarly presentations, in consulting with the doctors who would be offering clinics. But mostly I just wanted to see other people who looked like me.

I open the drapes of my hotel room window and look out over Charleston's rooftops, lifting my face to the summer sun. Standing in front of the mirror, I reach for my makeup bag. No matter how rushed or sleepy I am, the mask always goes on. It's as much a part of my morning routine as toothpaste or clean underwear. At breakfast I'll be meeting some of the people I've corresponded with online all year, people with stains like mine.

marked for life

I open my compact and my hand goes straight to the birthmark. Then I catch myself. With a tissue, I wipe the makeup off my stained cheek. How will the others respond to me if I hide the mark that connects us? I toss a deep rose cotton shawl, a birthmark-colored banner, over my shoulders. Then I walk out the door barefaced.

I step onto an elevator full of strangers wearing nametags, participants in a different conference. I stare at the floor, letting my hair fall over my cheek, so that the strangers won't see my face and I won't see the expressions on theirs. Then I force myself to raise my head, to look straight at them, to smile and say, "Good morning." Today should be different. Today I should bear my birthmark proudly, defiantly.

In the dining room, I approach the maître d'. "I'm meeting some people. I don't know if they're here yet." She looks at my face. "Oh, yes," she says. "I'm sure they are." She leads me to a long banquette at the back of the room. I'm trying hard to appear casual, friendly, to let nothing I do or say betray my nervousness. I am about to come face to face with the thing I have worked so hard to avoid. I've been bracing myself for this moment, wondering what the others will look like, wondering how I'll feel when I meet them.

I scan the table, searching for purple-stained skin. We introduce ourselves all around. "Where is your birthmark?" Lucy asks, and I am incredulous at the question. I pull my hair away from my face and swivel in my chair to show everyone. "It used to be much worse," I explain apologetically, as though I need better credentials to be accepted into the group. "I've had a lot of treatments. Where's yours?"

Lucy's birthmark covers most of her left leg and foot. Sitting at the table, it's impossible to tell that she has it. Margie's birthmark is on her face like mine, but it's nearly gone, replaced by ridges of scar tissue where a doctor burned it off in stripes.

Jimmy is beautiful. He has told us that more than half his body is stained, but the only visible marks are on his neck and face, on his hands, a tapestry of lovely rose patterns on creamy skin. He is not someone I want to turn away from, but someone I want to study, like an abstract painting. His pretty wife sits beside him. She pulls aside his shirt to show us the bumps on his chest where the stain has begun to progress.

Colette has made the trip from Paris. She smiles shyly at me. She is tall and stylish, her hair short and chic. She dresses with Parisian flair. But her face is the face I might have had if there had been no treatments, no experimental ruby laser, no pulse dye laser. Her birthmark is thick, dark, and cobbled and the heavy makeup she wears fails to truly conceal it.

Lucy says the birthmark that covers one leg upsets her so much she goes through three big boxes of powder each week, trying to cover it up. She says she wants to wear skirts and shorts like any other young woman. One day last month she felt dampness in her shoe and discovered it was overflowing with blood. Margie catches my eye. I know what she is thinking. How much easier it would have been to have a birthmark on my leg like Lucy, on my arm, my back, on any part of the body that can be covered with clothes.

We speak of doctors and treatments, of painful memories, of dealing with stares and cruel remarks. By the time the waiter brings a second pot of coffee, we've had all we can bear of such talk. The conversation drifts to shopping, restaurants, golf—the concerns of ordinary tourists.

The conference room is crowded with people milling about, talking in clusters. Searching for faces like mine, I see women wearing heavy makeup, men wearing beards to conceal stained cheeks. Many people have planned family vacations around the conference, bringing along husbands and wives, fathers, mothers, children. I stroll around the perimeter, scanning the crowd for birthmarks, as though looking for someone I know.

I choose a seat on the center aisle so that I can take photographs. In the row in front of me, nine-year-old Tracy bounces in her chair. Next fall she will start fourth grade. I can't take my eyes off her. It's as though nine-year-old Joie has come back to haunt me. Tracy has the same long, dark, curly hair, the same skinny body I had, and a stained face very much like my own. I want to protect her, to shout, "Somebody get that thing off before it hurts her anymore! Make it go away!"

I recognize her mother's name on the tag pasted to her dress. I've read her postings online, so I introduce myself, saying, "I looked just like your daughter when I was her age." She tells me that Tracy has had fourteen laser surgeries with almost no fading.

One by one, leading physicians, researchers, specialists in vascular anomalies address the room, juggling the remote control for the slide projector and the pen laser they use to underline their points with beams of red light. For the first time I understand exactly what the stain is, the malfunctioning or missing nerves, the veins that remain dilated and thicken, become flaccid with time.

A doctor shows us before and after pictures of tiny babies with stained faces. "The earlier you can work on them, the better the result," he says. "Many babies who are treated within a few months of birth have almost total clearing." These children will start school with nearly unmarred faces. It's too late for me. Part of my birthmark is gone, but the part that's left is as stubborn as an old bloodstain on a white sheet.

"If only those treatments had been possible for me when I was a baby," I murmur. Heads all around me nod in agreement. "It would have been a completely different life," someone says.

Another doctor shows slides of untreated port wine stains on sixty-year-old faces, bony overgrowths, hypertrophied soft tissue, dark purple, pebbled, hideous, hanging funguslike from distorted cheeks. I watch little Tracy, sitting very still now in the seat in front of me. What nightmare is this at the age of nine to see the monstrous thing your sweet face might become? Her mother quietly leads her out of the room.

Tracy has been diagnosed with posttraumatic stress disorder, the result of having been burned with the laser over and over again, held down by parents, grandparents, and nurses. Her mother wishes the doctors had been willing to use general anesthesia. Now Tracy is seeing a psychiatrist who does not recommend that she be forced to undergo further treatments.

Colette, Lucy, and I use the free time between sessions to get out of the hotel. In late July, Charleston is a steambath. Within minutes our clothes, our hair, our faces are wet. Colette's makeup melts. Walking down the narrow streets of the old city, I watch a smartly dressed woman look at Colette and quickly look away, pulling her small son by the hand, hurrying him along. Lucy is wearing long flowing pants, her birthmark safely hidden. I stroll along without makeup, hiding behind big sunglasses, my hair parted to cover my left cheek and eye like a veil, knowing no one will notice me while I walk beside Colette. In and out of stores, I watch salespeople try hard to ignore Colette's face. She makes it easier for them, chatting, charming them with her French accent. We all buy straw sunhats. Colette gives the sales clerk her camera and asks him to take a picture of the three of us, smiling faces shaded by wide brims.

When we return, Barbara Sparks, who is a vice president of Dermablend Corrective Cosmetics, has set up a display in the conference room. A slim blond with perfect features and a precision haircut, dressed in a stylish black dress, she has driven to Charleston from Tennessee, her trunk loaded with fifty gift bags full of makeup and cases more to give away. A crowd has formed around her, marked young women, old women, children, even a teenaged boy with a face stained like mine, all waiting for a chance at a free makeover. Someone mutters, "What can she teach us? She's flawless. She can't know what it's like to be us."

Barbara hears and shakes her head. "I've been there," she says. "I know what it was like to grow up with this. It wasn't easy." But she looks like the ultimate prom queen, the All-American dream of a girl, grown into a stunning woman. She traces a manicured fingernail over her chin and cheek. She says she has a birthmark there the color of an eggplant. The doctors have told her it's inoperable. I look at her closely, can't find even a shadow of darkness hidden under her impeccable mask.

"You are so beautiful," I tell her. "You should have been the most popular girl in school. I can't believe that your birthmark ruined that for you."

"Oh no," she says. "I was the ugly duckling. I hid in the corner. I never lifted my head."

She tells me that once she could wear makeup, her life changed. Behind the mask, she has become a different person, just as I have. With corrective cosmetics she transformed herself into such a consummate swan that she was chosen to represent Tennessee in the Mrs. America beauty pageant.

She got the job she has now by writing to Dermablend to tell them how their product had changed her life. She says she has made it her mission to help others with birthmarks like hers.

I am offering my own makeover sessions. I've bought every concealing makeup on the market, tried them all. Now they are lined up on the windowsill in my hotel room. I've announced that anyone who wants to experiment is welcome to stop by. Young, slender, and very pretty, Mandy comes to my room fully made up, so that her birthmark is invisible. She tells me that she couldn't bear to walk from her room to mine without makeup and that she's very nervous about showing her naked face to me. All her life, she's had to worry that the mask might slip; now I'm asking her to take it off. When she finally wipes her face clean, she reveals a round red spot on her cheek, the size of a silver dollar. "I wish my birthmark was as faded as yours is," she says. My birthmark is easily three times the size of hers. It still covers my cheek and most of my eye. But I understand that she doesn't see that. Her birthmark is the same to her now as it was before all the treatments she endured in her determination to obliterate it. Is my birthmark, like hers, so much larger to me than it is to anyone else? Am I cowering in the very big shadow of a very small monster? It is nonsense, of course, to think we can ever truly know ourselves, that is, in the sense of developing the sort of periscopic view that would allow us to emerge from the depths of self-protection and see ourselves as the rest of the world sees us.

On the hotel's mezzanine floor, teams of doctors sit at long tables browsing through treatment histories and photographs. These are the clinics, scheduled at fifteen-minute intervals. It's a chance to consult the leading specialists in the field. I nearly decided to skip my turn at the clinics, to go shopping, instead. I've already had so many treatments. I'm sure I've come to the end of that road. And I'm embarrassed about making a Big Deal. My own birthmark doesn't seem so important anymore.

I sit at the head of the table. Six doctors turn to look at me. Their expressions are kind, but I don't like being the focus of this sort of attention. Their eyes switch between my "before" photo and my face. They tell me I'm one of the lucky ones. I've

marked for life

had only partial fading, but they consider that to be an excellent result. Many stains don't respond to the lasers at all. They tell me that it's possible that the newest laser might fade my birthmark a bit more. It's worth a try. The doctors spend only a few minutes with me. My port wine stain is no longer severe enough to be interesting. I am almost embarrassed to have taken up their time, to have made a Big Deal about my birthmark.

Colette is waiting with Lucy on a bench in the hall. Sitting in a public space without makeup is terrifying for her. She has been anxious about it ever since she decided to come to the conference. How would she manage to get from her room to the clinic? How could she walk the halls, ride the elevator with the horror of her face in full view? So Lucy is there, trying her best to shield her. The French doctors have told Colette that her stain is too extensive to treat. It would be far too painful for her. It would take too many treatments, too many years. So she has watched helplessly as the stain progressed from flat and smooth to raised and pebbled, watched her skin grow thicker, darker. She has come to Charleston for hope. The doctors give it to her. They tell her that if she can come to the States for a period of time, there's a good chance her birthmark can be treated. But Colette is not convinced. She is afraid, she says, afraid of the pain.

Back in my room, late-afternoon sun blazes through the window, ricochets off the mirror, and strikes my face. A doctor has just told me, "It's not the first thing one sees when one looks at you." Am I like Mandy, hiding a stain that is no longer there? A smear of rosy red still mottles my eye and cheek and drips down toward my chin. But it looks different to me now. Spending time with people whose birthmarks are much more extensive than mine has released me from my ugliness, the way spending a weekend in the company of much older people once made me feel like a kid again.

My online friend Margie stops in to say good-bye and we compare our "before" photos, taken thirty years ago, before the progression of the stains, before the long series of treatments. We were two longhaired, twenty-something Jewish girls, with matching bloody handprints on our faces, as though we'd been touched by the same guardian angel.

I am ready to leave the conference. I don't want to be a person with a birthmark anymore. I want to turn my eyes away from my own face, look out. Look out.

I have been hiding for decades, masquerading as a clear-face. But I always knew that I was a fake, that behind the mask I was flawed, disfigured, marked. Now that I have finally met other stained faces, I realize that I am no more like them than anybody else. I have been an ordinary person all along, no stranger and no less strange than anyone.

My flight out of Charleston leaves very early in the morning. Half asleep but fully made up, I check out of the hotel and roll my suitcase to the side entrance, where the airport van is scheduled to pick me up. The lobby shops are closed, the halls deserted. I stand just inside the glass doors looking up at the sky, watching for the first light.

A woman I recognize from the conference comes up behind me, trailed by her daughter. I turn and smile. "I see I'm not the only one crazy enough to be leaving at this ungodly hour."

"Oh, we just have to get out of here," the woman says, pointing her chin toward the girl. "She's had a really rough night. We didn't sleep at all. She's been so upset. We had to call her father at two o'clock. He told us to get right home on the next flight. We were planning to spend the weekend sightseeing, but there's no way either of us would be up to that now."

The girl sits cross-legged on the floor, leaning against her suitcase. I think she may be eleven or twelve years old. "It was a horrible, horrible night," she says. How strange that this girl who has never met me before should be willing, even eager, to tell me that.

I look her over, trying to find a stain, but it must be hidden under makeup or under clothes. The only thing that marks her is the pain in her face. I see the history of my own pain there, the pain Mommy so rigorously denied, the pain I myself have avoided, kept secret, pretending, always pretending.

In the girl's face I see that the conference has been difficult for us all. For two days we have turned to confront the bloody marks that stained us. Now we are turning back, hurrying to escape, anxiously waiting for the van that will take us to the airplane that will take us far away.

The airport van arrives before I can find words to comfort that little girl, to comfort the little girl I once was. Silently, we drive into the steamy gray Charleston dawn.

A Face in the Crowd

> And I stared up at the raw spots on his cheek and thought, there is no safety anywhere; a humpback, a cripple—they all have the trigger that sets love off.
>
> GRAHAM GREENE
> *The End of the Affair*

I emerge into the dazzling L.A. sunshine and run to catch Marc in his red pickup truck before he gets kicked out of the white zone and has to circle the airport again.

Marc has known about the birthmark for only a few months. The night he found out, we were cuddled on my living room sofa, working on our second bottle of Merlot, lighting our cigarettes with the candles burning on the coffee table, sharing secrets. "I must really trust you to be telling you this," I said. He cocked his head and nodded. "Well, yeah!" His smile was kind, but almost placating, as though he was sure I was about to make a Big Deal about nothing. What could I possibly say that would surprise him? We'd been friends for fifteen years.

"I was born with a big purple birthmark shaped like a hand," I said, demonstrating with my own hand. "The palm and thumb part cover my left eye and cheek, and the fingers reach down toward my mouth."

"What! How old were you when it was removed?"

"It wasn't removed. I still have most of it."

"No, no. I would have seen it. How could I not have seen it?"

"I always wear makeup," I said, trying not to sound apologetic.

He examined my face in the candlelight. "Where is it? I want to see it. Are you wearing makeup now?"

I nodded.

"But why? Why would you wear makeup all the time, even with me?"

I lowered my chin to my chest, hiding. "Because I was afraid if you saw me without it, you'd think I was ugly."

He lifted my face, held it between two big hands.

"Joie, when I look at you, I see *you*."

Marc and I have good seats at the Hollywood Bowl. I'm happy sitting beside him, both of us swaying to the music. My birthmark is safely put away again, hidden under makeup, but the demon Purple Face, Scar Face, Ketchup Face, Kool-Aid Face, Miss Grape Juice Face no longer lurks beneath the mask, threatening to reveal herself. She has dissolved in the misty Charleston dawn.

I look out at the chorus of faces onstage, out over the faces in the audience. Thousands of faces surround me. Rows of faces descend in rings below me. Rows and rows of faces climb up to the top of the steep hill behind me. White faces, black faces, brown faces, faces of every race and combination of races, nearly eighteen thousand faces.

And I am just another one.